Memoirs of
a Stormy Life

Translated from the Yiddish by Eva Zeitlin Dobkin
Edited by Ira Altman

Memoirs of
a Stormy Life

May We Never be Tested With
That Which We Can be Punished

By

Harry Altman

Writers Club Press
San Jose New York Lincoln Shanghai

Memoirs of a Stormy Life
May We Never be Tested With That Which We Can be Punished

Published by Writers Club Press
an imprint of iUniverse.com, Inc.

For information address:
iUniverse.com, Inc.
620 North 48th Street
Suite 201
Lincoln, NE 68504-3467
www.iuniverse.com

ISBN: 0-595-09857-6

Printed in the United States of America

FOREWORD
(A Foreword by the Author)

"May we never be tested with that which we can be punished" is an old
Yiddish saying which is as apt as the light of day is real. No one can escape
the fate pre-ordained for him from birth to final breath. This conviction
has compelled me to describe my life story. A life filled with such difficulties that I couldn't escape them no matter how much I tried.

Although Memoirs of A Stormy Life is a personal autobiography,
the lay reader and the student of history will herein find an account of
events not yet described anyplace else. It may, for the aforementioned
reason, prove to be of considerable value to historians as they pore
over the accounts of Jewish martyrdom in the calamitous era of the
Hitler cataclysm.

The Jewish refugees of Poland had the misfortune of being lured into
Soviet captivity. They were herded into agricultural collectives, into
factories, and into the rural Soviets (kolkhozy, sovkhozy, zavody). They
were forced to do penal labor under the most horrific conditions of
extreme cold and hunger.

When, barefoot and ill clothed, they reached the very limits of
exhaustion, and could bear no more, they streamed towards Minsk
(the capital city of White Russia). Husbands, wives, and children
expressed their pain by lying down on the trolley car rails-disrupting
all trolley service.

The Russians hadn't seen so daring a show of protest since the days
of the Revolution. The boldness of it stunned the Russian people, and
caused the government to tremble. The chief officer of the Soviet,
"Comrade" Morozov came running. Mounting the steps of the Dom
Pravitelatvo (State Government Building), he invited the refugees to

gather in the clubroom for the deaf and dumb, which was situated nearby. He announced that those who didn't wish to work for the Soviets would be given unhindered safe passage to the Polish-held areas. However, once the demonstrators went inside the club for deaf-mutes, they weren't allowed to leave. Instead, they were led out of the hall by a back door into a yard where "Black Crows" (police vans) stood waiting. The NKVD then escorted one and all to prison.

Acceptance of a passport meant becoming the legal property of the Soviets. Those who refused to register were dragged from their lodgings in the middle of the night and sent off to Siberia to perform slave labor.

For fourteen long months the Jewish refugees suffered every manner of cruelty. Worn out by torture, they left the Siberian taiga with hope of reaching the warmer Middle Asian republics of the mighty Soviet archipelago of slavery. There, again, they endured the most horrendous living conditions till the day of their long-awaited "repatriation."

All of this is a chain of human suffering, as is not unknown to our people in our long history. It is totally unknown to those who believe the Soviet Union was a humane order. It was a regime that preached equality and freedom while practicing inhumane cruelty.

Those who fled from the unbridled persecution of the Nazis ran into the arms of the worst barbarians of the twentieth century where they were harassed more than any other people.

The Soviet Union was a despotic power, which enslaved a sixth of our globe and held other nations in fear and terror, as it fed the world lies, claiming to be the liberator and architect of a better world. Only someone who has lived in the Communist land of slavery could see through to the true countenance of the worst pretenders of our time.

Harry Altman
New York City

Chapter 1

I was barely three years old when I first began to be aware of what was going on around me. We lived in two rooms of the attic of an old four-story building at number 5 Niska Street in Warsaw, the capital city of Poland.

Close up against the wall of one room, stood a small bed, in which my mother, my four-year-old brother, Ben Tsion and I slept. The narrow bed could barely hold the three of us.

The passage from the door to a small cooking area was also very narrow. The clay stove had two burners on which my grandmother or my mother would cook our poor, miserable meals. Right next to the stove was a water faucet, and a half-meter below that was a black cast-iron sink, fastened to the wall, from which excess water ran off, and down which dirty water could be poured.

A massive oak table and six oak chairs stood in the center of the larger room. Lined up along three walls were three beds, for my grandfather, my grandmother, and one of my mother's brothers, uncle Moishe. From the back wall, the ceiling sloped sharply down to two windows (which should have been the fourth wall) at floor level. From the outside, the windows looked like immense doghouses growing out of the steep housetop not unlike most Polish dormers.

There were no toilets in the apartments of those days. A single water closet in the yard served all the tenants of the building, some four hundred persons.

It was dreadfully cold that winter, and we hadn't money for buying wood or coal.

At dawn, when grandfather rose for morning prayers, the first thing he did was cover us with his quilt to warm us up a bit.

I remember lying in bed crying day after day for I experienced nearly unbearable hunger pangs and suffered excruciatingly painful chilblains from my frostbitten feet.

Grandfather tried his best to comfort me and keep me from crying:

"Shh, shh, don't cry. Papa will come and bring you bread and shoes. Soon it'll be warm and you'll be able to play out in the yard with the other children. You won't be cold or hungry any more."

During moments of forgetfulness while I lay in bed, I listened to grandfather as he stood by the window reading aloud from the daily paper. World War I was in full swing at the time, and he was reading a report of soldiers who had fallen on the battlefield. We all held our breath afraid lest Uncle Simkhe, grandfather's eldest son, be among those recorded.

As I listened in the otherwise quiet room, I fell asleep until mother returned from peddling candy in the streets. On her way home, she would buy part of a loaf of bread and several potatoes with the few coins that she earned and then hurriedly cooked a thin, watery potato soup. When it was prepared, she would awaken us and we would all sit down to eat our poor little meal.

Grandfather Lev Silbermintz, formerly a well to do man, was the owner of a very large textile mill in Warsaw, at Number 5 Dzike Street, where it occupied a large building and surrounding houses. The factory was equipped with the most modern machinery, and employed hundreds of workers in the production of lace goods.

It never entered grandfather's mind that war could come and that "between a yea and a nay" his large fortune would be reduced to dust and ashes and he would be forced to endure great adversity in his declining years.

When grandfather was still well off, Poland was under Russia's yoke. When war broke out, the Tsar decreed that anyone in Poland who owned anything made of metal was to deliver it forthwith for use in the war industries. Those caught concealing the specified metals were to be severely punished. Immediately, people removed their brass doorknobs, copper fish dippers and various other objects and delivered them to the authorities.

Grandfather's machines had to be disassembled and virtually overnight his factory was in ruins. Grandfather managed to salvage two large suitcases overflowing with paper rubles. With these he thought he could survive the war. Before long, the Germans occupied Poland and declared Russian currency to be worthless. The two suitcases stuffed with rubles remained under the bed, and my brother and I and the other children of the building eventually used them for play.

At first, in order to provide for the family, grandfather sold various valuables from home, but he soon had nothing to sell. To make matters worse, grandmother became ill from all the hardship. She was confined to bed and the doctor had to call on her every day. When the situation became grave, mother decided she had to do something to lighten the heavy burden grandfather was carrying on his old shoulders. A neighbor suggested she sell some of the candy he manufactured, which was made of starch and saccharin, for it was difficult to obtain sugar during the war. Mother became the sole breadwinner but her earnings weren't enough to provide even minimal nourishment.

In the good old days, when grandfather walked about his immense factory, everyone looked up to him with awe and respect as though he were a lord. One day, a former *yeshiva* student, from the town of Grodzisk, about thirty kilometers from Warsaw, came to apply for work.

The young man's parents sent him to Warsaw to study at a *yeshiva* because he soon outdistanced all the other boys. Since higher education was unavailable in Grodzisk, the *melamed*, who taught them, recommended that the youth continue his studies in Warsaw.

When he arrived there, a new world opened up to him. After a few weeks at the *yeshiva*, he was attracted to a circle of revolutionaries. He gave up his studies and looked for some way to earn a living. He wished to be self-supporting so as to devote all of his free time to the ideas beginning to take shape in his mind. It was then that he arrived at grandfather's factory. Grandfather taught him to operate a bobbin machine in which thread was prepared for use on textile weavers.

Grandfather couldn't possibly have known that this *yeshiva* boy was destined to cause him so much sorrow and heartache that he would never be able to forgive him. The young man, Avrom Sholem Altman, was infected with the revolutionary spirit fashionable among young Jews of those days and started devoting all his energy to the socialist class struggle.

He first dedicated himself to organizing his co-workers. It didn't take long to establish a committee and compile a long list of demands for improving working conditions in the shop. When the list was ready, he headed a delegation for negotiating those new working conditions.

Although somewhat astonished, grandfather remained unruffled in the face of the organizing committee, and listened to their demands. When they finished, he spoke with deliberate calm, saying that there was nothing to negotiate about, and that if anyone was dissatisfied with existing working conditions, they were free to go home. No one would detain them.

The committee, with young Avrom Sholem at its head, wasn't surprised at grandfather's contemptuous reply and proceeded to call a general meeting. They decided to send grandfather a detailed letter describing their demands in full and allowing him a week to think the matter over. If he still rejected the workers' demands, they would go on strike.

When grandfather received their letter and read its specifications, he stormed into the factory and summoned all the signatories to his office. Once they were inside, he directed his daughter, Hendl, who was in charge of the bookkeeping, to pay each worker his wages and told them never to set foot in his factory again if they wished to avoid further embarrassment. He then returned to the factory, ordered everyone to interrupt their work and addressed them as follows:

"I've just dismissed all your representatives. They'll no longer be allowed to work here. If any of you are dissatisfied with your present working conditions, you may resign and I will pay you whatever you're owed. If you wish to go on working for me but still believe you're not receiving adequate compensation, you may appeal on an individual basis. I'll consider any request that's justified, but I'll not tolerate any instigators. Under no circumstances shall I permit noncompliance in my establishment!"

Dead silence. No one dared utter a sound. After several seconds, grandfather interrupted the stillness.

"So far as I can tell, you've nothing to say, so go on back to work. But remember, no rebels in my place, ever!"

The workers returned to their respective tasks with bowed heads. They didn't strike. They were afraid to lose their jobs and source of livelihood.

The fired committee leaders waited at the gate for the homeward bound workers and complained that it was unfair of them, having agreed to strike, to continue working. Their arguments fell on deaf ears, for the workers were afraid to lose their source of income.

Little by little, the committee members realized it would "take more than a few swallows to bring on spring." Since they were out on the street, they asked the other workers to persuade grandfather to take them back. After many interventions and apologies, grandfather agreed to rehire them except for Avrom Sholem whom grandfather considered the worst of the instigators.

Avrom Sholem was unable to find alternative employment. Perplexed, hungry, and threatened with eviction, he spent his days near the factory. When the workers saw him on their way home, they felt sorry for him, for his appearance aroused their concern. They asked grandfather to forgive the man, but he remained obdurate.

Grandfather had two sons and a daughter. He loved his daughter more than anyone else. She was the apple of his eye and he watched over her most attentively.

When Hendl went by the factory and saw Avrom Sholem in obviously desperate straits, her heart ached with pity. Coming up to her bookkeeping office and finding her father there, she described Avrom Sholem's sad state and pleaded with her father to forgive Avrom just as he had forgiven the others. She softened his heart, and he agreed to rehire Avrom Sholem.

Avrom Sholem didn't know how to thank Hendl for the favor she had done him. Due to her kindheartedness, he was back at work and living a normal life again. Any time she made her appearance, he greeted her with a thankful smile and whenever the opportunity presented itself, he complimented her extravagantly.

One day, when she came to distribute the workers' earnings, she stopped beside Avrom Sholem and their eyes met. Both their faces became suffused with pink. When she extended her hand to give him his wages, he timidly took her hand in his and, in a trembling voice, asked her whether she would consent to go for a walk with him on Saturday afternoon. His forwardness took her unaware and before she was able to recover her composure, he continued hurriedly to say that at two o'clock Saturday he would wait at the gate of her home. The romance of my parents-to-be had begun.

In the beginning, grandfather had no idea that his beloved daughter was going out with Avrom Sholem, *The Instigator*. After a while, however, he heard about the affair and flew into a rage. He couldn't bear the thought that his bright, darling daughter could disappoint him so and take up with a fellow he would never approve of. He often got into a row with her and threatened to discharge Avrom Sholem if she didn't immediately break off with him. But by then, mother was head over heels in love.

Her response to grandfather's threat was unusually sharp. If Avrom Sholem were dismissed, she would leave home and marry without parental consent. The feuding continued and it began to look as though it would never end. Grandfather was afraid to discharge my father lest he lose his one and only daughter.

Finally, Avrom Sholem and Hendl decided to put an end to the strained situation. They went to grandfather and announced that they wanted to be married the sooner the better. If he didn't give his consent, they would leave and have the ceremony performed elsewhere.

Grandfather's outcry was vociferous. He wept and shouted that he would never, while he was alive, allow that to happen. After they yelled at each other and cried a great deal, the young couple departed, slamming the door behind them. They took up residence with a sister of Avrom Sholem's who lived in Warsaw, at 16 Naviniarska Street.

Several days later, they had their marriage ceremony. It was performed without consent of the bride's parents, in the presence of the groom's party comrades and the sister with whom they were lodging.

Although my father had no situation at the time, he gave little thought to the matter of earning a living. Instead of seeking work and undertaking responsibility for his wife and himself, he spent nearly all his time with his comrades organizing worker cells dedicated to socialist ideals.

Shortly after the wedding, mother became pregnant. My brother, Ben Tsion, was born at the end of the first year of their marriage. Two years later, I came into the world.

Conditions became untenable for mother. We lived in a single small room with no means of subsistence. My father didn't take the situation to heart and mother had no choice, with two small children to support and raise, but to turn to her mother for help. Grandmother was very happy to hear from her daughter and proceeded at once to provide her with funds and other necessities. This she did without grandfather's knowledge, for he still couldn't forgive his daughter for having wronged her parents.

My father was still spending all day and half the night with his party members. Mother couldn't tolerate such an attitude toward herself and the family, all responsibility for which he had obviously shed. Sharp quarrels broke out between them and after one such dispute, my father left home altogether and, for a long time, no one knew of his whereabouts. Mother accepted her fate and made no attempt to find him.

Occasionally, grandmother would visit us. She realized how difficult our situation was and began to plead with grandfather to make his peace with his daughter.

"It is our own daughter and grandchildren in need after all, and we mustn't forsake them."

Grandfather perceived the justice of his wife's arguments and tearfully agreed with her. They came to take us to their home where we lived happily for several months. We were surrounded with so much warmth and love, food and luxury that we thought it would last forever. This brief happiness was soon to burst, like so many soap bubbles.

Our family's troubles began when Uncle Simkhe was ordered into compulsory military service with the Russian army. Grandfather was worried because his eldest son would be obliged to eat unkosher food. He was more concerned about that than with the fact that uncle Simkhe had never been away from home. However, that was the source of grandmother's deepest apprehension. She sighed and wept day and night over her eldest son's fate. Sorrow began to make its nest in our home.

Several months later, World War I broke out, and the Germans marched stiff-legged into Poland. These were the first of many heavy blows that fell upon us in rapid succession. Grandfather lost his factory, his house, and his entire fortune. All that remained for him was sorrow, poverty, and hunger. But these fearful circumstances were no deterrent to the onward, relentless march of time. Our difficult living conditions became too much for my beloved and ailing grandmother, and, just before Passover, she expired in her sleep.

Although I was only a three-year-old child at the time, I still remember the powerful impression her passing made on me. As for grandfather, this misfortune shocked him terribly. Overnight, gray streaks appeared in his pitch-black beard. His gentle blue eyes stared blankly into the distance, as though seeking a reason for the dreadful calamity that befell him. He was obviously choking on a horrible pain that he could neither swallow nor disgorge.

Since my brother and I were too young to attend the funeral, one of grandfather's sisters took us to her home. Grandfather was a *koyen*—a descendant of the high priests of Israel—and it was forbidden for him to be present in a house where there was a corpse, so he went with us. He seemed quite bewildered during the period of mourning and cried like a child over his great loss.

Once the Germans conquered Poland, life became somewhat easier. Because of the similarity of their languages, Jews were able to communicate with the Germans and began bartering with them. Mother, too, began smuggling meat into Warsaw from nearby towns and selling it to the housewives of the neighborhood. We subsisted on her earnings and life was now a bit less difficult. Our family's only wish was for a miracle that would bring uncle Simkhe back home safely from the front. If we could've heard anything of my father we would've thanked God for that too. Then perhaps the cruel war would've been less painful to endure.

When the Germans began meeting defeat, the Poles attempted to recover their independence from the ruins of Germany's losses. They fought valiantly against the weary Russian armies, which tried regaining control of Poland from the retreating Germans. The Poles were victorious in several decisive battles and they once again proclaimed an independent Polish state.

People began to sense that the war was coming to an end. Indications of stabilization were everywhere. Gradually, things did normalize, and people tried to adjust to a more orderly and peaceful existence.

A man who worked as a supervisor in grandfather's factory established his own large factory at Number 3 Bonifraten Street. One of the first things he did was to engage grandfather as supervisor. Grandfather was to perform the same duties that the new entrepreneur performed for him, and he was to receive a handsome compensation for his work. This seemed to grandfather a stroke of good fortune sent down from Heaven.

After he'd worked for several weeks, our lives took a noticeable change for the better. As soon as he received his first wages, grandfather persuaded mother to give up her trade and devote herself to taking care of the house and children. My brother and I were promptly enrolled in a Jewish school at Number 3 Nowolipje Street, where we enjoyed our studies and the tasty noonday meals they served us. Moishe, my younger uncle, obtained employment at the factory grandfather supervised. Since uncle Moishe gave mother money toward household expenses, there was quite enough for our needs. Mother took my brother and me to a tailor and ordered us new suits of clothes, and then took us to a shoemaker for new shoes. We were living the good life, "like God in Odessa."

On Friday evenings, grandfather would sit at the head of the table. Dressed in his brand new satin gabardine, which was tied with a heavy satin girdle around his hips, he raised the full *Kiddush* cup. He stood up to pronounce the blessing and, in his strong voice, sang the touching Sabbath melody. The rest of us listened most respectfully. After grandfather sipped some of the *Kiddush* wine, he made sure to give us all a taste. Then came the fish, the Sabbath loaf, and the soup with so many globules of fat floating on top that the light from the Sabbath candles played and danced on them. We joyously sang the traditional Sabbath songs as we waited for mother to bring the next course to our table.

One Saturday, as we sat at the table enjoying our festive meal, we heard a knocking at the door. Mother went to open it. There stood the postman with a red-lacquer sealed envelope. It contained a letter and some American dollars. Upon reading the letter, we discovered that it was from father who was in America.

The letter expressed profound regret for his mistreatment of us, and explained that it hadn't all been honey for him either, and that because of the war he was unable to establish contact with us. He asked forgiveness for the sins he committed and promised that henceforth things would be different.

I don't recall whether mother sent him an answer. What I do remember is that about a year later, as I sat in my schoolroom at my lessons, the classroom door opened to admit a stranger. In an uncertain voice, he inquired whether there wasn't a boy named Hershl Altman in class. The teacher called my name and directed me to step forward. I rose from my seat and advanced toward the teacher. The next moment, the stranger ran toward me and, before I realized what was happening, I was in the young man's arms as he fiercely pressed me to himself. He covered my face with kisses, and whispered over and over: "It's me, your father…my dear little child." For the first time in my life, I felt what it meant to have a father.

Father obtained employment as chairman of a House Painter's Association affiliated with the Left Poale-Zion movement. Their headquarters were at Number 38 Dzika Street, where they provided a restaurant for the workers. Many workers took their meals there as did we, where we partook of the appetizing food. Father brought enough money from America to rent a pleasant and comfortable apartment at Number 18, on the very same street where he worked.

We began an entirely new kind of life, that of a devoted family. During our free time, we enjoyed visiting the section of town known as Lashenkes where there were a number of magnificent parks. We would also go to the theater together.

In the summertime, father rented a place in the town of Falienitsa, on the rail line to Otwok, where we spent our summer vacations. We visited with relatives and friends and, from time to time, attended a literary reading or political lecture. Although political discussions bored me terribly, I was content to just sit between mother and father. On occasion, as I sat on one of my parent's laps, the tedious lecturer would put me to sleep.

At the age of seven, when I completed my course of study at the children's school, I was advanced to the Borokhov Folk School at Number 6 Dzika Street, where my brother had already completed two classes. The street was renamed Zamenhof Street in honor of Ludwig Zamenhof, the inventor of Esperanto. Esperanto was intended to be the language that all nations in the world would speak in the future, when there would be an universal alliance, and socialism would prevail throughout the world. That dream seems to have dissolved some time later and, with it, any interest that initially may have existed in a universal language.

Before long, mother became pregnant and awaited her day of confinement. I recall when her birth pangs began. Father hired a *droshky* and sent her off to the hospital. He then took my brother and me to stay at grandfather's house until such time as mother would return.

Grandfather had married again. His second wife had three children of her own. So, with the addition of the two of us, there were five children in their home. But my step-grandmother wasn't especially hospitable when grandfather asked her to take care of us.

After a period of very difficult labor, mother gave birth to a little girl. Shortly thereafter, it was discovered that mother contracted blood poisoning and that her life was in jeopardy. Two weeks later, she was still hospitalized.

Grandfather went to the hospital every evening, immediately after work, and sat at her bedside for hours. Father too, spent days on end in the hospital, keeping an agonizing vigil for her life.

As vividly as if it were happening now, I recall sitting at the table over my lessons when I became aware of mournful weeping rising to my ears from the staircases on the lower floors of the building. The crying increased in volume and grew more heartrending as it came closer to our door, as though the lament were climbing one staircase after another before reaching the last one. I began to tremble, realizing it was grandfather who was weeping. I rushed to the door. As I opened it, grandfather's wailing grew even more piteous. There wasn't need for anyone to tell me I was orphaned and that I'd never again see my beloved mother, the dearest possession, the most precious treasure a child can ever have. I experienced the bitter taste of what was to become a constant companion throughout the rest of my childhood, the fate of an orphan.

Father brought my newborn little sister to grandfather's house. The child was named Feygele, after my beloved grandmother. The baby was pretty and well formed, but born unlucky. She was orphaned as soon as she came into the world.

In those days, "baby formulas," were unknown. So it was necessary to find a woman nursing an infant of her own who would be willing to suckle our unfortunate little sister. Father contacted his family in Grodzisk and they found a poor woman in town who, for a consider-able fee, agreed to take care of my sister. And so, the baby was sent off to a home of strangers. Father lost no time in disposing of our home at Number 18 Zamenhof Street. He rented a room for himself, with another family, at Nowolipje Number 66, while my brother and I remained at grandfather's.

My step-grandmother was a very embittered woman and she harbored a vile attitude toward us. Father came to visit us from time to time and we complained to him. All he did to comfort us was to say that we wouldn't have to suffer much longer, which, of course, didn't alter the situation. When I could no longer endure my step-grandmother's mistreatment of us, I ran away.

I wandered across the Praga Bridge with a friend from school, and sat on the bank of the Wisla River until late at night, where the police noticed us. They took us to the Praga District Police Headquarters. When they asked us where we lived, I didn't give grandfather's address but that of my father. We spent the whole of that night on a hard bench in the police station.

Early in the morning, father was brought in to take me home. With tears in my eyes, I implored him not to send me back to my cruel step-grandmother, for I could no longer endure her mistreatment of me. We argued for some time before father agreed to take me home with him and see whether the family would take in my brother and me, assuming they were paid for their trouble. They agreed, and so my brother and I went to yet another home.

The family that took us in consisted of a brother and a sister about father's age, and an older woman, their aunt, whom they supported. A deaf mute, she was responsible for the housekeeping while her niece and nephew were away at work earning a living. After we lived in this place for several weeks, my father returned from work one evening with an entirely new plan for taking care of me.

"Tomorrow," he announced, "we'll both travel to Lodz, where there's an orphanage for children like yourself, and you'll have a nice warm home among children your own age. I believe that'll be the most suitable place for you. You'll be comfortable there and grow up to be a *mentsch* (a good person).

The orphanage was outside Lodz proper, in a village called Kali. It was under the auspices of the Poale-Zion Party, of which father was an early founder. He also worked with Ber Borochow, the guiding spirit of the Poale-Zion movement. For these reasons, father had no difficulty placing me in the institution.

My new home, a handsome new red brick building three stories high, with many rooms and verandas on three sides, stood in the middle of a cherry orchid. The wide main entrance, which had two beautiful glass doors, was at the rear of the building. From there a broad path led to endless thick green woods. To the right of the forest was a large lake where we went bathing and learned how to swim. The landscape was actually breathtaking.

One of the two pedagogues responsible for operating the orphanage was Avrom Kreuzler. He taught us Jewish history and literature. He also instructed us in the natural sciences and German as a third language. *Volksdeutsche* (ethnic Germans) inhabited the village and we needed some command of German in order to communicate with them. Our other teacher was a woman named Hershkovits, who taught us Polish, arithmetic, geography, and folk songs. In addition, she gave instruction in physical exercise and sports every morning. A German couple named Meisner was responsible for various physical tasks. They prepared the meals, did the cleaning and took care of the laundry. They also tended the garden surrounding the building.

The orphans, about thirty of us, carried out the lighter tasks. Our assignment was to study, work, and enjoy ourselves. Each week different groups of six children assisted with household duties. We helped with the cooking, served the meals and cleared the tables. Afterwards, we scrubbed the pots and washed the dishes, and straightened up the kitchen and dining room. Every bedroom contained six beds, one for each of six children. Each bed had a straw-filled mattress, a pillow stuffed with straw and a woolen quilt. Upon rising, each child was expected to make his own bed, and take turns tidying up the room.

Our daily routine was very strict. At seven in the morning, *Volksdeutsche* Meisner rang a heavy bell to awaken everyone. We were expected to rise promptly, make our beds, run to the washroom and wash up quickly, run out into the yard and get into line. Teacher Hershkovits then put us through our daily rhythmic calisthenics, after which we ran at a good pace for a distance of about two kilometers. These gymnastics were followed by breakfast. Lessons began at nine o'clock and continued until twelve. Lunch hour ended at one. Then came two more classes. At three o'clock we were free to participate in games. We played croquet, football, volleyball and various other games. During the summer months, we were taught swimming in the lake nearby. In inclement weather, Miss Hershkovits taught us Yiddish songs and accompanied our singing on the piano. Our playtime ended at six o'clock and was followed by the evening meal. The day's activities ended at seven-thirty, when we went to bed. This routine was readily acceptable to me in the summertime, when it kept me from thinking my own thoughts.

As the days grew shorter and the nights became longer and colder, making our poorly heated rooms uncomfortable, I shivered, my teeth chattering under the thin quilt of my little bed. Every winter, I got frost-bitten and suffered chilblains. As soon as I got into bed, my feet would begin to itch. Unable to endure the itching, I scratched until sores developed on my toes. In the morning, my feet would be so swollen I was unable to pull on my shoes.

On such nights, I remained sleepless for a long, long time. Wakeful and tormented by the cold and the itching, I felt sorry for myself and deplored my unhappy fate. Soon tears came flowing from my eyes, wetting my pillow. Night after night, I asked myself what had become of my family since mother died. Soon a painful longing for my recently deceased mother would begin to gnaw inside of me, as well as for my beloved grandfather and my dear brother Ben Tsion, to whom I had become so attached. I noticed a perceptible hatred for my father beginning to develop for having abandoned me to such merciless circumstances. Once again, he left me to struggle all alone in a cold world of utter strangers. Time gradually dulled my pain and suffering. Little by little I became accustomed to the conditions in which I was obliged to live.

After I'd been at the orphanage for about two years, my father, who hadn't come to visit me, in all that time, made a quite unexpected appearance. I remember that when he approached me, I froze in my tracks and stood staring at him in astonishment, my eyes vacant. I was unable to speak. I don't recall how long I stood motionless while facing him. I remember only that I felt a choking sensation in my throat and that through my tear-filled eyes all the world about me looked foggy, including my father, who appeared to be separated into a number of even strips as he stood there.

"Don't cry." I heard my father's voice as he attempted to calm me. He lifted me from the ground and pressed me hard against his breast. I still couldn't utter a word and repeatedly attempted to free myself from his arms. At last he put me down and asked in a gentle voice whether I wasn't pleased to see him after such a long time.

"Take me home!" I cried, suddenly aware that I'd regained my voice. "Take me home!" I repeated, even more loudly, as if to convince myself that I did indeed have my voice back.

"I don't wish to stay here any longer!" I began to sob violently, unable to hold back the tears that came streaming down my face. At that point my father put an arm around my shoulders and led me to a veranda where there was a table with two benches, one to each side. My father's words were loving as he spoke to me.

"Why don't you want to stay here?"

"I want to go home. I want to be with Ben Tsion. I want to see grand-father. I don't want to be alone among strangers."

I spoke briefly and quickly to convince him that I was hurt, and why.

"I miss everyone who was ever near and dear to me. Why'd you trick me into coming here and then not let me hear from you for more than two years?"

I yelled it all out in a single breath, and then fell silent. My father, too, was silent for a long time as he sat looking at me with sadness and compassion in his eyes. Finally, he spoke, quietly and slowly.

"*Kayne ayne hora* (may the evil eye stay far away from you), you're a ten year old lad now. Surely, you understand that you have no home. I haven't a home either, and have to live among strangers. Ever since

mother died, I felt this would be the best place for you. That's why I
brought you here. I still believe that until such time as I can take care
of you, this'll be best. You're well looked after and being taught to
grow up an educated man, one who'll find his proper place in the
world. No matter how much I may want to, I can't manage it in our
present circumstances."

After spending several hours with me, he said goodbye and returned
to Warsaw. After his departure, I felt even more forlorn. My sense of
loneliness and bewilderment intensified. Several months later, I
received a letter from my father in which he apologized for having kept
me waiting so long for news of him. He gave as his reason the fact that
he was abroad in search of better economic conditions but so far hadn't
found anything. He would write again as soon as he was settled. I
answered his letter immediately, but he didn't write again.

While I waited to hear from him, I suffered many difficult days filled
with disappointment that dragged on interminably and painfully. Two
years after my father's visit, the orphanage was obliged to close for it
had fallen on bad times.

Chapter 2

One morning, in autumn, a messenger escorted me to Warsaw. The journey was long and distressing. We started out on a tram from Kali to Lodz, where we boarded a streetcar that took us to the train. From the railroad station in Warsaw, we had to take two streetcars to get to where grandfather lived. It was late in the evening when we arrived at grandfather's house.

Grandfather was still living at Number 5 Niska, but in a smaller flat. It was on the third floor and consisted of one large room. The familiar large oak table and the heavy chairs stood in the middle of the room and four beds were lined up along the walls. The family consisted of grandfather, my step-grandmother, and her three children by her previous marriage and a little girl born of their marriage.

Our arrival was unannounced. The messenger explained that since the orphanage had closed and there was no record of other close relatives to whom I could be sent, there was no alternative but to deliver me to my grandfather who was obliged to take me in. My step-grandmother wasn't at all pleased to hear such talk and immediately demanded that the messenger take me to my other grandfather, my father's father, who lived in Grodzisk.

"You can see yourself how the seven of us are crowded into one room. There's really nowhere to put him."

Grandfather noticed my eyes fill with tears as I realized how superfluous I had become and that I was a burden even to my own relatives, who were haggling over me. He suddenly struck the table with his fist and, turning to his wife, said, in a loud voice, that she had better keep quiet.

"Put up the teakettle and serve something to eat. You can see how exhausted they are after their long trip. Then we'll all go to bed. There'll be plenty of time to figure how to get Hershl settled. We'll do whatever has to be done. After all he is my grandchild. God forbid that I let him be wronged."

Again, there were three of us sleeping in a single bed, my grandfather's this time. He and my brother slept at the head and I slept at their feet. Despite the close quarters, I felt far better in grandfather's house than I ever did in the chilly atmosphere of the orphanage. I could feel grandfather's warm disposition towards me once again. I loved grandfather dearly and longed for him all those many years I spent at the orphanage. Moreover, I was finally reunited with my beloved brother from whom I'd been separated for so long.

Ben Tsion was working and contributing towards my step-grandmother's household. I also learned that Uncle Simkhe was taken prisoner during the war, but he had returned, gotten married and now had two children. Uncle Moishe, who went off to Switzerland in search of a better life, hadn't been heard of for over two years.

After having been gone for so long, I again found myself sitting at the Sabbath table. The candles flickered inside their silver candlesticks while grandfather recited the *Kiddush* in that same strong voice and with the same melody I remembered from childhood days. Once again, I enjoyed homemade gefilte fish and Sabbath soup with all those globules of fat that reflected the candlelight like so many thousands of stars reminding me of the meals that my mother, of blessed memory, used to serve. I sang along spontaneously as grandfather chanted the Sabbath melodies with his usual heartiness. All of this warmed my spirit.

The Sabbath meal over, Ben Tsion motioned to follow him out into the yard, and I did so in silence not asking what for. Once outdoors, he quietly told me that he wanted to take me to the cinema. I was very pleased for I never went to the movies before and I looked upon my brother with eyes full of gratitude.

There were not as yet any talking pictures. Even so, the silent film impressed me greatly. I just couldn't fathom this mysterious art that produced such lifelike dramas on a dead screen. We had to read the titles very quickly in order to follow the story but that didn't keep me from being enchanted with cinematography.

On the way home, Ben Tsion told me how he came to be back at grandfather's house. When father took me to the orphanage near Lodz he already had a well thought out plan about what to do with us. One day, when Ben Tsion returned from school, my father told him that he was planning to marry the young woman with whose family they were boarding and that he believed it best for all concerned. A short time later, the marriage took place. My brother had no idea the extent to which his life was about to change.

For a while everything appeared to be going along normally, until my father went to visit me at the orphanage. When he returned from Lodz, things began to take an unexpected turn. Although Ben Tsion instinctively perceived that something was brewing, he didn't know what it was. My father and his wife were forever whispering and scrutinizing my brother as if to ascertain from the look in his eyes whether he had an inkling of what they were about.

Upon returning from school one day, Ben Tsion found the house door locked. Suspecting nothing, he stood waiting at the gate, hoping someone would arrive. After having waited several hours until nightfall, he became very anxious. Not knowing what else to do, he went tearfully to Uncle Simkhe's house. My uncle reassured him and saw to it that he had his evening meal. Later that night, he went back with Ben Tsion to see whether anyone had returned. When they arrived, the house was open. Our stepmother and her mute aunt were inside. When my uncle inquired as to my father's whereabouts, my stepmother replied that he moved out of the house and they didn't know where he was. Since she was hemming and hawing, my uncle knew she was lying. He became more insistent until, now quite irate, he seized hold of her arms and declared that unless she told him where my father was she wouldn't get free of his hands alive. Feeling the pressure of his hands on her arms, and seeing his face redden with anger, she realized he was in dead earnest. She stammered fearfully that my father had departed for Argentina. She and her aunt had gone to the station to see him off. That's why they returned so late.

"And what about his children?" my uncle asked. That wasn't something for her to decide she answered. They weren't her children and it wasn't her responsibility to care for them. At that point, my uncle had no alternative but to bring Ben Tsion to grandfather. When Ben Tsion graduated elementary school at fourteen, he went immediately to work. When I arrived, he'd been working several weeks and was beginning to feel independent, for he was earning enough to pay his own expenses.

I spent no more than two weeks at grandfather's. During the entire two weeks, my step-grandmother wouldn't stop her nagging, telling grandfather that he wasn't obliged to keep both his grandchildren so long as there was another living grandparent in Grodzisk. Why shouldn't the grandfather on my father's side also assume the burden of caring for one of his grandchildren? For the sake of maintaining domestic harmony, grandfather acquiesced and, at the end of my second week in Warsaw, he and Uncle Simkhe took me to the home of my grandfather in Grodzisk.

It wasn't easy for my Warsaw grandfather and uncle to persuade my Grodzisk grandfather to assume my care.

"It's true. I'm obliged to care for my orphaned grandchild. The trouble is, I haven't a wife and I live with my eldest daughter, her husband and three children. It's more than she can do to manage a household as large as ours. Besides, there's simply no place to put him."

My Warsaw grandfather then presented his counter argument.

"If you find it difficult to accommodate six people in as comfortable a home as this, you should appreciate how hard it is for me. With our grandson included, we'll have eight people in one crowded room. Honestly now, for whom would you think it easier? For heaven's sake where's your sense of justice?"

They argued for a long time. Finally, my father's eldest sister, aunt Ethel, intervened, saying:

"Father, I have three children. Let's assume I have four. He's still a child and he is my brother's flesh and blood. He mustn't be left all alone at God's mercy."

That ended the altercation, and so it was that I was taken to my new home in Grodzisk.

I now met my cousins for the first time. I used to hear of them, but never saw them. Aunt Ethel had three little girls. The oldest was Manya. She was two years older than I was. She was pretty and curvaceous with blue eyes and blonde hair. She was friendly towards me from the very beginning. The second sister, Rachel, was also a fair-skinned blue-eyed blonde. She differed from Manya in that she was slimmer. Rachel was three years younger than Manya. The third child was only three years old. She was very friendly and became quickly attached to people. No matter where we went, she wanted to go along. If we refused, she threw herself on the ground and screamed: "I want to go too! I want to go too!"

Manya's first act of hospitality was to take me out for a walk and acquaint me with the town and its environs. She led me to the frog pond that wasn't far from the house. From there we went to the Letnikes (the section of the city where tourists came for their summer vacations) and to the railroad tracks, and then to the wide-open road. We walked through Kalya Street to the market, and then to the water pump where water carriers obtained the water they delivered to the Jewish homes of town. From there, we went into a narrow street where the synagogue stood. She showed me a beautiful large building, the house of study, the

ritual bathhouse, and the small buildings where the followers of the
Rabbi of Ger and the Rabbi of Grodzisk went to study and pray. The
Talmud Torah was located in the *shtibl* of the Hassidim of Grodzisk. As
we went along, Manya greeted everyone who came our way and introduced me to them as her cousin newly come from Warsaw.

My Grodzisk grandfather, who was in charge of the Talmud Torah,
took me to see Yenkele *melamed*, who immediately enrolled me in the
Talmud Torah where my Jewish studies began. The teacher had no
problem with me because I had a good command of Yiddish, and was
well versed in Yiddish literature, being a graduate of the Yiddish
elementary school. Since he didn't need to teach me the alphabet, he
went right to instruction in Hebrew.

Just a few weeks later, I was praying competently from the *siddur*
and progressed quickly to studying the Pentateuch and Rashi's
commentaries. Before I had time to complete my first Pentateuch
book, I was permitted to join a group of students working on the
Gemara. Torah was being stuffed into me as though I was expected to
become a rabbi overnight.

Truth be told, I found Torah studies boring. At the orphanage, my
education had been in Yiddish and secular studies. Despite the fact
that my grandfathers were very pious, my upbringing up to the age of
twelve was non-religious. All that religious literature, and the old-
fashioned primitive interpretations of it, appeared to me to be backward and inconsequential when compared with the secular. I regarded
it a waste of time and gradually revolted against my rabbi and his
method of instruction.

When I encountered a passage my rabbi couldn't logically explain, I
interrogated him over and over again, asking a raft of confounding
questions. Instead of attempting a reply, he yelled at me: "Get on with
your studies you rascal, and don't ask so many questions."

On occasion, he let me have a lash of his thick strap, giving me something to remember for some time to come. In no way was I was going

to remain seated on that hard bench. The more I studied, the stronger the revolt in me grew until I decided I would study no more.

On the following morning, I rose early, as usual. Instead of going to *heder*, I met some boys my age with whom I had arranged to go swimming at an overgrown frog pond. We bathed and swam, and then decided to run out to the outskirts of town, where there were many fruit orchards. We picked all the apples we wanted and ate as many as we could. Engrossed in fun, we never noticed nightfall and that we had forgotten to go home.

It was after dark that I made my appearance. All the family was there and the evening meal was over. Grandfather greeted me angrily, shouting questions about why I hadn't been to *heder* and where and with whom I'd dragged about all day. I had no intention of making excuses and told him to his face that I no longer wanted to attend *heder*. This declaration excited even greater wrath. He slipped off his belt and began to strike me with it paying no heed as to where it fell. I pushed myself past everyone and out of the house.

I spent the next few hours wandering around town until past midnight. When I grew weary of straying about, I climbed secretly up to the attic of my grandfather's house, wrapped myself in some rags, and fell asleep. At daybreak, I slipped down from the attic and went to the outskirts of town. The parents of one of my friends were the proprietors of orchards in the area and I offered to help gather the fruit that had fallen from the trees. I ate some of what I picked for nourishment. At night, I shared a shed with the watchman who guarded the orchards. The shed was constructed of woven twigs and had a roof of straw which covered an earthen floor. We slept sharing a single quilt.

Subsisting on raw fruit gave me stomachaches and loose bowels and I realized that I couldn't go on living that way much longer. Weak with exhaustion, I laboriously made my way into town, where I remained near my grandfather's house. I figured that if someone in the family should "chance" to find me, I could finagle my way back home.

After lingering for several hours, I noticed Uncle Shimon appro-aching. I pretended not to see him but made certain he would see me. Several seconds later, I felt his strong fingers gripping my left arm and holding me firmly so that I couldn't get free. As I pretended to pull away, his hand tightened its grip and he inquired triumphantly, "Where are you trying to run to…and why did you run away in the first place?"

With tears in my eyes, I replied that I ran away because I no longer wanted to attend *heder* and because grandfather whipped me. My uncle let go of my arm and gently placed both his hands on my shoulders as he said:

"Listen Hershl, your grandfather is at the house of study for evening prayers. You can come home, wash up and have something to eat. I assure you no one's going to strike you again. And if you don't want to go to *heder*, no one can force you to. You'll be thirteen years old soon. That means that in just a few days you'll be a grownup responsible for your own actions. No one will be able to force you to do things you don't want to do."

I went to the house with my uncle. Aunt Ethel and the children were all happy to see me. I washed up and was given food to eat. Meanwhile, Uncle Shimon sent Manya to fetch Genendl, grandfather's youngest daughter, who lived close by. She came right over with her husband, Moishe. Grandfather had returned from synagogue by then, and every-one sat down at the table to discuss what to do with me in view of the fact that I refused to continue my *heder* studies.

Grandfather shouted that if I didn't go to *heder*, he didn't want to be under the same roof with me. He couldn't bear to see a *goy* (a Jew igno-rant of his Jewish heritage) grow up in his house. He added that his dis-appointment in me was all the greater because I had a good head on my shoulders and could grow up to be a rabbi. I refused to understand that I was throwing away a golden opportunity. After a long and stormy session, it was decided that I be put in the care of Aunt Genendl and Uncle Moishe who promised to teach me to be a tailor in their taylor shop. That way, in time, I would begin to earn my keep and become independent. I found myself in a new home once again.

Uncle Moishe and aunt Genendl lived in a nice apartment, the largest room of which served as the tailor shop. They had two children and my aunt was pregnant with a third. Although I came to them on condition that they teach me the tailor's trade, they began to teach me housework. The first thing they assigned me to do was fetch pails of water from the well. When I brought in a sufficient amount of water, they presented me with the slop pail and directed me to carry it out and spill its contents in a field at a considerable distance from the house. They worked out a daily routine that would keep me occupied from sunrise to sunset. I was expected to rise seven in the morning and purchase the day's supply of fresh bread. After breakfast, my aunt readied a list of things for me to buy at the grocer's. I was to go there on my way from delivering their eldest child, a little girl barely six years old, to school. When I returned from the grocery, the younger girl would be dressed waiting for me to take her for an airing. I was to keep her out until it was time for the noonday meal. The little girl was scarcely two years old and lacked the strength to walk so I had to carry her in my arms most of the time.

After the midday meal, my uncle sent me into town to deliver garments to his customers. On the way home, I was to buy items for the tailor shop: buttons, tapes, threads of various colors and other sundry supplies. By the time I returned the journeymen tailors had concluded their day's work and were preparing to go home, but that was when my work really started. When I cleaned up the shop, my uncle decided I hadn't done enough for the day. He taught me to rip apart old garments, which he would turn and sew together again, thus saving his clients the cost of new material. I found it all very difficult but I didn't have the boldness to protest. I did what I was told. Nevertheless, I resented having been turned into a servant and errand boy instead of being taught the trade.

My situation worsened appreciably when Aunt Genendl gave birth to her third child, for my burden became twice as heavy. What hurt most was that until then I was free on Saturdays to meet with friends and spend the day at the water's edge, rowing, swimming and having fun. This lifted my spirits and gave me the strength to endure the week's work. I always looked forward to Saturday. Now my aunt and uncle robbed me of my one day off as well. My aunt and uncle were still comparatively young and wanted to enjoy themselves. Every Saturday they went away for the day sometimes returning after midnight while I was left to care for the children. When I could no longer suffer the injustice, I turned to my Aunt Ethel and poured out all my bitter feelings. I implored her to do something to relieve me of my bondage.

Aunt Ethel was very good-natured and sensitive to people's suffering. We thought of her as the mother of the family and always turned to her for help. As soon as I finished telling her of my plight, she rushed me to her sister's house to put an end to my desperate situation. When we approached the yard, I told my aunt that I would prefer not to be present when she has words with her sister. I would feel very uncomfortable, and my presence might even aggravate matters. Aunt Ethel agreed with me and went upstairs by herself. I stayed down in the yard and impatiently awaited the outcome of her intervention. While I waited, I could hear the sisters trying to outshout each other. Although their yelling could be heard for a considerable distance, I couldn't make out the words. After some time, I heard Aunt Ethel hurry down the stairs. She was furious. She put one arm across my shoulder and rushed me along beside her, continuing her momentum. Half running and half stepping briskly, she began talking to me. She grew calmer and spoke with deliberation.

"From this day on you'll not have to be their servant and you won't have to be nursemaid to their children. I've put an end to all that."

I returned to grandfather's house with my aunt. Grandfather no longer protested my staying in his house, nor did he demand that I return to *heder* and continue my studies. His one stipulation was that I adhere strictly to Jewish law. That meant I would have to pray three times a day and accompany him to the house of prayer on the Sabbath. It also meant I would be expected to remain at home on Saturday afternoons and study the *Ethics of the Fathers*. None of this would be difficult for me and I promised I'd be careful to do everything properly just so I could remain at home with him.

When several weeks passed, and grandfather saw that I kept to my promises, he became respectful and loving. As for concern for the future, grandfather turned me over to Uncle Shimon, who was to teach me to spin lisle thread on the knitting machines in his little stocking factory.

I sat on a low stool all day long. I turned a large wooden wheel with my right hand while, with the left, I guided the thread as it wound from a pulley holding a skein of yarn onto a large wooden spool. I had to feed the thread regularly and evenly so that the thread didn't pile up to one side of the spool. If the thread didn't wind onto the spool evenly, it would catch at the "hilly" spot as it was being knitted into the stocking and would tear. When that happened, the unfinished stocking would fall out of the machine and the machine would have to be re-threaded. This represented a considerable loss of time and effort.

I did finally learn to do the work and serviced two knitting machines. I worked hard but all I ever received for my effort were my meals. My bed was a pallet of straw, which scarcely fit into the space between a closet and a large stove built of tiles. I had to use an old greatcoat of my grandfather's as cover. Every night, I would collapse of weariness and it would be difficult for me to get up in the morning. Uncle Shimon would wake me before anyone else because I was expected to say morning prayers before going to work. I had to say my prayers at the top of my lungs so that grandfather could hear that I didn't—God forbid—skip a single word in the prayer book.

Sometimes, when grandfather went into another room, I did skip, and whole verses at that. If I spent too much time at prayer, I would find it difficult to catch up with my work. On such days, the stocking knitters would snatch half-filled spools from the wheel and cause me to be behind all day. On more than one occasion, when I thought grandfather had left for the synagogue, I hurriedly took off my phylacteries so I could get right to work. Grandfather would suddenly appear from the other room figuring that I removed the phylacteries too soon.

"I see you only put your *tefillin* on to measure whether your head has swelled any!"

Despite all the hard work, my uncle's little factory failed to provide a sufficient income to feed our large family. The two machines I served didn't produce enough, so Uncle Shimon decided to borrow some money from the Jewish Free Loan Society of Grodzisk to buy a third machine, hoping to increase his revenue. Another machine meant a third more work for me. Instead of working twelve hours a day, I was now working sixteen. Uncle Shimon and Aunt Ethel also labored sixteen hours a day but the situation grew many times worse when it should have been improving.

Grandfather took ill and we used up more money in physician's fees than was coming in. The small town doctors were unable to diagnose his illness and recommended a specialist in Warsaw. The Warsaw specialist determined that the patient had stomach cancer. Grandfather became weaker day by day because he couldn't digest anything and immediately threw up anything he ate. He couldn't stand up and had to remain in bed. He became terribly emaciated, just skin and bones, and it was painful to look at him. He was bedridden for two long years until he quietly passed away.

All the Jews in town escorted him to his final resting-place. They all knew him and they hastened to pay their last respects. Not only was he the warden of the Talmud Torah of Grodzisk, he was also the reader of the law and leader of the prayers in the synagogue. He taught all the Jews of Grodzisk the passages of the Talmud and Mishnah. To this day, no one from the town of Grodzisk has forgotten the name with which he was most respectfully addressed: "Yitzhak Gabe" (Yitzhak, the warden).

After grandfather's death everything went downhill. Women no longer wore stockings made of lisle thread. Large modern factories for the manufacture of silk stockings sprang up and the small shops, in which eighty per cent of the Jews of Grodzisk had earned their livelihood, began to fail.

Uncle Shimon used to go to Warsaw once a week to sell the finished hosiery and bring back a supply of yarn. Now, instead of disposing of his goods, he was returning with half the bundles unsold. Anything that he didn't succeed in selling he had to offer at cost. Things soon came to such a pass that there was scarcely any bread in the house. We would buy various products on credit, but after a while the storekeeper found ways to refuse us any more on trust.

The situation was doubly painful for me. Not only did I feel as hungry as everyone else did, but I began to see myself as an extra burden to my uncle and his family.

One day, upon arising, I announced that I was going to go to Warsaw on foot and seek employment. With tears in her eyes, my aunt begged me not to go, saying that I wouldn't survive all by myself in the big city. But I was adamant. I told her she shouldn't worry. I wouldn't get lost. In any case, I was an unnecessary burden and the family would get along better without me.

My aunt took out their last morsel of bread and offered it to me for my long journey. I refused, insisting that she put it aside for herself and the children. Then I simply walked away from the town in which I had lived for three years.

Chapter 3

Late that night I arrived at the home of my Warsaw grandfather. My grandfather and my brother sat at the table reading a Yiddish newspaper by the light of a large kerosene lamp hanging from the ceiling directly over the table. When I appeared in the doorway, I was greeted with looks of astonishment. My step-grandmother immediately voiced an uneasy reproof.

"So you've run away again, have you?"

"No!" I responded immediately, but my glances were upon my grandfather and brother.

"I didn't run away this time. I left Grodzisk for good reason and with everyone's consent. After grandfather's death, I felt I no longer had a right to eat the bread of my father's sister and her impoverished family, especially when they have nothing to eat themselves. I ask nothing of you other than that you allow me to sleep here until I find work and am able to take care of my needs. I haven't anyone else to whom I can turn."

My brother ran up to me, put his arms around me and pressed me to him, his eyes filling with tears. Grandfather's eyes, too, were moist with tears as he approached me and we kissed each other.

"God forbid, no one's going to throw you out."

Then, turning his glance toward my step-grandmother, he said:

"If I can support your children, I can certainly take care of one of my daughter's orphans. No one can stop me from doing that."

My step-grandmother still wasn't reassured, but her tone was milder.

"And where do you propose to put him—on your head?"

"He'll sleep with me and Ben Tsion," grandfather replied, decisively.

I went to wash up. I then put on one of my brother's shirts, which he handed me, and lay down at the feet of my grandfather and brother to spend the night. In the morning, I rose with grandfather and my brother.

Ben Tsion kept his food separate from the others. He boiled up some tea, spread some jam on bread, and we shared his breakfast. He had decided not to partake of anything my step-grandmother cooked or served. By so doing he hoped to help maintain domestic peace in grandfather's home. I, too, Ben Tsion advised, should follow the same course for as long as I found it necessary to stay.

"So long as we don't touch anything of hers, things will be more or less peaceful."

I thoroughly agreed and assured him I would follow his example.

Before leaving for work, my brother handed me several *zloty* to buy food for the evening meal. If possible, I was to try to cook something. He said that there was no reason for me to feel ill at ease in the kitchen since he was contributing towards the cost of the coal used in the cook-stove. He even had his own pots and dishes. Our step-grandmother could have no complaints as long as he continued to pay for everything.

Grandfather made sure my step-grandmother didn't see him place several *zloty* in my hand before he went to work. I was to buy whatever I needed, he said.

I went out into the street, bought a newspaper, and turned to the advertisement pages to see if I could find work. I saw a notice for a boy seeking to learn the tailor's trade at a shop at Number 47 Mila Street. I immediately ran over to that address. The tailor measured me with his eyes and asked me how old I was.

"Fourteen," I replied.

"Where do you live?"

"At Niska Number 5"

"Do you have parents?"

"No. I live with my grandfather."

"Good," he replied. "Let's see what you can do. First of all, take the trash down to the waste bin in the yard. On the way back buy two dozen buttons this size."

He gave me some money and a sample button. I carried down the rubbish and brought him the buttons he wanted. On the way back, I figured him to be the same kind of businessman as my uncle in Grodzisk. "No bread would be baked from this corn," I thought.

Upon my return, he scolded me for having taken too long. I apologized, saying I would run faster next time. Feeling a bit bolder, I inquired as to how much I would be paid for a week's work.

"See here," he said irritably, "he's asking about money even before I know what he can do."

From the other room came the sound of a woman's voice and the hubbub of small children. The woman yelled out to her husband:

"Hayim, send the boy in here and have him carry down the chamber pot! It's full!"

The man rushed into the bedroom, brought out a full night pot, handed it to me and ordered me to take it down to the water closet in the yard. The stench from the potty assailed my nose and had me about to vomit. I rushed from the room pot in hand and slammed the door behind me. Then, with all my might, I hurled the chamber pot against the door and hurried down the stairs out onto the street, and continued running until I was far from the tailor's house.

In the days that followed, I tried many different jobs and found nothing I could stand doing that would pay enough to support my miserable existence. I finally obtained a position with a tailor who was to pay me three *zloty* per week. It would pay my expenses for only two days. However, in this shop I was to learn the trade. What's more, after work, I delivered the finished garments to our clients. The tips I earned amounted to twice what my employer paid.

Ben Tsion and I pooled our resources to pay for the food we shared. Our diet was the same day in and day out. For breakfast we had bread, prune jam, and tea. For the midday meal we went home for an hour, ate some bread and some herring and then took turns putting our mouths under the water faucet to take in as much water as we could to fill our stomachs. Whichever one of us came home first after the day's work, quickly peeled a few potatoes and made potato soup, which we ate with a piece of bread. We were satisfied with that and thanked God for what little we had.

My brother had joined the Palestine pioneer movement (Hekholuts), in which he was very active. On Saturdays, I went along with him to their meetings, where we joined with other members in dancing the *hora* and singing Hebrew songs. I kept asking him to tell me what happened to our little sister after she was sent away to be nursed by a stranger, but I never received a real answer. Finally, while walking home from a social gathering arranged by the Hekholutz, I pressed Ben Tsion on the subject, demanding that he tell me the truth concerning this mystery which gave me no rest.

Ben Tsion's eyes clouded over as he looked at me, indicating that he found the subject too painful to discuss. After a long silence, he coughed lightly, as if to clear his throat of the choking sensation that seemed to be there, and began to tell me the story in a trembling voice.

"Grandfather and the rest of the family thought you were too young to be told of the tragedy that befell our little sister. However, you're old enough now to know the awful truth. During the three years that she was in the care of the wet-nurse in Grodzisk, she was developing nicely. But when father left us, he stopped paying the woman. Like us, our little sister suffered with hunger as did her nurse and her own child. Feygele became ill of malnourishment and was sent to a Catholic hospital in Warsaw. She received treatment but was never discharged.

Uncle Simkhe would go there occasionally and would request permission to take her home, but the nuns said that since she had no home she'd be better off in their care. When he insisted, they said that only her parents could ask for her discharge and that an uncle had no right to her.

Grandpa didn't visit her because the walls of the hospital had crosses and paintings of Jesus hanging on them, making the institution an 'unclean' place. From his perspective, nothing could be worse. He just received reports from Uncle Simkhe whenever he visited, and, from time to time, he received a letter from the nuns, informing him that she was well and lacked for nothing. Then, after the nuns failed to write for a long time, there came a letter stating that the child had died at the age of six. Since she had no parents, they had taken care of the burial themselves. The matter was now closed, the letter said."

To my grandfather and uncle these statements seemed suspicious. My uncle went to find out where and when the child was buried. This time even grandfather went along to the foundling hospital determined to find out what became of the child. They were told that no information would be available to them until the nun in charge returned in two weeks and everything would be explained then.

When grandfather and my uncle returned two weeks later, they found the doors and gates locked, and to this day it hasn't been possible to ascertain the child's fate. Our family came to be convinced that the nuns stole the child, had her christened, converted and, as a result, she was lost to us forever—one more casualty of our father's merciless conduct toward his children.

Our poverty-stricken life continued. Ben Tsion was employed in the manufacture of women's pocketbooks and was earning a good deal more than I was. From time to time, he would help me by buying me a pair of shoes, a shirt, or a pair of trousers. Whenever he purchased something, he remembered to buy something for his younger brother for I would never have been able to get myself anything to wear from my own meager earnings.

As time went on, Ben Tsion's work situation improved. Soon, he earned enough to allow himself a Sabbath meal at one of the restaurants maintained by the various workers' party locals, and he would take me with him. One such restaurant was at Number 23 Karmelicka Street. It belonged to the Left Poale-Zion. Another was at Bundist headquarters, Number 9 Pszejasd. The Right Poale-Zion operated a restaurant at Number 14 Gensia. For sixty *groschen* one could obtain a sumptuous meal consisting of tasty soup, a good-sized portion of meat with two or three vegetables, a serving of bread, and dessert. Such meals gave us strength enough for a week.

One day, Ben Tsion returned from work with a letter in his hands and he was beaming. The letter was from father, who sent it to Ben Tsion's place of employment. According to my brother, here is what happened: One of the men who worked with Ben Tsion was a brother of the owner. He decided to go to Brussels, Belgium to live and to look for work at his trade. Some of his friends recommended that he apply to an acquaintance of theirs that owned a pocketbook factory. When he arrived at the address given him, the owner asked him many questions.

"Where are you from?"

"From Warsaw."

"Are you a pocketbook maker?"

"Yes, certainly. I learned the trade at my brother's factory in Warsaw."

The owner remarked that he had two sons who were probably living in Warsaw.

"At what address?" the young man asked. "Warsaw is a large city but perhaps I know them."

"I don't know, the older one should be about eighteen and the other one is two years younger."

"What are their names? Perhaps I've met them."

"The older one is Ben Tsion and the other one is…"

"Wait a minute! The older one is Ben Tsion Altman, the same surname as you. It must be your older son who works for my brother. And I do recall hearing him say that his father had gone away and that he didn't know where to look for him."

Of course, my father wanted our address, but the young man didn't have it. Instead, he gave him his brother's, and that was how the letter managed to reach us.

Ben Tsion opened the letter and began reading it aloud. It was written in a very moving tone, and he was forced to interrupt his reading several times in order to swallow the lump in his throat and brush away his tears. We listened silently, anxious to catch every word of what sounded like a confession of past sins.

"My poor, dear children," the letter began. "I still can't believe the great miracle that's occurred. It's as though a messenger from God has returned my children to me. You may be bare and destitute, but you are still in God's image. Oh, how much suffering and sorrow I must have caused you when I left you so many years ago. I'll never be able to forgive myself for the great wrong I've done you. Neither will I ever understand the wild madness that came over me and caused me to commit such terrible crimes against you. How could I ever have abandoned such little swallows as you were?

Ever since then, I've been driven to wander from place to place, over land and sea, but nowhere could I find a place to rest. It must have been heaven's punishment for my sins against you.

Please write to me and tell me whether you're in good health and what you've been doing. I promise you that from this day forward I shall do everything in my power to bring happiness and comfort back into your life, so that you may put all your suffering behind you."

We sent off a long detailed letter describing the miserable circumstances of our lives. A short time later, we received an answer in which several hundred francs were enclosed. This second letter recounted more of our father's wanderings up to the time he arrived in Belgium and settled in Brussels. His second wife followed after and brought some money with her, which they used to set up a lady's pocketbook factory. Eventually, his wife bore him a daughter who was now seven years old. He believed that he would soon be able to send us papers permitting us to emmigrate to Belgium so that we might finally be reunited and live as a normal happy family.

Ben Tsion and I used the money for some new clothing. We each purchased new suits, new shoes, new shirts and even new overcoats. Since the Passover holidays were approaching, we also gave our step-grandmother fifty *zloty* so that she might include us in her plans for the holiday. That way we could enjoy the holidays and make it unnecessary to go looking for a restaurant that served holiday meals.

The economic situation in Poland worsened daily. Workers in small Jewish factories were being discharged for there was scarcely sufficient work for the owners let alone journeymen assistants. For the same reason, I was obliged to look for new work for whenever I was discharged I had no choice but to immediately seek alternative employment.

At times, I would work for a tailor; another time I worked at pocket-books. I was once employed at constructing shipping crates for use in the export of goods and on other occasions, other things. During the intervals between jobs, I suffered from hunger.

When Ben Tsion lost his job, he went to Kielce to join a *kibbutz*. There he would learn agricultural pioneering skills (*hakhshara*) in anticipation of emigration to Palestine.

After many weeks of unemployment, I finally obtained a good position in a chocolate factory called "Pluto's." For this I was indebted to my good friend Yosl Martin. He lived in the same court as I did and his parents were very wealthy people who owned three men's clothing stores in Warsaw. Thanks to the efforts of Yosl's father, I was given a job to start at twenty *zloty* per week. A man with a family to support seldom earned that much. Whenever there was overtime work, I would bring home close to double the agreed upon amount.

However, there was a drawback to the position. My work at Pluto's was to construct thin plywood boxes in which chocolates were packed, and for that, I was needed only four months out of the year. During the other eight months, I was obliged to seek other employment.

Sometimes, when I was out of work, my friend Yosl would try to get his brothers, who ran the stores, to hire me on busy days. This gave me the opportunity to earn a little more. Several times it saved my life since there was little other work to be had.

Yosl's parents, his five brothers and two sisters were a very nice, refined family. Their apartment consisted of six lavishly furnished rooms. They had crystal chandeliers and couches of genuine leather. Heavy draperies hung in every room. The floors were covered with thick Persian rugs woven in magnificent splendid patterns. I spent many evenings at my friend's house during the long winter months. We played cards or dominos or just talked, telling each other stories or recounting our experiences. It felt pleasant and warm in the spacious rooms of their well-heated apartment.

Once I started to work at Pluto's, I began to spend more freely. I bought myself better clothing, joined a sports club called Gwiazda, and acquired a pair of hockey skates and a bicycle. I took ice-skating lessons, participated in bicycle races and spent more of my time enjoying myself. No longer wanting to be bothered cooking for myself, I began eating in restaurants regularly. For the time being, I was able to afford all those things. Moreover, my father would send me several hundred francs for the holidays and I would spend all of that money on clothing. My father was also in the process of filing papers that would make it possible for me to go to Belgium.

Three of us would routinely go skating together, Yosl, his sister Anka and me. Not only did we spend time on the ice together but we also went to the cinema or took a steamer to Mloczin, a two-hour trip out of Warsaw on a luxury ship along the Wisla, with music and dancing all the way. In Mloczin, we disembarked to walk in the fields and in the thick woods there. Several hours later, we would return to Warsaw on the same steamer.

After we spent a lot of time together, I realized that, quite involuntarily, I had fallen in love with the dark, gentle and attractive Anka.

She was three years younger than I was. Slender and pleasantly built, she had black wavy hair and glowing black eyes. The features of her light alabaster face were lovely and refined. Without my even having been aware of what was happening, she lit a fire in my boyish heart. However, knowing that we were of two different worlds, and that I would never find my happiness with her, I attempted to stifle such feelings, but in vain.

When I decided to distance myself from her, I asked Yosl not to take Anka along when we arranged to meet. That way, I said, we could count on having more time to ourselves during our free hours. After that, Yosl and I would go to Marymont, a new town that was being built just then. We would take the bus there and then go rowing or ride the swings and carousels. I did everything to try to forget her but the more I tried to forget, the more Anka appeared in my imagination in all her splendor, giving me no rest. I suffered a torturous longing for her and was unable to sleep. I sat up half the night writing poems in which I tried to express my yearnings and in which I celebrated her beauty and grace. I finally succumbed to Cupid, who shot his arrows into my young heart and wounded it.

It became a habit for me to wait at a gateway across the street from the Felicia trade school, which Anka attended. I waited on the corner of Nowolipka and Karmelicka. At exactly two o'clock, the girls came streaming out on their way home. When my searching eyes saw Anka leave through the school gate, my heart began beating so rapidly I was afraid it was about to leap from its place. I left my hiding place and followed her, at a distance, until she separated from her class-mates. Then I would suddenly appear before her as if I just came up out of the ground and would pretend that I bumped into her acci-dentally. We would then go home together. As we parted one day, I inquired whether she would like to go skating with me on Saturday. After a pause, she agreed.

Once again, we began to spend time together. We went to the Yiddish Theater, to the cinema and, on winter days, we spent time on the ice. I felt happy but unhappy, a mixture of two opposing emotions. I was happy when I felt her sitting close to me, our hands clasped. I was unhappy knowing that this dream would never be realized, that she could never belong to me because I would never be able to provide her the kind of life to which she was accustomed.

We were meeting without the knowledge of my friend Yosl or the rest of her family. Anka and I knew we were growing more attached to one another. With each day that passed, I felt more fearful that the closer Anka and I got, the briefer our happiness would be. Events did indeed take the turn that my intuition foretold.

To begin with, at the end of the season, I lost my job at Pluto's. When I was discharged, I was once again left high and dry. I was cut off from my brief moment of happiness just as surely as if an axe had been used. I upbraided myself for having lived so extravagantly while I was earning good wages and for not giving any thought to the dark days when I would have no means of subsistence. I wandered from street to street looking for employment, but found it impossible. I went hungry for days at a time. I was ashamed to meet friends for I was afraid they'd be able to tell. This was for me a prospect worse than death. My reluctance to come face to face with Anka was even greater.

At about that time, grandfather suddenly became ill. He suffered terrible abdominal pains. Half-unconscious, he was hurriedly removed to hospital and no one was allowed to visit him.

I recall when I went to the hospital to see him. I wasn't allowed to enter but could only stand in an anteroom and look in through a wide glass door. He was obviously in great pain. He noticed me and called me by name several times. I tore from the spot and was about to run to him when a nurse stopped me and pushed me out of the room. I could hear grandfather murmuring through his groans:

"My poor little orphan! My poor little orphan!"

The nurse informed me that my grandfather would have to be operated upon immediately and that it was time for me to leave. The next day, I learned that I lost my beloved grandfather and I was once again left wretched, forlorn and hungry.

On the way back from grandfather's funeral, uncle Simkhe noticed my appearance and realized how hungry, despondent and disconsolate I was. He took me home with him where I remained until the period of mourning was over. Then he took me to the home of my great-aunt Rochl Grinshpan, a sister of my grandfather.

Aunt Rochl was a widow and lived with her two sons at Number 71 Niska Street where they had one small room. Uncle Simkhe offered her ten *zloty* a month to provide me a spot to lay my head at night. He paid for the first month after which I was to take on the obligation as soon as I found work.

My great-aunt immediately purchased two large sacks, sewed them together, and made me a straw-filled mattress. She also made a pillow tick of a smaller sack, which she likewise filled with straw. I slept on the floor for there was no room for an additional bed. There already were two beds in that small room, one for her and the other for her two sons.

I would get up early in the morning and spend the day dragging myself through the streets of Warsaw to look for employment. I rejected the thought of writing to my father about my wretched situation so that he might send me some money in mid year and not just on those two or three occasions when he sent funds with which to purchase clothing. I was too proud to burden him and become dependent on him. Anyway, I didn't feel close enough to him. It seemed to me preferable to just die of hunger.

One day as I was walking along dejected and close to desperation, I encountered Yosl, who happened to be strolling along with two friends. He stopped me and immediately began to reproach me for having avoided him and for staying away from my friends.

"Everyone's asking for you and no one knows what has become of you. I don't know what to tell people when they ask after you. The only thing I can say is that I haven't seen you for several weeks."

Instead of answering, I felt my eyes overflow with tears. There wasn't need for me to tell my dear friend anything after that. It was all too obvious in my face, hunger having drawn it thin and sallow. Seeing my tear filled eyes, Yosl asked:

"Are you crying?"

"Yes, I'm crying," I answered helplessly, "I've just lost my grandfather, the most precious thing in my life."

But Yosl knew that couldn't be the whole explanation. He immediately took leave of his friends and led me into a coffee shop, where he ordered buttered rolls, some cheese, and coffee. After I ate and felt somewhat strengthened, I thanked him and we began a friendly conversation. I opened my heart to him and he heard me out with much feeling and sympathy. He told me the friends with whom he just parted were members of the Pioneers, the Communist youth party. He too joined the organization that was fighting for a society, in which everyone would be equal, where there wouldn't be rich and poor.

"And if we had a society like that in Poland, you would never lose your job, nor have to suffer hunger. You would always have what you need and enjoy a standard of living equal to that of every other citizen."

The Communist Party was illegal in Poland. Whenever a communist was arrested, he was given a jail sentence of many years' duration and underwent terrible torture while imprisoned. Despite such dangers, I was captivated by the beautiful avowals of liberty, equality, and brotherhood. I followed the example of my dear friend Yosl. I became a member of the Pioneer organization.

Before long, I threw myself into party work with fire and zeal and participated very actively in its work. We met every evening under the clock on Gensza Street at the corner of Zamenhof. From there, we went to a meeting at the home of a member. Each meeting was at a

different person's house so that the police wouldn't suspect us of communist activity.

We organized an educational unit, which met in the small office of a
coal company owned by the father of Mayer Zakshnayder (Mayer
managed the coal yard for his father). We met there two or three times
a week to teach ourselves world history, political economy and the history of communism. I got along well with my new party friends and
participated in all their demonstrations. I also carried out technical
tasks, such as pasting up posters on walls along the streets of Warsaw. I
hung small red flags bearing communist slogans on the electric trolley
cars, and distributed small receipt pads to be used in the raising of
funds to assist prisoners languishing in jail for their political activities.

The party assigned our unit to paste up placards in the particular
quarter where we lived. As soon as we received the posters, which bore
slogans against the government, we divided up the work. Yosl was to
carry the posters and have them ready for hanging. I carried a small
bucket of paste and a short brush with which I applied the paste to the
walls upon which Yosl then affixed the posters. The others in our group
stood watch at all four corners of the street intersection. If they saw
anything suspicious, such as an approaching policeman or secret agent
in civilian dress, they called out "Moishe." This was our prearranged
warning signal in case anything went amiss.

One time, we had only a few more posters to hang when we heard the
call: "Moishe! Moishe!" I was in the process of applying paste to part of
a wide structure shaped like an immense barrel. Kiosks were to be
found on many Warsaw streets, where they served as display stands for
all sorts of posters, theatre playbills and commercial notices. Almost
immediately, I saw a man in blue uniform positioning himself behind
me with the intention of catching either Yosl or me. I pushed Yosl aside,
shouting for him to run. Simultaneously, I shoved the pail full of paste
right into the policeman's face and began running like the wind, without looking back. I ran until I was out of breath. Still gasping, I stopped,

looked around, and saw that I put several blocks behind me. Observing that there was no one following me, I felt reassured and calmly walked over to where we agreed to meet should any such thing occur. I wasn't always so lucky.

There was another incident, which I recall vividly. I was participating in a huge demonstration to mark the anniversary of the October Revolution. Hundreds of us marched with red flags and transparencies bearing mottoes appealing to the populace and urging a revolution in Poland. Mila Street was crowded with communist demonstrators when suddenly hundreds of policemen came rushing out of the building yards. They had steel helmets on and were armed with guns, which they began to fire without warning, aiming directly at the crowds of demonstrators. Many a victim fell that day. Among the dead and wounded there was a Pioneer, a member of our section. His name was Leybele Sanik and he was only sixteen.

Demonstrators started running in every direction, each one hoping to escape into a nearby gateway. As they ran toward the gates, the police hit them over their heads with the stocks of their rifles. I also ran into the nearest courtyard and up the stairs to the top floor. The janitor slammed the gates closed behind us. When the police finished with the demonstrators on the street, the janitors opened the gates for them. In an angry rage, the police rushed up the staircases in pursuit of those who ran up to hide. Hearing the police hurtling up the stairs, we tore open the door to the attic, barricaded ourselves behind the door, and sought out a corner of the attic to hide in. But it was no use. The police broke down the door with their rifle butts, and then used the butts to hit us over the head as they drove us down the stairs onto the streets. In the street, trucks stood waiting to transport us to the prison known as "Danieliszewska." We were detained for forty-eight hours, interrogated and freed only after all charges were filed and a date set for trial.

The trial was held several months later in a courtroom on Miadowa Street. Two of my friends and I who were less than eighteen years old were sentenced to a prison term of one year but the sentence was suspended for three years. If, during that time, our conduct proved satisfactory the sentence would be lifted. If not, we would face a new trial and be obliged to serve the one-year sentence.

Ben Tsion returned from his pioneer training (*hakhshara*). His name was placed on a list entitling him to receive a certificate, which would make him eligible to emmigrate to Israel. But since there were great many applicants on the list, and the British government (the mandating power) consistently issued only a very few certificates, many of the pioneers (*halutzim*) would wait years for their turn.

Because my brother was a very loyal, idealistic *halutz*, he was engaged by the Warsaw Center for *Hakhshara* at Number 13 Orla Street to travel about the country for the purpose of organizing *kibbutzim* in some of the Polish villages. There the *halutzim* were to be taught agricultural skills in preparation for work in the *kibbutzim* or wherever they were to be assigned work in Palestine.

My brother would scout rural areas, where there were large land-holders, and tried to enter into contract with them regarding the employment of Jewish *halutzim* so that they might learn farm work. Such farms were called *hakhshara* farms. The *halutzim* worked hard for their meals and board and were satisfied so long as they had practice in the strenuous chores that would help them realize their dream of building a Jewish homeland. Because of his new profession, Ben Tsion traveled continuously so that I seldom saw him.

In 1934, he came to see me for the last time. He received his certificate and made all necessary arrangements for journeying to Palestine. I received his announcement with mixed feelings. Who knows, I thought, whether I shall ever again, in my life, see my brother with whom I've shared so much pain and suffering. On the other hand, I was happy that he finally attained his goal and was going to the much yearned-for land of his dreams.

I saw him to his train. Hundreds of *halutzim* were gathered there to bid farewell to the thirty or so fortunate enough to have been granted certificates. They sang Hebrew songs, linked arms and shoulders and danced the traditional *hora*, celebrating the final minutes of the departure of their comrades. I didn't participate in the dancing and singing. How could I have cared when I was seeing my brother off for the last time? I couldn't take my eyes from off my brother for even a moment that evening. I felt as if half my being was about to be torn away. I stood downcast as though my entire world had been destroyed.

When, shortly before departure, everyone began saying their good-byes, I clung to my brother with all my strength, showered him with kisses and, with a trembling voice, begged him to please: "Remember! Don't forget me!"

The crowd spontaneously began to sing the *Hatikva*, but I stood motionless, paralyzed. I felt as though the end was near. Ben Tsion was the last to board the train. He paused on the little step of his car, and looked at me with pity in his eyes. The train commenced to move to the strains of *Hatikva*. Instinctively, I ran alongside Ben Tsion who was still standing on the step. He had one hand on the railing and kept waving to me with the other until the train developed speed and disappeared into the darkness of night.

Chapter 4

After a considerable time had passed, my sadness began gradually to dissipate and my mind reawakened to the reality of continuing life. With even more enthusiasm and zeal than before, I threw myself into party activities. My sadness and longing for my brother was swallowed up in the storm and whirl of that life.

I obtained employment again and would come home tired every evening. Nevertheless, after a hurried meal, I would return to the street where my party co-workers were waiting. Late at night, after we performed our party-mandated duties, I would lie down wearily on my straw mat and sleep through the night like a stone until morning light woke me to a new day of work. Time ran its course in this difficult routine.

I received letters from Ben Tsion regularly. He wrote that he was an agricultural worker on a *kibbutz*. During the day, he labored in the field under the burning sun. At night, he stood guard, gun in hand, to protect the *kibbutz* from attack by marauding Arab assassins.

Eventually, my father sent me the long awaited papers that would facilitate my entrance to Belgium. However, to obtain a visa to Belgium, I needed to attach a character reference addressed to the Belgian Consulate. And that's where my difficulties began. Since I was awaiting trial, the court wouldn't allow me to obtain the recommendation. I had to wait the full three years of probation before I could be exonerated and entitled to a reference. I ran from one governmental office to another and wrote numerous appeals but to no avail. I became discouraged and almost gave up hope of ever leaving Poland.

During the winter months, I again went to work for Pluto's and earned good wages. When that work ended, I was always able to find work with a box-maker named Motl Steinlauf, in whose shop plywood barrels and crates for use in exporting various kinds of goods were manufactured. He employed a number of young men my age. Singing and fun always accompanied the work.

At noon, we gathered around the great, round stove furnace at which the wood was shaped into curved staves for making barrels. We all ate our meals there and maintained a jolly mood by joshing and bantering with one another.

One of the factory employees was a niece of the owner. She was four-teen years old and still in school, but she came after school to help her uncle by tending the telephone and performing clerical duties. Andzia was a gorgeous young girl. All the young men vied with one another in complimenting her and attempting to set up a rendezvous. But she refused them all.

As we sat about the stove eating our midday meal, each man would brag that he had as good as received a promise from Andzia that she would go out with him. Everyone knew, of course, that these were idle boasts. One day, as we sat around the stove fooling around in this manner, I spoke up:

"Give me till Saturday and I'll set up a rendezvous with the pretty Miss Andzia."

Everyone laughed loudly and made fun of me. After going on in this vein for a while, they began to demand that I make a wager and not just brag.

"Very well. I'll bet if you insist."

"Bet a week's wages," someone called out.

"A week's wages is a bit much, but I'll risk a day's earnings."

They took me at my word and the wager was on.

I thought about how I might win the bet. At that time, the new talkie *I'm In Heaven* with Ginger Rogers and Fred Astaire was playing at the magnificent Passage Theatre on Senatorska Street. I went there and purchased two advance tickets for a Saturday performance. The next day, I went to the office where Miss Andzia worked. I showed her the tickets of admission, and asked her to see the movie with me on Saturday afternoon. I said that if she refused, I'd be out the price of a ticket and that it would be a shame to waste a ticket to such a wonderful movie.

At first, she wouldn't hear of it. After much discussion, she said she had never been out with a boy before and didn't want to go out with me either. "I understand," I replied, "but there's a first time for everything, so why not me? I'm only asking just this once so as not to lose the bet."

I assured her that she wouldn't come to harm, and that I would call for her at home and take her back after the performance. She answered that she couldn't make any promises till she got her mother's permission.

"Very well," I responded. "Do ask your parents and let them know with whom you're going and where I'm taking you."

On the following day, as I stood at my workbench, Andzia came up to me blushing, and whispered in my ear. At two o'clock Saturday she would be at the gate to her house and if I arrived promptly, we could go out together. When the fellows in the shop saw us whispering, they wanted to know what we were about. I refused to say for fear that one wrong word might spoil everything.

After the film, we took a long walk home. The spectacular singing and dancing had us so enthused we kept talking about it all the way. As we said goodbye, I asked whether she would be reluctant to meet with me again. "No," she replied, with a smile and thanked me for the pleasant afternoon. I attempted to kiss her but she blushed and eluded my arms. Turning away quickly, she rushed up the flight of stairs to where she lived.

On our days off, we took walks together and visited with some of my friends or we took a tram to some of her friends. We gradually grew closer and what started out as a joke became serious. Three years later Andzia became my dear bride with whom I've lived happily ever since.

I began to visit her at home where I met her parents and her two sisters. The older one was Bella, the younger, Halinka. Andzia was between them in age. They all lived in a single room on Number 71 Dzelna Street, which was too crowded for a family of five. When she graduated from school Hanele (Andzia) went to work as a milliner.

She decided to save her earnings, and when she had acquired several hundred *zloty*, she gave the money to her parents so they might rent a larger place. They expended a great deal of time and effort in finding a larger and more attractive apartment at Ogrodowa, Number 28. It had three pleasant, spacious rooms and all the latest in accommodations. I went there every day after work and spent the entire evening in Hanele's company. On Fridays or Saturdays we invited our friends up for *bibkes* (little get togethers), and entertained ourselves far into the night.

After spending three years in Palestine, Ben Tsion managed to take an airplane trip back to Poland. He stayed several weeks so that we could have some time together and enjoy one another's company. I introduced Hanele, her parents and her sisters to him. He liked them very much and teasingly took to calling Hanele "Little Goat." One day, he took us to a photographer's studio and had us all photographed, and took some of the portraits along with him for remembrance.

Shortly after my brother's return to Palestine, my stepmother came to visit and find out why I was unable to obtain the character reference needed for a visa to Belgium. Hanele, her family, and I went to the railroad station to meet my stepmother. Then we got into a taxi which she directed go to her old address at Number 66 Nowolipje, where her mute aunt still lived, and where she intended to stay the eight days of her visit. While we were still in the taxi, she made it plain that she wasn't satisfied with us. She asked bluntly why I made a commitment to this girl, when I was "neither here nor there." Her remarks hurt us deeply but, for courtesy's sake, we made little of them, rude as they were. We drove up to the house and I carried her suitcases up and arranged to be there again early the next day to talk everything over at leisure.

On the way back to Hanele's house, we talked about our guest, who hadn't made a good impression on any of us. I tried to make excuses for my stepmother saying she was tired after her long journey. She was impolite because she was nervous. After some rest, she would surely take a different tone. When I came to pick her up the next morning, she was well rested. She asked that I take her where she could buy some Jewish salami. She remembered its taste from her old Warsaw days, and had a yearning for some. We could talk there.

I took her to Smocza Street, where we found a table at Havele's Famous Wurst Place, and made ourselves comfortable. My stepmother launched into an account of herself and my father. From my father's letters, I already knew of the things she mentioned. What I didn't know was that my father had changed occupations. Ladies' pocketbooks were no longer in fashion and he therefore opened a factory for the manufacture of ladies' hats. He was successful at it and was earning a good living.

When our conversation turned to my going to Belgium, she began by repeating what she said in the taxi the night before. Why did I tie myself to a girl before becoming established? What's more, she said, after I got to Belgium, I would encounter great difficulty in obtaining permission for the girl to come and join me. Her manner of speech was insulting but I refrained from giving her a sharply worded response. Instead, I tried calmly to convince her that there wasn't any obstacle to my going to Belgium because I wouldn't be a burden to anyone there. Not until I could support myself would I even think of having Hanele join me. On no account, would I ask anyone for help and I would appreciate it if she wouldn't speak of it again.

My stepmother had a plan for obtaining a character reference for me. She had contacts in the Socialist Party of Poland (PPS) which had elected several deputies to the Sejm. She turned to these deputies with a request that they act on my behalf and obtain the necessary document. Wherever she went she met deaf ears. The reply was always the same: We can't change the law for one individual. Someone advised her to consult an attorney who was very prominent in the Department of Justice. The lawyer took on the case for a large sum of money. My stepmother paid it promptly and received assurances that in the space of three months everything would be attended to.

Hanele's parents invited my stepmother to an evening meal so that we might spend several hours with her before her return journey. I was very pleased with the fine reception they gave her. From my stepmother's attitude, however, it was clear that she thought little of it. Before she left, I asked what she thought of Hanele's family. She replied that Hanele was a fine, pretty girl, but her parents? "Fiddlesticks! as the Jewish proverb says, 'after you've taken the cow out, slam the stable doors shut!' "

Her remark shocked me as if I'd been doused with a bucket of freezing water. I could tell that when I got to Belgium my stepmother would cause me no end of trouble. But what else could I have done but ignore her remarks? I had to escape the poverty of Poland where it would have been impossible to build a future for Hanele and me. The lawyer did finally obtained a recommendation for me and I began excitedly to prepare for my journey to Belgium.

Leaving Hanele was very difficult. Not until that moment did I realize I loved her with every fiber of my being. The nearer the day of parting, the more I felt I couldn't live without her. My only consolation was that this was something I had to do to build a better life for us.

I recall how in the taxi that took us to the railroad station, we sat close together as though we were one. Hanele's eyes were moist and brimming with tears as she strove with all of her might to hold them back so as to keep me from breaking down. She tried to prove she was strong enough to endure our separation.

On the station platform, when I put my arm around her and kissed her before boarding, she clung to me and began to sob, begging me not to leave. Drenched with tears myself, I attempted to calm her but couldn't. She continued to sob making me feel as if my heart was being slashed with sharp knives. When the train began to move, I finally tore myself away and boarded. She ran alongside, crying and calling out my name. For the duration of the twenty-four hour journey, I couldn't cease thinking of our difficult parting. My ears rang with the sound of my dear Hanele's weeping.

When the train arrived in Brussels, I saw my father through the train window. He stood waiting for me with his wife and daughter. A taxi was hired. My baggage was loaded on, and we drove to my father's residence at Number 18 Rue Grisar.

My father occupied several rooms of a small two-story building that entered onto a yard. Just opposite the house stood another two-story building, which was my father's hat factory. On the first floor was an immense room with eight stampas, on which hats were shaped and blocked to style. In the same row but closer to the door, was the hydraulic machine on which finished hats were pressed. In the back stood a large buffing machine on which felts were scraped and given a shiny nap. On the long right hand wall there was a large table at which a variety of textiles for soft toques were cut. A number of sewing machines were fastened to yet another large table. There were machines for sewing straw, for stitching felt hats, and even a machine for attaching brims. A powerful motor tied by long cables drove all of them. On the second floor was a massive long table. Girls sat along both sides of it shaping the toques and trimming the blocked hats. It was a pleasant surprise for me to see such a large factory equipped with the most modern machinery and to find out that my father was so obviously well established.

After I rested a few days, he took to teaching me the trade. He had me stand at the heated stampas and learn to be a stretcher. I, as the back stretcher, would take the felts down from a sort of kettle, one at a time. Using both hands, I would pass them to the stretcher up front, who also took hold of each one with both hands. Then the two of us would pull hard on the wet felt and position it on a hot form. When the felt was in place, the front stretcher quickly pulled the top part of the steam press down on it and, using a foot pedal, made sure the two parts fit tightly together. We repeated this process until all eight machines were filled. At that point, we hurried back to the first press and removed the dried hat before the extreme heat burned it. After removing all eight felts, we began the process anew. This went on all day.

For the first few days, I found the work very difficult. While pulling the wet felts onto the hot forms, I scalded my fingers and frequently had to work with my fingers bandaged. At night, I collapsed with weariness on account of the endless running. Also, every muscle of my arms ached from pulling on the felts, with all my strength, all day long. In time, I became accustomed to the work and didn't even feel the heat on my fingers. When they healed they became callused and no longer bothered me. My muscles stopped aching, and the whole process began to seem like a game.

I worked an entire four-month season receiving only bed and board, with the exception that, on the Sabbath, my father would allow me a few francs to cover expenses, such as shaving supplies or even an occasional ticket to the movies. I used the money to buy writing paper and postage stamps and wrote Hanele every other day. After work, I sat down and wrote very long, detailed letters describing my day's experiences. I stressed how much I missed her and assured her it wouldn't be long before we'd be together again. I wished to keep her from losing faith and kept writing until all hours of the night. This irked my stepmother, and she would incite my father to try to put a stop to our correspondence. She claimed it was difficult for me to get up in the morning and I would find the work too taxing because I hadn't enough sleep.

I finally realized what she was driving at. My stepmother wanted to keep me from building my future on her turf. My suspicions were first aroused during conversations at the dinner table. My father pointed out that the next world's fair was going to be held in America, and that it would be easy for me to obtain a tourist visa at that time. Once there, I could find a way to become a legal resident. Life is better and pleasanter in America than in Brussels he said. I rejected all such suggestions and asked them to stop offering advice I would never accept. Instead, they ought to consider paying me for my work. That way I could start saving money and bring my girl here. Then, perhaps, the two of us could settle down and begin to lead a normal life.

Only after much insistence did my father agree to pay me. I was to begin obtaining wages at the start of the "straw season." Since the "felt season" was ending in a week or two, my father would teach me to sew on straw. He really kept his word this time. As soon as the last orders for felt hats was filled, he sat me down beside him at a straw machine and spent many days instructing me how to work straw. When the straw season began, I had become quite a hotshot. At the end of the week, I received my first wages and was overjoyed with the princely sum of five hundred francs. This was more than I ever earned in my entire life.

I immediately sent a letter to Warsaw and enclosed the whole amount. I wrote Hanele that the five hundred francs were to reimburse her parents for the loan they made me before I left for Belgium, and that she was to use the remainder to buy herself a nice present. I finally became a wage earner I told her and, from now on, I was going to save all my *groschen* for the day when our dreams would be fulfilled. I was intent on bringing it about as soon as possible vowing that it wouldn't be long before we found our happiness.

The more I worked and saved, the more disturbed my stepmother became, apparently sensing that I would soon be sending for Hanele. She dogged my every footstep, and no matter what I did, no matter how well I behaved, she was never satisfied: I left things lying around instead of putting them where they belonged. Or I was a few minutes late getting to the table for the evening meal, or I wasn't polite enough to my half-sister. There were countless such petty accusations and they tried my patience.

Occasionally, my father and stepmother would visit friends or acquaintances of theirs that had daughters my age. Upon returning home, they would praise these girls to the sky and hint that a young man like myself ought to consider taking one out for a walk once in a while, or to the movies. I cut such conversations short right from the start by introducing other topics. Not only did those girls not interest me, they bored me. I compared them to my Hanele and found the difference so great as to be laughable. Such thoughts brought on a great longing for Hanele, and to ease my pining, I immediately wrote to express the strength of my feelings for her.

Since my father was a celebrated leader in the Zionist movement, he was always able to see to it that whenever there was a dance for the Zionist-Youth I would have a ticket of admission. Sometimes, he went with me hoping that if I became acquainted with one of the girls there, I would eventually give up my girl. The more pressure they exerted, the more I was moved to do the opposite.

By the end of the season, I saved enough money to send for Hanele. Because I wasn't yet a permanent resident, I was unable to bring it off myself. I asked my father to sign a statement that he was in need of a hat designer. On that basis Hanele would have been able to obtain a visa to Belgium. When my stepmother learned of this, she became furious. She openly expressed the fear behind her opposition. She was afraid that once Hanele arrived, she and I would take over the factory. She would never allow my girl to join me, she shouted.

"I also have a child," she raged. "After all, my daughter should have some say in this matter! I knew this is how things were going to be. Once he brings her here, he'll want to take over and make fools of us all!"

She went on and on in that vein. Barely in control of myself, I answered her accusations as calmly as I could manage:

"Can't you see how laughable your complaints against me are? All I'm asking for is a piece of paper that makes it possible for her to enter the country legally. I'll even sign a notarized statement that I require nothing more of you. When Hanele arrives we'll marry, and I'll move out. If you wish, I'll stop working for you. We can earn our bread elsewhere."

I couldn't convince her of the honesty of my intentions. She continued to make a scene and it seemed there would never be an end to it. Finally, I said:

"If you'll not do this small thing for me, I'll be obliged to have a stranger do it."

My words so enraged my stepmother that her lips were actually foaming.

"Since you're threatening to go to strangers, you may as well take your things and get out now!"

Hearing that, I began to pack my suitcase. My father, seeing I was in earnest, tried to dissuade me, saying:

"You had better give some thought to what you're doing."

I responded by telling him that I hadn't come there for them to step all over my feelings.

"If after all these years you really meant to compensate me for all the pain and suffering you caused me, but now refuse a mere trifle which would help me be united with my girl—who is more precious to me than anything in the world—I shouldn't spend another minute under your roof."

Without so much as a "goodbye," I walked out of the house, slamming the door behind me.

I rented a furnished room with a Belgian couple and then sent a letter to Warsaw. In it, I detailed all that had occurred between my parents and me. A few days later, there was a reply from Hanele that my going to Belgium was probably a mistake to begin with. From my stepmother's attitude the few days she spent in Warsaw, anyone could tell that no good would come of going to her house.

Hanele's letter was a separate one from her mother's. With warm and tender words, her mother advised me not to take anything that happened to heart and asked me to return to Warsaw:

"For a long time now, we've thought of you as our own child. A loving home awaits you here always."

Upon receiving the letter, I thought I really should go back for there was little good to be expected from my estranged parents. Before leaving however I wanted to embarrass my father before his party comrades who were so proud of him. They regarded him as a saintly idealist and looked up to him with greatest respect. Yet, as a father he was most cruel.

I went to the Zionist Alliance headquarters where I met some of his closest comrades and introduced myself. They looked at me in astonishment refusing to believe I was his son. Although I had been in Brussels for more than a year, none of them were aware he had children other than the daughter whom they knew.

I briefly described my father's "positive merits." I told them of my many years of abandonment and all he had done to me since my arrival in Belgium. They listened in suspense. They didn't want to believe that their leader, Sholem Altman, could have had the heart to do such things to his own children. When I concluded, they remained speechless. Realizing my story must have sounded unbelievable to them, I hastened to add:

"You don't have to believe anything I told you, though it isn't even a tenth of what he's done. I ask you, his friends, to summon him before a tribunal wherein you may become acquainted with every detail of what I've said. But please do it before I leave for Warsaw."

As I was speaking, my father suddenly appeared. Bewildered, he asked me what I was doing there.

"I want us to go before a tribunal," I replied, "a tribunal of your comrades, so that the verdict may be as favorable to you as possible."

Perplexed and disconcerted, my father had no choice but to agree to my demand and chose a half dozen of his comrades to hold court. We went into his office and the trial began.

After a brief review of what I already told them, I presented my complaint. I cited his refusal to sign Hanele's immigration papers and of my threats to make the request of strangers. For those few words, my stepmother drove me from their house. I was now unemployed and living in a furnished room with strangers.

My father listened calmly, never once interrupting. When I was done speaking, he realized there was more I could say. Therefore, during a pause in my narration, he commenced speaking to prevent me from continuing.

"There must be something you want of me or you wouldn't have come here to see me tried. Why don't you just go ahead and say what you want?"

I summoned up the courage to go on speaking:

"Since there can be no peace for me in my stepmother's house, I will return to Poland. I believe that to be my father's and certainly my stepmother's wish, and I will do them that favor. But since my father is well off, it's no more than right that he pay me enough to establish a small business of my own. I shouldn't have to go hungry as I did before coming to Belgium."

"So, how much do you want?" my father shouted impatiently. The whole affair was very irksome to him and he wanted to be done with me as soon as possible.

"I don't know how much you're in a position to pay," I responded. "Let your friends determine the amount. Whatever they think sufficient to become established in Warsaw will be acceptable to me."

They asked me to leave the room so that they might discuss specific amounts. After talking it over for quite a while, they called me back in and declared that they reached a unanimous decision. The amount agreed on would be approximately four thousand *zloty* Polish currency, to be paid in two installments. I was to receive half the amount in three days, and the other half at the end of the season, which would be in six months. I accepted their judgment and began preparations for my departure. I purchased a train ticket and, at the appointed time, went to meet my father. He had the money ready and our parting was chilly. I took my suitcases and was off to Warsaw.

When I arrived at Hanele's home, I found her parents and her two sisters there. Hanele was still at work. She was employed to trim hats with a firm on Gszibowska Street. My decision to return was made so hastily that I didn't have time to reply to the letter I received from Warsaw. Hanele's parents had no idea when to expect me. Nevertheless, they gave me a warm reception.

I could scarcely wait for Hanele to return from work and find her unexpected guest. Finally, there was a ring at the door. I ran to open it and caught Hanele in my arms, as I covered her with kisses. At long last, I recovered my greatest happiness.

After several joyous days, we returned to a grim reality. The economic situation in Hanele's home wasn't good. Her parents owned a "trim shop" where even in good times they had difficulty making a living. The economic crisis tore gaping holes in an already debilitated economy. Poverty was even greater among the Jewish population for the Polish government treated Jews like stepchildren and taxed them twice the rate as Poles. Heavy taxation and lack of customers consumed everything that Jews possessed.

I arrived in Warsaw just before the Christmas holidays, a time when some goods might have been sold and a little money earned. But Hanele's parents' store was empty. They hadn't anything to sell. Their creditors were reluctant to allow them any additional goods because many of their clients had already gone into bankruptcy. The crisis was bringing total ruin to the country.

My mother-in-law to be arrived home worried and told us that people came to the store but she had nothing to sell.

"If I can't sell anything during Christmas, what can I expect to do later on?" she asked.

I immediately withdrew some money and made her a loan of it so that she might purchase some goods and stop worrying. I also thought about a business for myself. What could I do with the money before it was all frittered away?

Hanele worked and saved what she earned, while I ran around for days trying to find something that would yield a decent living. I discovered the best return for my money would be the income from a fruit store. I went all over Warsaw looking for one that would provide a decent income.

In the meantime, heavy clouds were gathering on the political horizon. Hitler came to power in Germany and marched on Austria, capturing Vienna. He demanded the Sudeten region of France, and the free city of Danzig in Poland. The entire country began to live in fear of an approaching storm. Jews were especially apprehensive in view of the terrible trouble that Hitler's hordes had already brought them in Germany.

Immediately after they gained control, they declared a boycott of all shops owned by Jews. Then came the notorious, murderous frenzy of *Kristalnacht*, when they demolished Jewish shops and plundered and robbed Jewish possessions, desecrated and burned Jewish synagogues and other holy places and, finally expelled all Jews who were Polish citizens. On a cold and frosty night when everything was covered with snow, these Jews were driven, man, woman and child, into the forests of Zbonszyn. There, many perished of hunger and cold before the Jewish Committee, itself impoverished, reached them with some bread, and warm quilts to somewhat alleviate their terrible situation.

Hanele's older sister was keeping company with a young man who lived in the same building. His name was Hayim Sukman and, like me, he was looking to find some means of livelihood before getting married. Concern for an independent income was the primary reason young couples put off getting married or starting a family.

Couples went together for years before they felt economically secure enough to marry.

In those days, many young men learned the trade of "chauffeur-mechanic." Bella's betrothed was one of them. He intended to buy a taxi after he learned the trade. However, a taxi cost nearly a thousand *zloty*. That was a small fortune which very few young men possessed, Hayim included.

Hanele's mother was very eager to see Hayim and Bella married. This led her to suggest that I purchase a taxi and work in partnership with Hayim. We would then both have an income. I told her that I didn't care to own a taxi and that I would rather have my own fruit store than go into partnership with my prospective brother-in-law. I knew that when one goes into business with a relative there's bound to be trouble sooner or later.

I finally discovered a very attractive fruit store. It was on Salna, a lively street that was always filled with passersby. I observed the store several days in a row and noticed that it had many customers in the course of a day. It seemed an ideal investment for me. I took Hanele and her parents to see it so that I might get their opinions. They were very enthusiastic. So we went into the store to talk about purchasing it.

The owners were willing to sell and the price they asked was well within my means. I gave them a deposit and promised to pay the remainder when the transaction was completed. When it came to framing the agreement, the seller requested a clause providing for an eight day period in which to consider the sale. If during that time either party decided against completing the transaction, my deposit was to be returned. I left happy and I prayed to God that the owner wouldn't change his mind. I looked forward to having my own business at long last.

Chapter 5

A few days later, newspapers carried the headline story that the Germans were massing great numbers of troops on the borders of Poland, filling everyone with dread. It was becoming obvious to everyone that war was inevitable.

I hurried to the store and got back the several hundred *zloty* I left as a binder. I figured that during war currency gets devalued. So on that very day, I accompanied Hanele's mother to her creditors where we bought up as much merchandise as possible.

A stampede had begun. People were buying up whatever was to be found especially if it was edible. Prices were rising by the hour. We tried to purchase products that could be stored long term without spoiling. We bought staples like flour, potatoes, rice, beans, onions, sugar, and even jars of pickles.

We emptied a back room, filled it with the products we bought, then locked it to ward off "the evil eye." Wide pillar-like supports for the ceiling of the bathroom created recessed spaces. We filled them with the fabrics and trimmings we bought and nailed plywood covers over them creating the appearance of a continuous wall. We then painted the plywood to match the color of the wall.

The first day of September 1939 began as any other. On that day the government scheduled exercises to instruct citizens in the procedures with which they had to become familiar. Every courtyard had young volunteers assigned to prevent panic and maintain order by guiding tenants into building basements whenever the sirens sounded. Bella was a volunteer and she was stationed in our courtyard.

At eight in the morning, all the city sirens began to sound. Bella hurried to put her identifying armband on and went down to perform her duties. We refused to go to the cellar for the exercises seemed ridiculous to us. Instead, we went to the window from which we could watch the war games. We heard the buzzing of planes all across the sky and saw anti-aircraft ordinance exploding in their vicinity but none of the salvos hit the aircraft. We admired the clever imitation of war we were witnessing with Polish planes playing enemy and shot at in a manner deliberately designed to miss.

How astonished we were when Bella came running up the stairs with fear filled eyes and told us that the war had begun. The planes were German scoutcraft on reconnaissance over the city. I attempted to calm everyone by saying that what Bella heard on the radio was part of an elaborate governmental scheme to persuade people to take the exercises seriously. I then hurried down into the yard to ascertain how much of what Bella said was true.

Since we didn't have a radio, I searched for where I could hear a broadcast. I didn't have to look long. It was decreed that radio owners place their receivers in a window and turn up the volume so those citizens who didn't possess radios could also be apprised of what was happening.

My blood froze as I heard what was fast becoming a terrible reality. The first governmental edict was for reservists, discharged soldiers and all men classified as being in either the "A" or "B" category report to centers designated in their military status identification booklets.

Wide strips of paper were pasted on windows to prevent the glass from shattering should a bomb explode nearby. Every crevice around the windows was sealed to keep gas from seeping into the building in case of a poison gas attack. Under no circumstances was anyone to turn a light on at night. There were many other such directives.

My military classification was "C," so I wasn't being called up for the time being. Hayim, on the other hand, was classified "A" and was mobilized right away. With heavy heart, we escorted him to the train. He was sent directly to the front.

On that very day, German bombers began flying over the rooftops of Warsaw and, with a terrible droning sound, rained bombs upon them. With a dreadful groan, house after house fell apart like a deck of cards. Hundreds of people were buried alive under the ruins. Even those who sought shelter in the cellars perished under tons of rubble.

Soon there were radio reports of German troops advancing with lightning speed upon the soil of Poland and approaching the gates of Warsaw. All men aged seventeen to fifty-five were commanded to obtain shovels and gather in their yards.

At dawn, we were led outside the city to dig protective ditches for its defense. As we dug ditches in the suburb of Wola, a number of German planes appeared. They swooped low and began firing machine guns. We threw ourselves into the trenches in total disarray. The Germans flew lower and continued to sow death. Not having anything to defend ourselves with, we made ourselves as small as we could by pressing our bodies up against the earthen walls. We tried to shield our heads from flying bullets with the scoops of our shovels.

Hayim's older brother, who was in the trench with me, escaped certain death when one of the bullets struck the shovel covering his face with a resounding ping and bounced off again, falling on the ground beside us. Many people were wounded and killed that day.

When we returned home, we found Hanele, her parents, her sisters, and Hayim's parents waiting for us at the gate. They wept with joy to have us back alive. The radio had broadcast an account of the "massacre" of defenseless trench diggers. They spent the entire day waiting for us, fearing for our lives.

In no more than a week the Germans encircled all of Warsaw. The Polish government made preparations for defending the city. Trolley cars were overturned while streets were barricaded and cut off to prevent troops from getting through. Every courtyard was filled with armed soldiers who fled from the front after they failed to fend off the advancing Nazis. They attempted to defend Warsaw street by street and house by house.

It was impossible to bring provisions into the city and this caused widespread hunger. It was decreed that any bakery still left intact bake bread with flour provided by the government. The queues that formed were kilometers long and one had to stand in line all night to obtain a loaf of bread. Everyone in our household took up a spot. Even so, not all of us succeeded in bringing bread home for by the time our turn came all the loaves were already snatched up.

It was especially difficult for Jews to purchase bread. If a Pole noticed a Jew standing on a bread line, the Pole pulled the Jew out and as likely as not gave him a thrashing while shouting: "It's on account of you Jews that we lost the war! For that, you mustn't have Polish bread!"

It was our good fortune that both Hanele's mother and her little sister looked very much like Gentiles. For the most part, they were able to bring bread home without running the risk of being victimized by anti-Jewish outbreaks.

Life became evermore difficult. When the Germans neared the city, they set up emplacements of heavy artillery and aimed the guns at the heart of Warsaw. People standing at overnight bread lines were felled by the artillery attacks hammering the city. During the day, German planes dropped incendiary bombs on buildings, turning the city into a mass of fire. Tenants mobilized and carried pails of sand up to the roofs and stationed themselves on top of their houses. The moment a flame bomb hit, they dashed sand upon it to extinguish it. This wasn't an easy thing to do, for as soon as the bomb landed, it spread fire as though it was fluid and very quickly covered a large area.

The soldiers stationed in the courtyards of Warsaw made the situation even worse. When enemy aircraft flew overhead, they showed their "bravery" by shooting up at the planes. The Germans, noticing the source of the shooting, turned back and destroyed the building along with the soldiers.

Things came to such a pass that we were in mortal danger if we remained in the apartment. We were certain that if a bomb fell on our roof, we wouldn't be able to run down from the fourth floor to the street in time. We decided that we would have to go lower down. On the ground floor, near the gate, there was a synagogue. We would move in there. Should a bomb hit, we might have a chance to escape, since we would be only a few steps from the street.

We each took a small valise filled with provisions and a quilt and carried them to the synagogue. We put our blankets down on a small area of the floor to prepare a place to sleep. Gradually, the synagogue came to overflowing with people who lived on the upper floors and who reasoned, as we did, that it would be much safer to be lower down.

I found a bench beside a window and decided to make my bed on that instead of on the floor. That night was the worst that Warsaw experienced during the entire war. The cannonade of the big guns continued all through the night. The fear engendered by the artillery reverberations left everyone breathless. The entire city was enveloped in flames and smoke. Everyone huddled close to someone. In dread anticipation, we hoped to meet our expected, terrible end in the embrace of our loved ones. I lay alone on my bench and sadly watched as Hanele clung to her mother and sisters and shuddered at the sound of a collapsing building or a bomb exploding.

Suddenly, we heard a horrible crash and then the rumble of cement falling from the adjacent houses, some of it into the synagogue. Shattered glass fell from all the windows. The impact was so powerful that the air pressure threw me like a light piece of wood from off my bench. Everyone let out a terrible scream, thinking the bomb hit me. Fortunately, I wasn't seriously hurt. The house, which stood two meters distant from the synagogue, had been badly damaged however.

After that, we decided to go down into the cellar to spend the rest of the night. Sleep was out of the question. The bombardment never ceased, not even for a minute. Deathly afraid through it all, we remained in the cellar until about ten in the morning, when it became quiet. Not knowing what to make of the unexpected silence, we were afraid to move from our spot lest our movements reawaken the bombardment. We could hear, through the small cellar windows, the beginning of some movement in the yard. Someone went up from the cellar to see what was going on and returned with the news that Poland capitulated. We stretched with relief, gathered up our belongings, and began to leave the cellar. We went out into the fresh air and home.

It didn't take long to discover the city's water system was damaged. There was neither electric power nor gas for cooking. People began to run about the city searching for something to eat but were unable to find anything anywhere. The city lay shattered. Nearly all the houses either lay in ruins or were engulfed in flames and clouds of dust. Firemen and civilians attempted to extinguish the fires by throwing shovelfuls of sand on the burning ruins.

Across the street and opposite our house there were piles of lumber. Carpenters used to buy wood there for their work. The Ulan troops of the Polish army, who were supposed to defend Warsaw, were quartered in the lumberyard along with their horses. During that last terrible night, a bomb struck there, set the stacked wood on fire and injured some of the horses. The soldiers promptly shot their wounded mounts. When people saw the soldiers shoot the horses, a wild stampede broke out to cut large pieces of horseflesh, some of it from animals still half alive, and take it home to be cooked and eaten.

Since we were without water, I took a large kettle from the house and inquired whether anyone would go with me to the Wisla to fetch water. Hanele and Bella volunteered and we set out on the long walk to the river. On the return journey, we saw our first Nazis: several generals, smartly attired in high, shiny boots that glinted in the sun. They wore well-fitted elegant uniforms, swastika bands on their alcoves, and snow-white gloves on their hands. As they stepped down out of their stylish convertibles, they asked us the way to the council house.

The next morning, large notices in German and Polish were posted all over the city. They announced that the Germans were holding ten of the most prominent citizens of Warsaw hostage, detained until the entire city was cleaned up. This was to be done in a week's time, when the German Army would make its triumphant entry into Warsaw. Should the task not be completed in the specified time, all ten hostages would be shot and the citizenry severely punished.

Every day, there were new posters bearing new decrees. Fear took possession of all the citizens, and of the Jews, especially, since most of the orders were plainly intended to harass them. People, mostly Jews, were rounded up to clean streets and fight the fires at the gas works, where the coke that was used for fuel in the production of gas, burned for eight days after the surrender of the city. All efforts to extinguish it failed, for thousands of tons of coke were involved. Jews were forced to labor twelve hours a day without interruption and under the worst conditions. It was impossible to breathe for the burning coke gave off choking fumes. People became faint from the combination of poisonous gas and weariness.

When bakeries finally resumed baking bread and people again formed lines outside the shops, the Poles quickly learned one German word, *Jude*. As they stood in line, they used their index fingers to point out Jews to the SS. The Poles pronounced the word "*Jude*" with a savage pleasure. With barbarous fierceness, the SS officer would drag the Jew from the line, strike him with the butt of his rifle until he was bloodied. Of course, the victim lost all opportunity of obtaining a loaf of bread.

Since it was very difficult to buy food, I put a knapsack on my shoulder; put on a cap, such as the gentiles wore, and took the electric train (which by then had resumed operation) to Grodzisk. From peasants that I was acquainted with, I bought some chickens, ducks and geese. I had them slaughtered, stuffed them into my knapsack, and took them back to Warsaw with me. There, Hanele's mother sold some to relatives and kept the rest for us. This was a risky undertaking for, as a Jew, I could have paid with my life. However, the young take all kinds of risks without giving much thought to what they're doing.

Jews were seized on the streets of Warsaw as a matter of course and forced to do heavy labor. A dozen or so SS officers, armed with rifles suddenly appeared and seized every Jewish passerby, whether young or old. Those taken were lined up in a row on the cobblestone streets and led away to clean streets or clear away the ruins of bombed buildings.

For the time being, women weren't being rounded up, so I never went out alone but always with Hanele. Whenever I saw SS approaching, I rushed through the nearest gate while Hanele remained on the street until the danger was past.

One day when such a seizure was in progress, I ran past a gate and continued on up the stairs of the building. When I went up several flights, a man opened his door. I warned him that people were being captured in the street and not to dare go out. I asked him to allow me to hide in his home until the soldiers stopped taking people. He let me in. We stood behind the curtains at a window and observed everything that took place on the street. We saw the SS beating Jews and forcing them into a group that was led away to do convict labor. When they gathered their quota, they marched away with them. I went back into the street and found Hanele waiting for me.

On the way home, we discussed the terrible conditions under which we were being forced to live. We concluded that we had better get away because it would be impossible to endure such suffering and persecution much longer. The sooner we left, the more certain we would be of saving our lives.

Before Hitler's hordes decided to attack Poland, they took the precaution of making a pact with the Soviets that would improve their chance of success. The Soviets were to invade Poland at the same time as the Nazis, and share in the war booty. The two robber-nations made plans for Germany to attack from the west as far as the Bug River, while the Russians would capture eastern Poland up to the same river, where they would subsequently fix their respective boundaries.

Poland couldn't withstand the pressure of these two mighty armies. After resisting hopelessly for three weeks, Poland could no longer endure their merciless attacks and capitulated. When the marauding Hitlerists, together with their Soviet ally, achieved their end, they temporarily opened the borders on both sides of the river so that there would be a free exchange of "refugees" who fled to save their lives. People began to stream from one side of the border to the other to return to their homes and be reunited with their relatives. It was during this time that a Polish soldier, who fought alongside Hayim, arrived and brought us news of him. He told us Hayim was alive, in good health and uninjured and that he was in Bialystok, a city on the eastern bank of the Bug, which was taken over by the Russians.

When Bella heard that Hayim was alive, she was so happy and excited that she wanted to rush across the Bug to the Russian side, and look for him. Since I was already determined to go to the Russian side in order to survive the war, we decided we would all go together. Hanele's mother didn't want her girls to go to a foreign country with boys they weren't properly married to. So we hurriedly called our relatives together, friends, and acquaintances, and Hanele and I were married at the home of a rabbi. I had to make my mother-in-law a solemn vow that as soon as we found Hayim, I would see to it that he and Bella were married before they lived together. A friend of ours, who also just returned from army duty, joined our little group to go to the Soviet side with us, as did Hayim's two brothers. There were eight of us willing to make the one hundred fifty-kilometer journey.

The rabbi who married Hanele and me lived across the street, at Number 27 Ogradowa. There was still no electricity in the buildings. Our wedding ceremony was performed in darkness broken only by the light of a few small tallow candles. There was not much in the way of refreshments for the guests. Using some flour we had from pre-war days, my mother-in-law baked a cake, which was served with small glasses of cherry brandy that we put up the summer before.

The very next morning, after the ceremony, at six o'clock, we left the house with our friends. They spent the night in our house so that we wouldn't lose time. We were thus able to start out together. The morning was dreary, as though weeping over our fate. Halinka, Hanele's twelve-year-old sister, insisted on accompanying us to the outskirts of the city.

After we walked for a while, we found ourselves approaching the large synagogue at Number 3 Tlomacka. We stopped there to observe the damage to the immense lion sculptures at the entrance to the great synagogue of Warsaw. The two lions were still upright in the ruins, but they were decapitated and their shattered heads lay mixed with the other debris.

As a light shower began to come down in the gloom, we suddenly realized that Hanele forgot to take along her snow boots, which she would be able to make good use of. Halinka volunteered to run and fetch the boots if we would wait where we were for a while. She arrived breathless with the overshoes, and we dissuaded her from going any further. As we bade her a heartfelt farewell, she started to weep bitterly. Her tears affected us all, and the manner of our parting dominated our mood the rest of the way. That was the last time we saw her alive. Along with her mother, and many other Jews, she was murdered in the Majdanek concentration camp.

The men in our party were weighed down by the rucksacks on their backs. We filled the sacks with a three-day supply of bread and food. We, each of us, also carried two shirts and a few other things we would need on the way. The women carried small valises containing only the most essential items of clothing. We did everything possible to lessen the load on our long journey.

As we had estimated, we traveled fifty kilometers the first day. Just before sunset we found a peasant whom we paid well to cook us an evening meal and bed us down in a stable, where fresh hay had been piled. In the early dawn, we set out to continue our march.

To keep from losing our way, we followed the railroad tracks. After walking for half a day, we came upon some German soldiers working at repairing the line. Thinking we were Polish, they greeted us and asked whether we understood German. I replied that I understood. They then asked where we were going. I explained that we were refugees from the east bank of the Bug and that we were returning home. They informed us that half a kilometer farther we would come upon the train, which brought them there. We would certainly be let on board and, on the return journey, be taken to where the Bug flowed. We thanked the men and hurried to traverse the half-kilometer.

To make things easier for Hanele, Hayim's brother Ignac offered to carry her valise. He didn't have much baggage of his own and would be able to handle the valise better than she could.

We did indeed come upon a train of several cars loaded with tools for track repair. When the soldiers noticed us, they greeted us politely and helped us get on board. The train then proceeded at a slow pace in the general direction of the Bug. As the train moved along, the soldiers observed each of us carefully. Some of them doubted that we were gentile. After carefully scrutinizing us, the Germans decided that Ignac must surely be Jewish. In truth, he did have a specifically Jewish appearance. The soldiers approached us and started to ask questions.

"Who are you?" one of them asked in German.

"Refugees from the other side of the Bug," I replied boldly, "and we're returning home to our parents."

"And who are you?" said another one, pointing to Bella and Hanele.

"These two girls are my sisters," I replied just as boldly as before.

"And all the rest?"

"All people going home, like we are," was my response.

Since they already decided Ignac was Jewish, they turned and addressed him directly:

"*Du bist ein Jude ja?*" ("You're a Jew, yes?")

Ignac turned deathly pale and was unable to answer. They took this for proof that they weren't mistaken and they all began to shout: "*Jude raus!*" ("Jews out!")

Trembling, Ignac jumped up with Hanele's valise still in his hand and leaped from the moving train. Watching him jump, we all turned to stone. Fortunately, the train was proceeding slowly and we could see that Ignac landed on his feet. This was reassuring. He probably hadn't been hurt, Thank God! The Germans were now laughing loudly amusing themselves at the expense of the "fainthearted" Jew.

Although we were deathly afraid, we arrived safely in the town of Malkin, which lies along the Bug. We roamed the town looking for Ignac, for we wanted him to be with us when we crossed the border. We didn't want him to lose us.

It wasn't until after noon the next day that Ignac appeared. He was exhausted and without either his baggage or Hanele's satchel, which contained a new heavy wool sweater, her two best skirts, blouses, and other feminine garments. Hanele was left with nothing other than what she was wearing, except for a few small things I was carrying for her in my knapsack.

Ignac told us what happened to him after he jumped the train: As he walked along the road towards the Bug, some Germans caught him, took everything he had, and then beat him badly. Bruised and hungry, he could scarcely drag on. He arrived in Malkin twenty-four hours after the encounter and was very happy to have found us again. We stopped at a peasant's house, ate a meal, and slept the night. We then paid the man a few additional *zloty* to hitch up his horse and wagon and take us to the border.

When our documents were being examined at the border, we had yet another scary experience. The German border guards weren't conversant in Polish. So they had a Polish peasant fronting for them with whom they made the following pact: Whenever Jews crossed the border, he could take whatever they had of value, and then share it with the Germans later on.

Our friend, the discharged Polish soldier, had a gentile appearance. His flax-blonde hair and short pug nose wouldn't have led anyone to suspect that he was Jewish. His name, too, was typically Polish: Josef (Uziek) Razkosznik.

When he left with us, he brought a brand new bicycle with him, which he held onto all the way from Warsaw. Now, at the border, the interpreter-peasant decided he'd like to have the bicycle together with all of Josef's and his wife, Hella's belongings, which were attached to its frame. After our papers were examined, we were permitted to cross the border. Uziek was the last to undergo inspection. When the peasant thought to confiscate this great bounty, he took hold of the bicycle with both hands and tried to take it. He pulled the bicycle toward himself. Uziek then pulled it back with all of his might and a great tussle began. The German guard, who was just about to let Uziek through, asked what was going on. The peasant, in exultation, replied: "*Das ist ein Jude*" (This is a Jew).

Uziek didn't lose his composure. He seized the bicycle with one hand, and with the other he waved his identification papers in front of the peasant's eyes and shouted at him in Polish: "Bang yourself on your head you stupid peasant! Is Uziek Razkosznik a Jewish name?" He spat at the peasant and grabbed the bicycle, as he hurried across to the other side. The German ridiculed and mocked the peasant and took him to task, certain that the man made a mistake.

Chapter 6

Once we were on the Russian side, we went to the railroad station, where we saw thousands of refugees waiting since early morn for a train to take them to Bialystok, a major city. Late that night, a freight train arrived filled with people coming from the east. When they disembarked, yelling and pushing arose as the crowd rushed towards the freight cars. They were afraid they would be left behind to spend another night at the station, for the train couldn't accommodate them all.

In the midst of all the noise and pushing, we heard a familiar voice calling our names. I turned my head to see who it was that was trying to attract our attention, and saw Hayim elbowing his way through the crowd. As he pushed his way closer to Hanele, who was separated from me by a few steps, he put his arm around her and, beamingly, asked: "Where's Bella?" I pointed her out to him. "There she is!" The crowd carried her along so that she was a meter closer to the train than we were. When we all scrambled up onto a freight car and were together again, Hayim gave the following account of how the miracle of our meeting came about.

"I couldn't wait to get a letter or some news of you" he began, scarcely pausing for breath, "so I decided to go to Warsaw. In fact, I just arrived from Bialystok on this train. And then a wondrous thing happened. As I descended from the train, I looked for someone I might recognize from Warsaw, but found no one. I was about to leave the station when the crowd began pushing and clamoring to get on board the train."

In the noise and confusion, he recognized familiar voices calling my wife's name and then mine. He tracked the voices from within the crowd and soon caught sight of Hanele and me. With all of his strength, he pushed his way towards Hanele, and that was how he found us. If that hadn't happened, heaven knows whether we would ever have met again.

When we arrived in Bialystok, the city was a teeming beehive of tens of thousands of refugees running from every city and town in Poland in an effort to save their lives. The Soviets transported hundreds of refugees to the outskirts of the city by military truck and sheltered them in the barns of Polish farms. We made request of the Soviet militia to house us somewhere within the city. They complied with our request and assigned a militiaman to go with us to help us find quarters.

The Soviets issued an order requiring all families occupying a dwelling of more than two rooms to make an extra room available for the temporary housing of refugees. With the help of the militiaman, we found a room with a Jewish family. We all stayed in one room. It had but two beds, so that some of us were obliged to sleep on the floor.

On the following morning we made inquiry as to where we might find the home of a rabbi, for we were intent on fulfilling my mother-in-law's wish that Bella and Hayim have a proper wedding ceremony. We found a rabbi, a very old man with poor vision. He explained that he would gladly do the *mitzvah* (act of charity) of marrying the young couple. But he couldn't because he was unable to write a *ketubah* (certificate of marriage) on account of his poor eyesight, and there weren't any printed ones to be had. I said that I could solve the problem. I took out my own *ketubah*, and copied it word for word on a small piece of paper, except that I inserted Hayim and Bella's names and the new date. After I carefully read it back to the rabbi, he performed the wedding ceremony in accordance with the laws of Moses and Israel.

One day, as I walked along the streets of Bialystok, I bumped into my cousin Manya, who fled from Grodzisk, together with her husband,

Leyzer, and her two-year-old daughter. She told me how, for the time being she was living with our uncle, my father's younger brother Benyomin, who married a woman from Bialystok.

Manya escorted me to my uncle's home. My aunt lived in two small rooms with her three children and her old mother. My uncle hadn't been home since the outbreak of the war, when he was inducted into the army. When the Soviets took over Eastern Poland, the Russians took him captive. My aunt had some letters from him in which he informed her that he was being held in a camp deep inside Russia and that there were many other Polish prisoners there where they were forced to perform hard labor.

Hanele and I inspected the small apartment and had difficulty understanding how so many people could fit in for, with Manya, her husband and her child, they were now eight. Learning that nine of us were sleeping in one small room, my aunt proposed that Hanele and I stay with her until our situation became clearer. We couldn't understand how even more people (ten) could sleep in such crowded conditions.

"You'll adjust to it," my aunt insisted.

"It's preferable to living among strangers."

With her husband away, and three little girls and her mother to care for, my aunt was leading an impoverished life, but she was, by nature, a very generous and compassionate person. She prepared a place for us on the floor, although in reality there wasn't any room. Half our bedding was under the table; the rest occupied the last bit of floor space so that there was nowhere to walk at night. If we got up, we were obliged to step on the bedding.

In order to obtain sustenance, we went to the *toltshak* (market) and engaged in trade. We bought and sold from hand to hand. Hanele and I took on separate roles. I would roam the market, where Russian soldiers came to sell the clothes off their very backs—their shirts, underwear and other items. I bargained hard to have them accept a lower price than they were asking. When I felt I couldn't do better, I bought their goods and turned them over to Hanele, who sold them at a small profit.

Assuming separate roles was a device for avoiding the strictures of Soviet law. Trading, which they termed "speculating," was forbidden. If they found me buying something, I could say I was purchasing it for my own use. Similarly, if they questioned Hanele's selling, she could say it was her property and she needed to sell it in order to buy bread.

We didn't do badly for our efforts. We earned enough for food and other expenses. Nevertheless, we weren't satisfied, for there was no future in it. We hoped to settle down in peace and await the end of the war. We knew we couldn't remain in Bialystok, which the Russians considered a border city, especially since thousands of additional refugees arrived daily, and the city was overflowing with people.

The Russians hung radio loudspeakers all over the city, from which propaganda would pour all day long:

"Stalin has opened the gates of the golden fatherland to all workers and farmers. If you're willing to work, you'll be allowed to settle and you will obtain jobs immediately. Work will be made available in thousands of our Soviet shops, on our rich farm collectives (*kolkhoz*) and in our factories (*sovhoz*). You'll no longer have to roam the overcrowded streets of Bialystok. You'll enjoy a beautiful life of freedom, filled with happiness and contentment. All those wishing to take advantage of this bounty should come and register. Troop trains will be leaving daily to transport registrants to Russia free of charge. All registrant's needs will be provided for, and they'll be assisted in establishing a home, if they are but willing to work."

Hanele and I thought that it mightn't be a bad idea for us to try out this Soviet brand of happiness. We registered and, as we were directed to do, reported at the railroad station the very next morning with all our belongings. We were loaded onto trains for departure to Soviet "paradise."

When the Soviet troop train began moving along the tracks on the Russian side, we were struck by the evident poverty of the peasants. Fields that stretched for hundreds of kilometers were neglected or abandoned. The little huts that glided past the moving train were all made of an earthen-like clay. They had straw roofs and tiny windows, an indication of the gloomy life of those who lived therein. The peasants that we saw harvesting the last crops of the season appeared to be as forlorn as their huts and the ground they worked on. They all wore a sort of dull black uniform. Their jackets were torn, their trousers, made of the same material, were shabby. Large, white cotton batting stared out at us from every torn and worn spot. The dreary scenery caused our hearts to sink. We felt regret for having willfully entered "the kingdom of the poor."

The train stopped several times to take on Red Army troops who signaled it along the way. They packed themselves into the overfilled cars, which were more suitable for transporting cattle than transporting people. As soon as they came aboard, the soldiers sat down on the floors of the cars and began singing communist propaganda songs and asking us to sing along with them.

The first stop was at the White Russian town of Polotsk. The engineer announced that anyone who cared to was free to visit the town because the train would remain at the station for half an hour. He cautioned the passengers not to be late returning for the train would leave without those who overstayed. Hanele and I got off the train.

The town intensified our feelings of regret. There was widespread poverty such as we had not been accustomed to seeing even in Poland. While there was great poverty at home, it was paradise compared to what we saw here. The small two-story houses were all built of wood, and they stood half in ruin. They were peeling and shabby just like the tattered clothing the townspeople were wearing.

From a distance, we could see (a *larok*) a small store outside of which there was a queue of hundreds of people waiting to buy sugar. We couldn't understand why so many people had to stand in line in order to purchase a little sugar. Several policemen were stationed to see that no one enter out of turn. When one of the policemen noticed us approaching, he called out: *"Eto bieszentsi oni dieset let sakhraniye videlyi!"* (These refugees haven't seen sugar for ten years). He politely led us to the door of the *larok* and let us in without our having to wait on line. When the storekeeper was about to hand us a kilo of sugar, I told her I didn't need that much. Two hundred grams would do because I was traveling, and I could wait to buy more later when we were settled. Everyone stared at us as though we had come from another planet and had lost our way. We didn't know then that months might pass before we would see sugar again.

At midnight, we arrived in a still larger town in White Russia. Women, wearing white aprons, were waiting for us at the train. They stood beside military field kitchens from which they distributed sweet hot tea, sugar buns, and liverwurst. Each person took a portion and returned to the train to sit down and eat what was a tasty meal for someone who had gone hungry all day.

The liverwurst caused Hanele to have stomach cramps and fever and I was unable to help her in any way. We had to spend the night in the crowded train and were obliged to wait until morning for a doctor.

Early in the morning, when the town was just rousing itself from sleep, a military band marched up to the train and played *L'internationale*. A political lackey then mounted a platform and delivered a long and boring propaganda speech in which he praised the generous father of all nations, their dear comrade, Stalin. Stalin, who delivered us from Polish *Panczizna*, invited us to a happy, joyous existence in his great, beloved fatherland to share in the fortunate life enjoyed by all Soviet citizens. Following the politician's speech, the band played *Daroga Strana Maya Radnaya* (My Beloved Fatherland), and then, finally, the process of unloading the people from the train began.

Military trucks drove up and everyone was ordered to get into one. We were transferred to the town's school building, except for Hanele, who was taken by passenger car to hospital. I was given assurances that as soon as she felt better, she would be sent to join me.

At the school, we were given a towel and a piece of soap. Then we were lined up and led to a bathhouse to wash up after our journey. On the way to the bathhouse, we noticed that the streets weren't paved. Deep puddles pockmarked the roads. Long boards of about fifteen centimeters wide were laid out as a substitute for sidewalks. We had to traverse them very carefully to avoid slipping off into the mud. We slid off the boards more than once, landing in mud over our ankles.

The bath was in an old, neglected wooden building. It hadn't showers or tubs such as we were accustomed to. Instead, there was a long bench on which stood a row of wooden pails. Above the bench, along the entire length of the wall, there were two pipes with faucets attached. Hot water could be drawn from one pipe and cold from the other. We stood naked next to a pail, filled it with water, and, hurriedly, soaped ourselves. Then we rinsed off with the water in the pail. After ten minutes, we were sent out to make room for the next group of people waiting in line. After bathing, we were led back to the school.

In the large school auditorium, we were again asked to stand in line, this time to be registered. We were asked our names, birth date, and occupation. Next, we were handed a token together with thirty-five rubles, which we were to exchange for a meal at a city restaurant. We hadn't eaten a comparable meal for a very long time, and we weren't to dream of eating such a meal again for more than seven years. We slept on the bare grounds of the school.

The following morning, different factories and collective farms sent trucks to pick us up. Lists of names were read out loud and the designated persons were loaded onto the trucks and driven to their respective workplaces. I was among the last to be assigned because I was waiting for my wife to return from the hospital. When Hanele did finally appear, only twelve people were left of all the hundreds who were at the school. The official in charge telephoned a collective farm situated about fourteen kilometers from Liyasna and a truck was sent to take us there. The *kolhoz* to which we were sent specialized in the production of milk.

Since none of the twelve of us had the slightest notion about tending cows, we were handed shovels and put to work digging long ditches in which drainage pipes for the farm would be laid out. We were also assigned two rooms, one for women, the other for men. We were handed coarse sacks and told to fill them with the straw that we would find in the barns for the purpose of making mats on which to sleep. We also received a quilt with which to cover ourselves.

The supervisor of the *kolhoz* hired a Russian woman to work in the farm kitchen where she was to prepare one meal a day just for us. It was to be the midday meal, and it consisted of potatoes and barley to which she added some sauteed onions and a piece of bread. For breakfast and the evening meal, we received additional potatoes, four hundred grams of bread, and a half-liter of milk. Insofar as food was concerned, we had no cause for complaint for the members of the *kolhoz* received less than we did. They were, of course, very envious of us on that account. On the other hand, we found the work very taxing for none of us had ever in all our lives worked land before. Moreover, the shovels we used were heavy and dull. For the first few days, our hands blistered. During the next few days, the blisters burst, leaving the palms of our hands, as well as our fingers, covered with raw wounds. In some cases, our hands healed quickly and hard calluses replaced the blisters. In other cases, the open wounds began to fester and refused to heal.

Hanele complained that she could never become accustomed to living in this forlorn rural area. She was a big-city girl accustomed to relaxing after a long day's work by going to the movies or reading a book. Here there was nothing but hard work, after which all one could do was collapse with weariness. The infected wounds on her hands kept her from falling asleep at night and in the morning, still unrested, she was forced to repeat the same monotonous routine.

Following a frightening experience, we decided we'd have to get away to a large city. What happened was this: At the end of the workday, the women would stop fifteen minutes before their husbands and depart for home to prepare their meals so that it would be ready when their men arrived. On the day in question, Hanele took her usual route across a field where cattle grazed. Because it was a grey day with a light rain falling, she put on a bright red kerchief to protect her head from getting wet. As she hurried towards home, I stood at the edge of the field and watched her lengthen the distance between us. I could see the cows grazing contentedly as they chewed their cud. I also saw a bull clawing the earth with his hooves and raising his head repeatedly in Hanele's direction, and then suddenly taking off after her. I didn't know why the bull turned wild, but I could see that he was running at Hanele with increasing speed. I immediately recognized the danger she was in. I dropped my shovel and started racing towards her. As I ran, I shouted over and over again:

"Throw the kerchief from your head! T-h-r-o-w a-w-a-a-a-y your k-e-r-c-h-i-e-f!"

Seeing that the bull was now only about four meters from Hanele, I ran with even greater speed and determination, calling out to her all the while. She finally turned her head and saw the bull charging towards her in full force. With both my hands, I motioned for her to throw the kerchief from her head. At last, when the bull was only about a meter away, she pulled the kerchief from her head and tossed it aside, as she began to run. The bull rushed towards the red piece of cloth, caught it on his horns, and ground it into the earth continuing to do so until it was all in shreds. I hurried over to lead Hanele from the field and had great difficulty calming her. Whenever she thinks of her harrowing experience these many years later, a shiver still passes through her.

I assured her that we would no longer remain in the *kolhoz*. Rising early the next morning, we walked off to Liyasne, where we met our friends Uziek and his wife, Hella. We all decided to leave for the city of Vitebsk.

Uziek was experienced at stitching boots and soon found work in a shoe factory. On the very same street, we found another factory, one that manufactured boxes. I made immediate application with the supervisor, who happened to be Jewish. I told him that I was familiar with the work having been employed in the manufacture of *yashtshikes* (boxes) in Poland. He took me aside, tried me out, and seeing that I could do the work, retained me. He assured me that I needn't worry about having run off.

He wrote a letter for me, which I took back to the *kolhoz*. In that letter, the supervisor of the box factory explained that constructing boxes was my trade, and that the factory was in great need of my skills. He requested the *kolhoz* to release me from my employment as an unskilled laborer and grant me permission to work at my own trade. Upon reading the letter, the supervisor of the *kolhoz* let me go. And so we packed what few belongings we had and settled down in Vitebsk to work at the *Tarnev Zavod* (box factory).

Since I was familiar with the work, it wasn't difficult for me. However, for Hanele it was real torment. The snow and bitter White Russian winter had arrived. Hanele was assigned work in the freezing yard. Her task was to lift heavy boards onto her shoulders and carry them to the factory where the crosscut saws would shape them into box-size lengths.

Sometimes, when it snowed overnight and the boards froze together, it was impossible to separate them come morning. Hanele wasn't dressed properly for she hadn't brought any warm clothes from home. It was impossible to find any for sale in all of Russia even if one had the money with which to make the purchase in the first place. Consequently, she was always cold. Her hands were frozen and swollen, and she caught a cold with a hacking cough. She was constantly crying on account of her misery.

It cut me to the heart to see her in such terrible condition. I made request of the factory supervisor that he do something to alleviate my wife's torment. I asked that he give her work inside the factory so that she wouldn't have to spend her entire day out in the awful cold, particularly since she was too lightly clothed, not having any warm garment to shield her.

"She won't last the winter unless you do something," I told the director.

"If she knew how to hammer boxes together, I could let her work inside," he replied.

I seized upon his words. "I'll teach her. No one's born a box maker. The skill has to be acquired. Let her start now and she'll soon be as adept as the others," I pleaded.

He agreed to let me begin teaching her the next morning, but it wasn't easy. When she positioned the nails to drive them into the box, she would miss and smash the hammer against her delicate fingers and lacerate them so badly that they would need bandaging. But she preferred going around with bandaged fingers than being frozen all day long in the cold factory yard or carrying heavy boards on her slight feminine shoulders.

Our situation was no better with regard to our living quarters or the meals we received. We were quartered in an *opsheszitza* (group residence). Such collective residences were common to Russian factories, collective farms and rural soviets. In these immense rooms that were reminiscent of enormous tents, they would place beds right next to one another so that, as in a huge barracks, the workers slept in close proximity. A room could house from twenty to one hundred thirty workers, depending upon the length of the *opsheszitza* building.

We were assigned two beds in just such a room, which housed about thirty workers. Since all of the other occupants were men, Hanele found it difficult to live there. Her bed was in a corner up against a wall. When she needed to wash herself, she had to hang a quilt that would screen her from the eyes of the men.

Every day, a woman came in to clean. She built a fire in the large iron stove, filled a huge kettle with water and saw to it that there was boiling water available for providing the only "refreshment," of which there is more than plenty in Russia. It was called *kipitok*.

Every worker would receive four hundred grams of bread (about a pound). The bread was as heavy as clay. It contained more water, straw and bran than it did flour. This loaf was to suffice for an entire day's meals but was scarcely enough for one.

At six o'clock in the morning, the factory whistle woke us and summoned us to work. We rose swiftly, washed, and went out to obtain our allotment of bread after which we drew a cup of *kipitok*. That was the extent of our breakfast. At ten minutes to seven, the factory whistle blared again, at which time we set out for the factory. We were expected to begin work at exactly seven o'clock.

There was no such thing as a regularly designated day off, such as Saturday or Sunday. All over Russia people worked five days then rested on the sixth so that one's day off didn't always fall out on the same day of the week. It could come on a Thursday, a Saturday, or a Sunday, for example.

The recess for the midday meal was from twelve noon to one o'clock. When the whistle blew at twelve, the workers made a wild dash for the *stolova* (kitchen restaurant). There they formed a line to redeem a token at a little window and obtained a plate of thin soup made of sour, green tomatoes. This was known as *rasalnik*. The stronger pushed their way up to the window and would quickly have their tokens exchanged for soup. The weaker didn't even manage to buy their tokens before the whistle blew again summoning us back to work. They had to return without having eaten their small portion of *shtshi* or *rasalnik*. Work ended at four o'clock.

After work, everyone hurried out onto the streets of Vitebsk to rush from store to store in search of something to buy. Unfortunately, all the stores were bare. If by chance, some store had goods to sell, a line a mile long would form there. As likely as not, after you managed to get into line and wait for hours, it was announced to your face that everything was sold out. People often went away disappointed.

The greatest irony of the Soviet hell is this: You sweat and grub for a mere ruble, the reward for your labor, and you pay six to ten times the value for anything you buy. To make a purchase, you stand in long queues for hours and hours. And then, you're told that you're being "given" the item, not that it's being sold. Whenever you go past some line, you don't ask: "What's being sold?" but rather: "*Tshto dayut?*" (What's being given?)

At first, because there was so little food to be had, we divided up our bread, eating half for breakfast, and saving the rest for the evening meal. An emaciated young Russian, Vanka occupied the bed next to ours. He apparently noticed where we hid our bread and after we left the barracks to go to work, he stole it. When we returned famished, our bread was nowhere to be found and we went to bed hungry. Fortunately, that situation was short-lived.

We kept insisting that the supervisor quit requiring a woman to live in a man's barracks. He finally conceded and assigned us a small cottage.

The cottage was built like a summer bungalow. Its wooden boards were so old and dry that their cracks allowed the wind to blow through. A single room and a tiny anteroom were all there was to it. The furnishings consisted of two beds moved close together, two mattresses, a clay stove and a crude table and bench made from planks of wood.

Still, we were glad to make the change since it promised us a little corner of privacy. It soon became clear however that before long we could freeze to death there. There was no coal for heating. We tried to use the sawdust and shavings from under the crosscut saw. When this material burned, it created a great deal of heat. But since wood burns quickly, I had to get out of bed every half-hour to gather additional shavings and sawdust to make sure the fire would last the night. Otherwise, it became as cold indoors as outside.

One night, after a particularly tiring workday, we lit the stove and went to bed. We fell into a deep sleep and overslept, so that we didn't get up in time for work. We were awakened by a terrible clatter at the door and when we finally opened our eyes, the supervisor and several workmen were standing beside us. They had broken into the house thinking that we froze to death. It took us a long time to come to. Scarcely able to stand, we drank glass after glass of hot *kipitok* until we sensed some warmth in our limbs. By then more than half the day had gone by.

Bella and Hayim, who stayed behind in Bialystok, wrote us a letter informing us that it was impossible to stay in that city and decided to join us in Vitebsk so that we might keep from being separated. Upon receipt of their letter, we wrote them not to even consider coming. Living conditions in Vitebsk were unbearable and we were ourselves in fact planning to return to occupied Poland. We told them that we would explain everything fully when we arrived. However, they didn't receive our warning in time. They were on their way before our letter reached them.

At the same time, we told Uziek that we were planning to run off and return to Bialystok because living conditions were just too difficult. Uziek declared that although they were better situated than we were they didn't wish to remain by themselves. He and Hella would feel too alone for we were their only friends. If we go, he and Hella would go with us.

When my brother-in-law and sister-in-law arrived and slept overnight in our cold cottage and heard what difficulties they would face in Vitebsk, they decided to return to Bialystok with us. We let Uziek and Hella know that we were leaving immediately. We wouldn't wait one more day. We packed our few belongings and went to the supervisor to tell him that we were escorting our sister and brother-in-law to the train. As soon as the train departed, we would return, we said.

We waited at the train station for a very long time. The longer we waited the more anxious we became. We were afraid of being caught by the NKVD who would surely send us back to the Tarnev factory. So we took the very first train leaving for the western occupied territory even if it wasn't scheduled to stop in Bialystok. We wanted to get away from Vitebsk as soon as possible. A train pulled in, a direct express that was destined for Minsk, the capital of White Russia, and we climbed on board.

Chapter 7

When the train stopped at Minsk, we saw thousands of Polish refugees at the railroad station. Like us, they had run away from Russian factories and collective farms. Everyone had a story of the horrible conditions under which he or she was forced to work and they all wished to return to the occupied territory in the west. They came to the capital to get permission to return. The borders were sealed and no one could proceed without a permit. They told us that they had been waiting around for weeks but permits weren't being issued.

It was the winter of 1940 and soldiers were streaming to and from the Finnish front where the war was in full swing. It was an unusually hard, cold winter with terrible snowstorms and we hadn't any place to stay. To warm up a little on those frosty, cold days, we went to a municipal cafeteria known as *Fabrika Kuchnia* (Kitchen Factory). We bought a cup of coffee and sat down at a table, where we remained as long as we dared. We didn't often manage to stay long, for the seats were needed for actual diners. If the attendants noticed our sitting there for any extended time, they chased us out. We went from one section of the cafeteria to another until we had no choice but to depart.

Outdoors, the cold made our noses and ears itch unbearably while the biting wind penetrated to our bones, for we were none of us dressed warm enough. Half running, to keep from going stiff, we would move from street to street. I carried our few belongings in a rucksack on my back, which made it all the more difficult for me to drag myself about in the streets of Minsk.

One day, we met a man I knew in Warsaw who was fortunate enough to have obtained employment and was living at a boardinghouse. I asked him if he could help us by getting permission from his landlady to leave my rucksack with her so it would be a little easier for me to get around. My acquaintance made inquiry of the woman and she agreed to keep my pack in one of her rooms. I expressed my thanks and then begged her to allow my wife to spend the night. The woman wouldn't hear of it because it was strictly forbidden to take in refugees. The penalties for doing so were severe. And yet, no one was allowed to be out on the streets at night.

We went to the railroad station and mixed with the soldiers waiting to change trains for their respective journeys. The station was always packed with both soldiers and civilians. But we couldn't stay at the depot for long. It was always under guard by the police who recognized us by our clothes and they would mercilessly turn us out into the streets. We were arrested on more than one occasion and taken to the headquarters of the military police. They would write up reports in which we were described as vagrants roaming the streets without passports, running away from work. They gave us twenty-four hours to leave the city and return to the factories from which we'd run away. They told us that if we were arrested again we would earn long prison sentences. We were actually pleased to be sitting in headquarters for the few hours of interrogation. The long bureaucratic protocols and threats gave us little concern.

Sometimes, when we had nowhere to sleep, we went to the railroad station where trains that were in need of servicing were parked on the side rails. We sneaked into a car and spent the night on a seat or in a berth. There was a considerable risk connected with sleeping on those trains because the local thieves made it a practice to rob refugees of what little they still possessed. The thieves would remove coats from off of anyone who in his sleep used his coat as cover. They would pull the shoes from off their feet and would steal anything else that was accessible.

Once when we were sleeping in a berth, we were awakened by a horrific scream. Still sleepy, we hurried down from our berth and rushed to see from whom the cries were coming. We got there just in time to see a Russian hoodlum running out of the car carrying the sleeve of a coat in his hand and disappearing into the darkness of night. It seems that the owner of the coat, while still asleep, sensed that his coat, which he was using as a blanket was being pulled away. He held on to it with all his might, but the thief also pulled mightily and the sleeve came off in his hands. Alarmed by the noise, the thief ran off with the sleeve still in his hand. At least the young man saved the rest of his coat. But it was something of a tragi-comedy to see the poor fellow walking the streets of Minsk wearing his one-sleeved overcoat.

Our situation worsened from day to day. People literally sold the shirts off their backs just to get by. The homelessness and cold plagued us relentlessly. We knew something drastic would have to be done soon or we would all perish from cold and hunger. It would have to be so dramatic it would arouse all of Minsk. We decided to lie down along the streetcar tracks and prevent the trams from running even if this should cost us our lives. Life as we were living it no longer had appeal anyway. The idea spread like wildfire and it was decided that at noon the next day everyone would gather on Kirov Street at the entrance to the Dom Pravitelatvo (State Government House). We would stage a mass demonstration to demand exit permits. If our demand failed to be met, we would make sure to carry out our threat and lie down on the rails in order to prevent the trolleys from running.

The day was cold, sunny and clear. Thousands of refugees, including women and children, were soon massed on the wide steps leading to the immense government building. The police, who were quick to notice that something was brewing, made an attempt to disperse us. As if with one voice, we began to shout: "*Mi hotshym domoy!*" (We want to go home) "*Mi hotshym domoy!*"

Crowds of Soviet passersby stopped with wide-open eyes, their mouths agape at the daring spectacle. Soon hundreds of policemen arrived and scattered the Russian spectators. When they turned to chase us from off the steps, we rushed down to the trolley car tracks. Men, women, and children lay down on them and the cars couldn't proceed. As we lay there, we repeated our demand: "*Mi hotshym domoy!*" "*Mi hotshym domoy!*"

Government officials including the head of the Regional Superior Soviet, came out of their offices and stood watching, stunned by the boldness of it all. When they recovered somewhat from their shock, one of them brought a megaphone and shouted:

"*Tovarishtshi bieszentsi!* (Comrade Refugees) Come gather at the steps. Comrade Morozov wishes to speak to you!"

We stood up and approached the steps. The megaphone was passed into Morozov's hands as he shouted for us to listen to what he had to say.

"Comrade refugees," he began, "Why this uncalled for demonstration? We wouldn't force you to stay here. If you don't wish to remain of your own free will, you'll be granted free passage to the western territories. I've already ordered a commission to register you and issue the required permits. You should go immediately to the Clubhouse of the Deaf-Mutes, about ten meters from the Dom Pravitelatvo. When you get there please file up in an orderly line and whosoever wishes will be given a permit for his or her return to the West."

The audience became a huge crowding throng with everyone trying to be first to reach the Clubhouse of the Deaf-Mutes. I was suspicious and didn't believe a word of it. I was afraid that it might be a trap. Turning to Hayim and Uziek, I said:

"Why don't just we men go in and see whether they're telling the truth? If they are, one of us will go and call the women in. If not, why get them trapped too?"

We were the last to go in. As soon as we entered, we were surrounded by armed police who wouldn't allow anyone in or out. As I suspected, we were lured into a trap. They began registering us immediately. We were asked to give our names, occupation, date and place of birth, our place of employment in the Soviet Union, and our reason for running away. The last question we were asked was:

"Would you be willing to go back to where you worked or would you prefer to return to the West?"

"To the West" I replied with determination. I was then sent to another room to join others who had responded as I had. Those who wished to return to the factories or the collective farms were sent to a different room where they were told that they would soon be supplied with train tickets back to where they had been employed.

The registration continued far into the night. When it was finally over, we were led out through a back door into a large yard where huge black trucks were already waiting for us. The trucks were windowless except for a small, iron-barred pane on the back door. On each side of the door sat an armed guard. We were crowded into these trucks, which the Russians called "black crows," and carried off to prison.

Upon arrival, thirty-five of us were packed into each cell, like chickens in a crate. The cell just barely held us, and contained but one cot. Up near the ceiling there was a single barred window, three-fourths of which was obstructed on the outside by a sheet of tin so that very little light came through. Obviously, there wasn't any likelihood of obtaining a night's sleep. There was scarcely room enough to sit on the floor. Six of us however could sit on the bed. So, every twelve hours six of us, chosen by lot, would take turns sitting on the cot. The rest would sit close together on the floor and doze off occasionally. The only small measure of comfort to be had was to sit on the soft straw-sack on the cot. Unfortunately, that wasn't to be more than once a week.

Once a day, we were led outdoors for a ten-minute walk. We marched around a circular steel tower in the prison yard. Atop the tower stood a prison guard holding a machine gun, which he aimed at us. We had to keep our hands clasped behind our backs as we walked in single file forbidden to utter a word to anyone. Once a day, we were permitted to go to the washroom to wash or take care of our needs. If anyone had additional need of the water closet, he wasn't allowed to go outside but had to use a large receptacle, which stood in a corner of the cell. Each morning, when we were escorted to the lavatory, a different pair of men took the waste bucket along. They emptied and rinsed it and took it back to the cell.

At about nine o'clock in the morning, the cell door was opened and every prisoner was given a hunk of bread and a cup of black, bitter coffee brewed entirely of chicory. That was our breakfast. At about five-thirty in the afternoon the cell door was opened again and we were given another hunk of bread with a thin, measly soup that contained a little barley. This was our second meal of the day. Once the "evening meal" was consumed, we made preparation for the cruel sleepless night to come.

The nights were unbearably exhausting. We had to crowd together and sit on the floor, our hands around our knees, our heads resting upon them. Not only did we have to endure the crowding but also the insufferably cold temperatures. The most difficult thing of all was the stabbing pain in the soles of our feet. This was due to the fact that we sat the entire night with raised knees and couldn't stand up to allow the blood to circulate. Getting up stopped the pain but if anyone tried to get to his feet, he disturbed the others who were dozing, creating a considerable disturbance. If someone had to go, he would have to step over them on his way to the bucket. The resulting commotion awakened everyone and many a curse was directed at those who dared cause the rest of us to lose the sleep we all constantly craved. If we managed some sleep, it would only be prior to midnight for there was none to be had thereafter.

Promptly at midnight, all hell broke loose. The cell door was opened and a guard began reading off a list of initials, not names. Anyone who didn't respond was promptly dealt a violent blow. When the guard said, "*Na bukva 'A'* " (letter A), he meant "Altman" and I was expected to step outside and line up next to the cell door. "*Na bukva 'B'*" meant "Bernstein," and so on. When those called were all lined up, we were led through the long prison corridors into the yard. "Black crows"awaited us there, and then took us for a fifteen or twenty-minute ride to the headquarters of the NKVD. We were escorted up a staircase and then taken separately into a small room that contained a desk and two chairs. An NKVD agent sat in one chair and I was told to take the seat opposite him. Then the interrogation began. It went on until precisely five o'clock in the morning when I was led down the stairs and taken back to prison.

The initial interrogation consisted of a series of questions intended to elicit my entire life history up until my coming to the USSR. Who were my grandfathers? Who was my father? What was my background? The examiner badgered me until the grey of dawn. By the time I was back in my prison cell, it was six o'clock and the daily routine of the institution commenced. I didn't dare take a nap for sleeping during the day was strictly forbidden.

Exactly the same thing happened every night. The interrogator looked at the report he'd written the night before and ordered me to relate the story of my life again from A to Z. Occasionally, he made a note in his papers. I assumed he was recording a remark that contradicted something I said the night before. I decided that on no account would I let that happen. So I began to weigh and measure every word I uttered. On succeeding nights, I spoke as though reciting from a *siddur* (prayer book). Several nights later, realizing that I was speaking too quickly and mechanically as if I was reading the *megillah* out loud, the interrogator broke into a smile and said, "Enough. I've heard exactly the same thing from you day in and day out."

He tried a different approach. He inquired in a suddenly familiar fashion how I was being treated in prison. "You know better than I do the answer to that question," I replied.

"Instead, why don't you tell me why I'm being tormented like this? What terrible crime have I committed that warrants my incarceration? And, while you're at it, perhaps you can tell me as to the whereabouts of my wife, my sister-in-law and her husband. Why isn't he in my cell?"

He laughed out loud.

"I can't tell you where your wife is, but your brother-in-law and his wife aren't as foolish as you. They signed up for work and were sent to a factory in Orsha where they're working and living happily like every other Soviet citizen. If you sign that you're willing to return to work in Vitebsk, you and your wife will be released as well."

I told him that I categorically refuse to return to work in Vitebsk under the terrible conditions that obtain there.

"If that's your position" he continued, his voice turning serious, "you've no one to blame but yourself. Nor have you cause to complain for we haven't better facilities for tramps and parasites such as yourselves."

Night after night, I was dragged in for interrogation. I was tortured like this for thirty days.

On what proved to be the last night that I entered the NKVD agent's office, he politely directed me to my seat and asked, "Do you wish to see your wife?"

"Certainly, I responded. "That's my fondest wish." As I spoke, I doubted his sincerity.

"You may see her on one condition. You must first sign a statement saying that you'll give up being a parasite and return to work."

"I've worked all my life and I've never been a parasite. Nor do I want to be one here in the Soviet Union. But the dreadful, inhumane conditions with which we were rewarded for our labor forced us to run away. Under no circumstances can we return to work under the same or similar conditions."

A rather lengthy pause followed. Then he asked with some uncertainty, all the while measuring his words:

"If we find work for you here in the city, will you and your wife be willing to work?"

"If conditions are even halfway decent, we'd be happy to."

My questioner thumbed silently through his report for some time. Finally, he asked:

"How old were you when you first learned to be a tailor in Poland?"

"Thirteen," I responded.

"Have you learned anything about the trade since then?"

"Not much," I replied.

"Can you operate a sewing machine?"

"Yes, I can do that."

"What would you say to being employed in a *Shvayni Zavod* (tailoring factory) here in the city of Minsk? The plant produces greatcoats for the Red Army. Would that be all right? Are you prepared to sign a statement saying that you'd do such work conscientiously?"

"Certainly," I said.

He slid a sheet of paper across the desk for me to sign. Then he called a military attendant to take me back to prison. As I reached the door, the NKVD agent added that I would be hearing from him soon. I was filled with a confusion of feelings, a mixture of doubt and hope. The hours dragged on and I wondered whether it was true that I would be released. Could it be that I'd soon be seeing my dear Hanele of whom I hadn't heard anything for a month now? Or were they having sport with me and deliberately giving me false hope?

Daylight appeared. I heard the cell door being unlocked and I shivered in anticipation. When the door was opened, we hurried out to the washroom. Half an hour later, the lock was turned again. Breakfast was served and I still saw no sign of the interrogator's promise being fulfilled. When it was nearly time for us to be turned out for our daily airing, the cell door was unlocked once more and I expected to be going for our usual "walk." But instead of rushing us out, the guard called my initial as he had on all the interrogation nights before:

"*Na bukva 'A'*!"

"Altman!" I called back.

"*Bieri barakhla y wystupay*!" (Take your things and step outside).

Everyone in the cell was amazed. I waved my hand in a gesture of parting. Their envy-filled eyes accompanied me as I went through the door and out of the cell. I was led through the long prison corridors toward the office. When the office door opened, I saw Hanele standing there flanked by two prison guards. Her face was as yellow as wax and her cheeks appeared swollen as though she was suffering from dental abscesses. I rushed over, hugged her and covered her face with kisses. I was choking with tears, happy that we finally found each other.

We soon went to work at the overcoat factory. I was assigned to ironing military coats. Hanele was taught to make buttonholes and then to sew on the buttons. We slept in an immense dormitory barracks especially constructed for the *Shvayni Zavod*. Here, men and women had separate accommodations. But now we didn't see much of each other. The factory operated on three shifts and Hanele never worked the same shift I did. If I worked during the day, she worked at night. If I worked at night, she worked during the day. We met only during days off (*Vikhodnoya*). We took our meals in the factory dining room where the food was better than in the municipal cafeteria. We earned more than the city's residents for we mastered our new work quickly and produced more than the expected norm. We were placed on the list of the *stakhanovtses* (exceptional workers) and, as such, received additional pay.

The NKVD kept watch on everyone in the barracks and took note of when they went to work or returned. We believed the NKVD kept closer watch on us than on the White Russians. The extra rubles we earned were spent on a trip to the movies or to a theater and occasionally on something that was being "given" (offered for sale) in one of the city's shops. Hanele only now told me the terrible things she went through at the time we were tricked into entering the Clubhouse of the Deaf Mutes.

When we left the women outside and entered the clubhouse, they saw dozens of militiamen surround the building, a sight which frightened them to death. They didn't know what to do. After some discussion, they figured that no one would be permitted to come back out. They were afraid to be without us and decided to share our fate. So they attempted to enter the club but the militia barred their way. They pleaded to be allowed to be with their husbands but to no avail. The guards were ordered not to let anyone pass. There was nothing to do except wait and see how the matter would end.

They waited until long past nightfall but no one came out, not even after all the lights in the building had been extinguished. They couldn't imagine what was going on inside. They went up to the door and knocked. No one responded. They listened but it was quiet as a grave. At that point, they realized that we must have been led out by a back door. In tears, they went to the police station to inquire as to our fate. The police replied cold-bloodedly that they sent us to prison for roaming the streets without passports. They were told that if they didn't leave the city at once they too would be arrested. The women began wailing loudly declaring that they wouldn't leave without us. They promised the police that if only they released the men, they would make sure that everyone left Minsk.

There was a Jewish officer at the police station who evidently felt sorry for them. He ordered sweet tea with buttered rolls from the mess hall and invited them to eat. At the same time, he tried to comfort them saying that their husbands would be released shortly. He warned them not to defy Soviet law though. When assigned work, one can't quit on one's own accord. Out of compassion, he saw to it that they not be driven out into the unbearably cold streets.

In the morning, my brother-in-law and Uziek arrived at the police station with railroad tickets. They were going to Orsha to work. When Hanele inquired as to why they were released while I hadn't, they explained that after much torment they realized they couldn't get anywhere with the Russians and yielded, agreeing to work wheresoever they were sent. They suggested that Hanele go with them until my release. She declined the offer saying that she believed that if she left, she would never see me again. And so they departed without her. She remained in the station house hoping that I would be freed. On the following day, the NKVD led her and several other women, similarly situated, to prison.

After she'd been there for several days, she was stricken with terrible abdominal pains. She began to moan and call for help. The guard, doubting that there was anything seriously wrong, yelled into her cell, threatening to throw her into the dungeon if she didn't stop complaining. There, he said, she could lie all alone, like a dog.

The pain didn't subside. She lay all night long with parched lips, screaming in agony. In the morning, when everyone was hurried into the washroom, she was in such pain that she couldn't stand up. She was forcibly removed from the cell and shoved into the washroom where she fell unconscious on the filthy floor. When all the other prisoners returned to the cell and were counted by the guard, he saw that one was missing. Going into the washroom, he found Hanele lying on the floor. When he tried to get her to stand, he noticed that she was lying in a pool of blood. He immediately sent for the prison nurse. The nurse, finding that Hanele's pulse was very weak, began to shout: "Hurry! hurry! call First Aid! she's dying!"

When she regained consciousness, she was in a hospital and there were several doctors at her bedside. They told her that she lost a great deal of blood. The physicians found that she was pregnant and that, as a result of mistreatment, she miscarried. She was in imminent danger of dying. They had to perform emergency surgery and ordered blood transfusions to keep her alive. Now it would be up to her to see to it that she regained her strength. The doctors prescribed a nutrient rich diet and told her to make an extra special effort to eat. She wouldn't initially have much of an appetite for she was anemic but she should force herself nonetheless.

When Hanele took stock of where she was, she saw an armed militiaman sitting beside her bed observing her every move. Seeing that there were other women there but that none of them was being guarded like a criminal, she broke into tears bemoaning her unhappy fate.

Although she was being provided nutritious food, she found herself unable to swallow even a bite of it. The officer shouted at her to eat saying that if she didn't she would be returned, weak as she was, to prison. There she wouldn't be catered to with such bourgeois fare.

She remained in hospital for a week but without much improvement. The policeman handed her clothing to her and led her back to prison. She wasn't returned to her former cell but was assigned to a cell in a section of the prison where the sick were held. A doctor came to examine her on a daily basis. He prescribed various vitamins and generally saw to it that she improve. One day, she was summoned to the office of the prison and told to wait.

"What am I waiting for?" she asked the two men guarding her.

"Would you like to see your husband?" they replied.

"I don't believe you," she answered. "This isn't the first time you've lied."

They burst out laughing at her words. Then the door opened and to her great surprise she saw me.

We wrote to Hayim and Bella. In their return correspondence they informed us of rumors that in the city of Kiev permits were being issued to anyone wishing to return to the occupied western areas. Many had indeed departed and were already on the other side. Those who received letters from them confirmed the truth of those rumors. In a second letter, Bella told us that they themselves had arrived in the occupied Polish city of Kowel and that we'd better make certain to hurry there lest we be too late. We began a secret plan of escape.

I rushed over to the railroad station to purchase tickets to Kiev, the Ukrainian capital. Although no one was permitted the sale of tickets without a *komandarovka* (special permission to travel from one city to another), I found that placing a few extra rubles in the palm of the ticket agent's hand would get me tickets without it. Taking the porter aside, I offered him a couple of rubles and asked him to get me two tickets to Kiev. He went through a back door into the ticket booth and promptly returned with tickets good for passage one week from the date of purchase. Earlier date tickets were sold out. Actually, it was better for us to have to wait the week because we still had to draw up plans for running away. We couldn't afford to arouse suspicion as to what we were up to.

On the following day, I packed our things in a valise I'd been using to carry soiled clothes to a washwoman. On a number of previous occasions, the NKVD looked inside to make certain I wasn't carrying contraband. As I carried the valise out of the barracks, an NKVD agent wanted to know what was inside. "You know what's inside, laundry," I said. Fortunately, he didn't ask to inspect its contents. I hurried on to the railroad station where for a few rubles I rented a locker. Most of our things were soon out of the barracks and with nothing to carry, stealing away wasn't difficult. On the designated day, we rose as usual and pretended to be going to work. We walked to the railroad station instead. The train departed on time and we arrived in Kiev as planned.

Chapter 8

At the railroad station in Kiev, thousands of refugees were already standing on line. We got on line ourselves and on the same day obtained travel permits to depart from Kiev to Kowal.

Kowal was swarming with people. In addition to the resident Jews, there were thousands of returning refugees who had gotten their fill of Soviet paradise. At great jeopardy to their lives, they scarcely made it into Russian-occupied Poland.

By contrast with people living in Russia, those in Kowal lived a relatively good life. They had all sorts of things to trade. Although the stores were practically empty, the black market provided everything that anyone could want. It was a veritable cornucopia of things to eat and the Russians were buying in quantity. They spent their rubles as though they were "pouring peas from a sack." For with the very same rubles, which they could buy nothing other than their meager food quotas in their own country, they purchased everything that was for sale in Kowal, a new experience for them.

In greatest demand were watches, for which they willingly paid the highest prices. They came home from the border towns with bags filled to overflowing with precious commodities and sold them for ten times their value. These "mad" bargains in smuggled goods gave rise to an exaggerated even legendary conception of the wonders of life in capitalist countries. The Russians held their breath as they listened to the tales spread about by returning Soviet soldiers.

The Soviet authorities regarded this phenomenon as dangerous. Alarmed that their citizens were being carried away with these stories from across the border, they decided to eliminate the threat. They ordered placards to be hung on the walls of the city directing all refugees to register during the course of the next three days. They would be asked whether they wished to return to the German-held area of Poland or, alternatively, receive Soviet passports to obtain employment deep within the Russian mainland. Since Kowal was a border city, it was to be cleared of refugees for they posed an undue burden on the occupation forces.

People filled the registration stations. Most of those electing to return to the German held territories were Poles. The German registration agents scrutinized their papers. Poles were permitted to return to live under German occupation but Jews were barred and immediately referred to Soviet officials for processing, bound for the Soviet Union.

Uziek and his wife managed to get back to Warsaw because in both appearance and name they seemed typically Polish. Hanele and I, and Bella and Hayim ignored the registration thinking it would be better to wait and see the outcome of this new edict. We rented a small room, originally a storefront, and the four of us set up housekeeping. My brother-in-law and I did a little trading in the marketplace and we all subsisted on the meager earnings it brought us.

The owner of our apartment had a daughter who was employed as a secretary in the offices of the occupying powers. The girl was friendly to us and, from time to time, she would bring news of official plans affecting refugees who registered but weren't in a hurry to apply for Russian passports. One day, upon returning from work, she came to our room and told us that a decree was issued in Moscow directing all refugees who hadn't yet obtained Russian passports to be forcibly expelled that very evening. She warned us against spending the night in our room. The city was to be cleared of refugees in one full sweep.

Convoys of troop trains were waiting on the outskirts of the city to take everyone away.

Although none of us registered, we were badly frightened and worried over what to do next. We decided to spend the night in the orchard behind our host's house. We took out our quilts and pillows and bedded down on the grass under the trees, hoping to escape becoming victims of this terrible decree.

We lay quietly on our bedding, expecting the worst. We were unable to shut our eyes, and kept straining our ears in the stillness for the slightest rustle that might indicate impending trouble. We didn't have to wait long. First, we heard the sound of a truck approaching. Then came the pounding of rifle stocks against the closed shutters of our little abode. The sound of furious shouts reached our ears: "*Atvariti, miznayim je zdies biejentzy jewiot!*" (Open! We know refugees live here). After shouting several times and banging liberally on the doors, they were convinced that there was no one inside. The truck started up again and its sound gradually dissipated into the night. We could scarcely wait for morning.

When we emerged from our hiding place, the streets of Kowal were unrecognizable. Instead of the noise of thousands of people, we were greeted with the silence of a burial ground. The city was emptied as if hit by an epidemic. Occasionally, a Red Army soldier would pass by, his clumsy boots echoing dully in the emptiness as if pounding on some hollow metal casket.

We would slip into our apartment like frightened mice and lock ourselves in. What should we do now? We spent the day measuring and weighing every remaining option. It was impossible to continue living as we were, of that we were certain. Sooner or later, we would be caught and our punishment would be severe. There was nowhere to hide. Were we to go out in daylight, we would be recognized immediately. We were unable to sleep for yet another night and spent the entire time in obsessive discussion about the danger hovering over us and in calculating our chances of survival. We decided to voluntarily surrender to the authorities and share whatever fate awaited the other refugees. Whatever our suffering, it would be easier to endure together with others.

When that second sleepless night was over, we packed our belongings, opened the door to the little store as wide as we could, and waited for someone to notice us. Three Red Army officers came by. We called them over and told them we were refugees. We heard that all the refugees were taken away. The soldiers must have accidentally missed us, we said, but we didn't want to be exempted. We wanted to share whatever fate awaited the others and we were surrendering voluntarily.

Two of the soldiers immediately took up guard over us. The third went to call for a truck to take us away. A short time later, a truck arrived and we got on with our slim possessions. We were taken to the outskirts of the city and left off in an enormous building. There, sitting on the floor, were thousands of refugees, their bundles beside them, awaiting an unknown fate.

We were registered separately with separate questionnaires. Then large trucks arrived. We were loaded on board, together with our bags, like so many geese, and taken to the railroad yards outside the city limits where long trains of freight cars stood waiting for us. Forty people, baggage and all, were stuffed into each of the freight cars, the doors of which were then bolted shut from the outside. Two armed Red Army officers were assigned to guard each car. We had no idea where we were being taken. The train dragged on slowly. As we read the names of the stations along the way, we realized that we were going farther and farther north. The further we traveled, the firmer our conviction that we were en route to the white bears of Siberia.

Drained and tired, after three weeks of exhausting travel, we arrived at last in the Transfer City of Asino. Most of those being sent to Siberia were first brought to Asino and then taken along the Chula River to various settlements in the Siberian taiga. We were ordered to sit down and wait for a boat of transport. Night fell, damp and chilly. The grass was cold and wet with dew and we began to shiver. Spreading our two quilts between the four of us, we huddled together to keep warm. We covered ourselves with our coats and made an attempt to nap.

Suddenly, clouds of mosquitoes attacked us. We tried pulling our coats up to cover our heads, but to no avail. The insects came through even the smallest opening and bit us terribly on the face, neck, hands, legs and anywhere else that was accessible. It was impossible to chase them away. An awful struggle between man and mosquito lasted all night and it was enough to make one lose one's mind. We jumped up and ran from one spot to another, hoping to find shelter from the attack, but there was none to be had. As far as the eye could see there was nothing but wild taiga, endless overgrown forest, where a human being couldn't even set foot. In our frantic struggle, we grabbed up our quilts and wrapped ourselves in them. We twisted in every direction in our fear-filled attempt to keep from being eaten alive by the vicious parasites.

We looked like black ghosts dancing in the gloomy night. The mosquitoes cruelly attacked every millimeter of our bodies and relentlessly sucked our blood till we could hardly stand it. We couldn't wait for morning, hoping for relief from this dreadful nightmare. In the dawning light, we were able to see in one another, the outcome of our nocturnal ordeal. Our lips, hands, and legs were all swollen, and our faces were so puffed up, our eyes could scarcely be seen.

The boat that was to take us finally arrived. It was an immense barge, black and dirty. As many of us as could fit were packed in, like so many cattle. After several trying hours we arrived in the town of Ziransk, in the region of Novosibirsk. The Soviet slave traders were there waiting for us. They immediately started to sort the newly arrived human merchandise for forced labor.

Since my brother-in-law was a chauffeur-mechanic, he was called to step away from the group and stand to one side. We told the officials that we were a family and wanted very much to stay together. We pleaded with them not to separate us. They pushed us aside and shouted at us with dripping sarcasm, saying that they weren't concerned with families. They would permit wives to accompany their husbands, but no one else. Hayim and Bella were told to stand in line with several others and taken away to a destination unknown. The rest of us were directed to load our things onto waiting horse-drawn peasant wagons. We were then lined up in pairs and ordered to march behind two armed soldiers, and in front of two that brought up the rear. Our column was comprised of mostly the elderly, women and small children. Some of them didn't have sufficient strength to keep up the pace and lagged behind. The two soldiers at the rear urged them on, sometimes striking them with their gunstocks to muster their last bit of strength.

It began to snow although it was only September. The snow was heavy and wet. It wasn't the kind of snow we were accustomed to seeing in Poland, neat, sparkling crystals that looked like so many variegated stars. What fell from the skies here were irregularly formed "sheets" that soon transformed the ground into puddles of mud which were so sticky that walking became increasingly difficult. In front of us was a professor from the University of Krakow, an elderly gentleman who had apparently reached the limits of his strength. We saw that he was about to topple over, so Hanele and I approached him and we each took hold of one of his arms so we could hold him up to walk him. The poor man could no longer stand however and had to stop. When we pleaded with him not to give up, to continue walking, he refused. We had fallen behind the other marchers and the rear guard began to yell and curse at us in the coarsest Russian possible. We pointed to the old man to show that we were holding him up to keep him from falling. They then showered us with even worse verbal abuse than before, and angrily pulled him from us. When they attempted to set him on his feet, he fell full length into the mud. Seeing that he was in serious condition, the guards ordered us to help them lift him up and get him to the horse and wagon that came up behind us.

At dusk we arrived at the village of Seminovka, forty-two kilometers from Ziransk. Tired, wet, and hungry, we were led into a huge wooden shelter. We, were each handed a small ration of black bread. We were told to pour our own *kipitok* from a steaming kettle and sit down on the bare clay floor to eat. Afterwards, badly chilled, and still in our wet clothing, we lied down, on the floor, to sleep.

Early in the morning, we were driven outdoors, where the guards announced that we didn't have much further to go. It was a matter of eight kilometers more. There, in the village of Prokharuvka, we were to build a new city. If we became loyal workers and met our quotas, we "would receive everything." At the conclusion of these remarks the order to march was given, and our column started out again. In something over an hour, we arrived in the village of Prokharuvka. We entered a large mess hall, where we were served small bowls of *shtshi* (sour soup made of green tomatoes) and another four-hundred-gram portion of bread.

After the meal, we were again directed to line up and were led two kilometers farther on to a brand new village which had been given the name "Sukhay-Log." Alongside a wide road, were new, but still unoccupied, little shacks that had just recently been built. Six to eight people were assigned to each shack, which consisted of a single large room that was completely bare. There was no sign of furniture anywhere, no bed, no table, not even a bench to sit on. We complained to the official in charge of the new settlement: How will we sleep? Where will we sit? How can we be expected to live without anything but the four walls? By way of reply, he showed us a pile of boards and another pile of logs lying outdoors. He said that he would provide an axe, a saw, a hammer and some nails per shack and give us three days to get settled before putting us to work.

Besides Hanele and me, those assigned to our shack included an elderly couple and a woman with a one-year-old child. The NKVD had sent the father of the child to some unidentified location, depriving the woman of her husband and the child of its father simply because the man had voiced a complaint regarding the inhuman conditions the three of them were being forced to endure.

I lost no time bringing in the wood and obtaining the tools and nails from the official in charge. First, I cut some of the boards and put together a bed. After that, I built a table and two long benches to put alongside it. I had to admire my own handiwork, it looked that good. When our co-tenants saw how well I did, they asked that I make beds for them as well. I didn't refuse them. By the end of the day, our abode assumed a more habitable appearance. Some of the people in nearby houses also requested that I make things for them, and I had more than enough to do for the three days helping my neighbors get their homes in order.

We all went out to where the tall, wild grass was growing behind our houses. With our bare hands, we gathered up the grass, which was still wet from the first snowfall and brought it into our huts. We spread it on the floor to dry, then laid the dry "hay" over the boards of our beds. Some people were fortunate to have something to cover the hay with. Those who didn't, slept on the dry grass without covering it.

On the third day, the official in charge called us into the dining room of Prokharuvka and delivered a speech in which he explained that our work would be to cut down trees. In the spring we would put the downed trees into the Chulym River and let the current take the logs downstream to Omsk and Tomsk. In the large sawmills of those cities, the logs would be cut into boards, which would then be distributed to the lumberyards of the wood industries. We would be compensated for our work on the basis of how much of our assigned quota we produced. Anyone fulfilling one hundred per cent of his quota would receive six hundred grams of bread. Anyone fulfilling eighty per cent of his quota, four hundred grams. The less one produced, the less bread one would receive. The lazy wouldn't get to eat bread at all. Anyone who produced more than one hundred per cent of his quota would be named a

Stakhanoviets and would be entitled to receive special tokens, which he could use in a special dining room for exceptional workers. There he could buy a ragu (a stew that was more bones than meat) or a "meat cutlet" (that was more fat than meat).

"Naturally, the lazy won't be allowed to enter the dining room for the *Stakhanoviets*. Let me warn you all to forget where you came from and urge you to work energetically at building your new home. You'll erect a city here, which will be your city. You'll become citizens and enjoy every privilege enjoyed by all Russians. The sooner you become accustomed to the idea that this is your home, the easier it will be for you to acclimatize. Understood? If there's anything you don't understand, you may put your question to me, and I'll try to clear it up."

I stood up, raised my hand to attract the official's attention, and began to speak:

"Comrade *natchalnik*, a little while ago you mentioned that we ought to forget where we came from, forget our homes and never think of them again. How can we forget? The cruel war tore us from our homes, forcing us to leave behind those we hold dearest. Some of us left our parents. Husbands left their wives and children. We were separated from our warm, comfortable homes where, for better or for worse, we would have lived out our years in familiar surroundings. And then, suddenly, such an awful change! We were cruelly dragged to distant, frigid Siberia, suffering inhuman conditions all along the way. We're impoverished and unclothed, and now we're being forced into slave labor, to do work that none of us ever learned to do. What sins have we committed, to deserve this?"

Everyone assembled broke into applause. Suddenly frightened and stunned by my own words, I sat down, thinking I'd gone too far, and that I might pay dearly for having done so. When the crowd settled down, the commissar banged his fist angrily on the table. His overstuffed face turned red with rage as he roared in wild fury:

"We do not tolerate this sort of thing! We've a place for counterrevolutionaries who preach parasitism. Our Red Army soldiers are fighting on the battlefronts, and giving up their lives to rid the world of fascism. It is their blood that has freed you from Polish feudalism. We've extended our hands in brotherhood and made free men of you. And you repay our good will with rebelliousness. You can forget about our ever letting you return to your accursed Poland!"

Silence reigned in the hall. A deep depression fell on everyone. My dear Hanele's voice was tinged with fear as she reprimanded me for being the only one to speak up on our behalf. She was very much afraid that the commissar might take revenge and send me away so far that no one would ever know what had become of me, just as they had done to the husband of the woman who was living with us.

Early the next morning, when the sirens blared in Prokharuvka, everyone hurried to the square. We were divided into brigades consisting of eleven persons each. Ten individuals were to do the work, while the eleventh was named *diesatnik* (one in charge of ten workers). It was the *diesatnik's* responsibility to see that the members of his brigade did their work and, when the workday ended, to assess and record how much of its assigned quota they had filled.

When our brigades had been issued their saws and axes, a convoy of several armed soldiers conducted us to a forest several kilometers away to show us how to fell a tree. Deep notches were made low down on the trunk so that the tree would fall to one side. Two workers then used a long saw on the opposite side of the notches. The tree crashed, ending in a loud snap as it separated from its trunk. Next, other workmen approached and used their axes to chop off all the branches. Then several people most of them women, dragged the severed branches out of the woods to an open field and burned them. The workmen who chopped the tree down now returned, measured the trunk, and cut it up into prescribed lengths so as to avoid waste. The length of the trunk determined the spacing of the cuts. The logs were moved and laid side by side in orderly stacks. Finally, the *diesatnik* measured the circumference of each log, marked the thickness on a cut-off end with his hammer and chisel, and recorded the information in his book. After work, he brought his report to the camp office where the total amount of work the brigade had completed would be calculated.

Despite our returning home weary from a full day's work, we were obliged to go out into the woods after dark and gather firewood. We had to toil in the forest even on our days off to amass enough for the hard winter to come. We had to get it done before snow covered the ground, for the snow never melts in those regions prior to the month of May.

Life was extremely difficult. Our ration of the black, clay-like bread wasn't enough for even a single meal, yet we greedily consumed all of it first thing in the morning with our hot *kipitok*. That little bit had to sustain us throughout the arduous workday.

In the evening, after work, frozen, hungry and exhausted, we were barely able to drag ourselves the few kilometers from work to the mess hall. Once there, all we could buy was a bowl of *shtshi*, or *rosalnik*, which consisted of water with a few bits of floating sour green tomatoes or pickles. We poured it into our stomachs in a vain attempt to still the incessant gnawing hunger that ate at our insides.

The deeper into winter we went, the more trying our living conditions became. The garments with which we left home began to fall apart from wear. Whenever we sewed tears in one spot, new ones appeared in another. There was nothing with which to patch the holes. We couldn't find so much as a rag for the purpose. There was nowhere to shop and nothing to buy with the paltry few rubles we earned for our slave labor, save the ration of bread and the watery, mock soup. It was worse than that, for we hadn't even shoes to wear on our feet.

According to Soviet law, anyone sent to Siberia was to receive a pair of felt boots and a quilt jacket before being put to work in its forests. Of course, we never received anything of the sort. We tried holding our dilapidated shoes together with strips torn from our ragged shirts.

There was no way to obtain shirts either. By the time we had been in Russia for a year and a half, we had no shirts at all. Fortunately, I was still able to wear my cotton-wadded jacket, which I received when I worked at the *Shvayni* factory in Minsk.

When winter was at its worst and temperatures dropped as low as forty to fifty degrees below zero Celsius, and the snow covered the ground to a depth of two to three meters, it was impossible to go to work in the woods. On days such as these we were given shovels and put to work clearing a path to the well from which we drew our water. To fetch the water we turned a crank, which let a pail, fastened by a long chain, down into the well, and then cranked the pail up. Everyone spilled a little water beneath the crank handle and the icy cold caused the accumulated spills to freeze over, one on top of the other, until they formed a hill of ice the height of the well.

One day as she went to the icebound well, Hanele slipped while cranking up the pail of water. As she fell against the pile of ice, she let go of the crank handle. It continued to revolve as the full pail descended and the handle struck her on the head repeatedly, rendering her unconscious. Fortunately, several women found her lying there insensible and bleeding. They carried her to our hut and resuscitated her. It took her many long weeks to recover from the painful blows of that day.

Chapter 9

Sometimes we were hit with raging snowstorms accompanied by fierce, biting winds, and our little shacks would be completely covered with snow. One day we arose and were about to leave for work. When we looked out the window, we saw that we'd been buried alive.

We put on our outer clothing, and opened the door (which, fortunately, opened inward), but we couldn't see the sky. We worked very hard to clear an opening out of our "grave." It took us half a day just to fashion a short footpath near the entrance so that we would have someplace to relieve ourselves. There could be no thought of going further.

We were buried in the snow for two days. When we tried to light a fire in the stove, we were nearly asphyxiated because the chimney was filled with fallen snow and the smoke backed up into the house. We had to keep the door open to let the fumes out. Now the freezing cold caused us to suffer even more. It was a long time before the smoke wended its way out through the chimney so that we could shut the door.

We filled pots and buckets with snow and put them on the stove to melt the snow for water. After two days, some people dug a path to our house and freed us, permitting us to go out onto the village road.

The long winter dragged on like an endless nightmare. Despite the dreadful cold and deep snow, we were driven mercilessly into the woods to fell trees. Before we could put a saw to a tree, we had to clear the snow around it for a distance of three to four meters in order to have where to run when the tree began to fall. The merest breeze could change the direction of the fall, in which case failure to run in the opposite direction could well have resulted in death. Just clearing the snow to make such an escape route required half a day's work. Consequently, it was impossible to fill the prescribed work quota and we received only two to three hundred grams of bread. During the winter months, many people died of cold or hunger, or both. Falling trees killed some. We could scarcely wait for spring to arrive.

In May, at last, the snow began to melt. The coming of spring, we hoped, would improve our situation. It soon became evident, however, that the season brought along some brand new hardships.

In Siberia, everything comes on suddenly. Just as winter arrives all at once, so does summer. No sooner does the snow begin to thaw than it melts completely, seemingly overnight. The heavy snow cover is in a flash transformed into deep mud and water puddles. The appearance of these large pools and deep mud holes were accompanied by billions of mosquitoes, arriving in great cloud formations to devour our bodies.

During the winter months, we managed to keep our shoes bound together and bandaged, and our feet dry because the ground and the snow were too frozen to leak into our shoes. But slogging through the mire in the spring made our shoes heavy with moisture and made our lives miserable.

To protect our faces from the mosquitoes, we were supplied with linen hoods. These hoods covered the entire head and neck, and had a thick black inset in the front through which we were supposed to be able to see and breathe while we were being protected from the tiny parasites. We tried wearing the hoods and soon discovered that they helped us no more than cupping would a dead man.

In Siberia, the mosquitoes are so miniscule that they can get through the smallest opening. We found better use for the linen, making patches of it to cover the holes in our shabby clothing where our skin showed through. Apart from the tiny mosquitoes, there were also many so-called "horse flies" coming from out of the Siberian forest. When they beset someone and bit him, they not only sucked blood until they were ready to burst, they left a round hole at the spot where the blood was sucked. This hole usually filled up with pus and it would be weeks, sometimes even months, before the wound healed.

One tremendous horsefly somehow got through to my left foot and bit me on the instep, where one's shoelaces rub. Two days later, after tramping in the mud, I found that my foot had become so swollen I wouldn't be able to work. In the morning, I dragged myself to my job with great difficulty and went immediately to the overseer to show him why I couldn't work. He examined my foot and agreed that I wouldn't be able to work for three days and sent me to the doctor to have him attend to my foot. The doctor lanced the wound and pressed out some matter. He applied a clean bandage and told me to spend the next three days in bed, after which I was to report to him again.

When the three days had passed, I went to see the overseer again. The physician was there and urged the overseer to release me for several additional days because the wound was far from healed. The official took a look and said: "*Nitshevo* (It's all right), you'll be able to work." The doctor differed with him saying that by going to work I ran the risk of having more dirt enter the open wound, causing it to worsen. The official, unconvinced, insisted that I go to work. After some additional exchange, it was agreed that I be given easier work. The overseer handed me a notebook, a pencil, a chisel, a hammer, and a ruler. He appointed me a *diesatnik* of a brigade and sent me off to work.

My new work wasn't difficult. When the workers finished for the day and had arranged the logs in neat piles, I measured them and made entries in the notebook recording the length and breadth of both ends of each pile. I also saw to it that my brigade kept on working.

It was customary for the overseer to ride by on his horse once or twice a day to see if everything was in order. When he came by on the first day of my new assignment, he dismounted, tied the reins to a tree, and called me to him:

"*Kak diela?*" (How's it going?)

"*Nitshevo*," (All right) I replied.

"Do you understand your responsibilities?" he asked.

"Certainly," I answered.

As we walked along conversing, we moved quite a distance away from where the brigade was working. Going a bit farther into the woods, he sat down on the ground, bid me to sit down and began to question me: Where was I from? What was life like for people in Poland?

I told him that in Poland a worker was free to choose his employment and employer. He can purchase whatever he wishes with his wages. Bread isn't rationed. Those with sufficient income could purchase anything they wished because food, clothing, furniture and all sorts of other things were readily available. All one needed is money. With money one could buy whatever one's heart desires.

He listened to me with both his mouth and ears wide open. Then he said:

"*Ye znaiu szeshti gramatni*" (I know you're an educated person). I realized that from the very first day you arrived. I admired your courage in challenging the routine speech I give to newcomers. I could've punished you severely, but I respect courageous people. That's why I've assigned you less strenuous work. But what you've just told me is unbelievable. It sounds like a tale from the Arabian Nights. I can't believe there's any country on earth that provides its citizens with such luxurious living conditions as you describe. Either you've just invented it or you're lying."

"Listen to me, Comrade Khatyeyov. Poland isn't the greatest country in the world, but compared to living conditions here, even an impoverished worker, indeed even a dog, lives better there than an overseer does here."

He arose, smiling, and, as if he were talking to himself, murmured: "*Tu vriash, Grisha, tu vriash.*" (You're lying, Grisha, You're lying).

We returned from work that evening to find an unpleasant surprise waiting for us. Four NKVD officers in full-dress uniform, with gold braids on the epaulets of their overcoats, sat waiting for us on their well-fed horses, which were in fully decorated harness. When everyone in the village returned, we were commanded to line up and face the officers. Our overseer arrived hastily and counted us to see that no one was missing. A mortal fear came over me. I felt something terrible was about to happen. The ground beneath my feet began to shake for I expected the worst. I thought that I had brought trouble upon myself with my big mouth.

Still sitting on his horse, one of the NKVD officers began to read from a list of names and ordered each person whose name was called to step out. When he called six names, the riders paired off, two in front and two behind those selected, and marched them off in the direction of the district town of Ziransk. After the six refugees were led away by the NKVD, our commissar read us a short lecture. He warned us that the same thing would happen to us if we dared incite others or if we were dishonest in our work. He then ordered us to disperse.

That night I couldn't shut my eyes. I wondered where they dragged off those six unfortunate people. What did they do to deserve to be taken so suddenly from our midst? As I thought of them, a shiver passed through me. If they were being punished for incitement, I should have been the first to be taken away. Why did they pass me by? I decided henceforth not to utter any but the most essential words to the overseer, lest I provide him with an excuse to find fault.

When I went to work the following morning, I was in a state of shock. About midday, the overseer came riding by as usual to check on our work. I tried to keep from looking in his direction and pretended not to see him. But, he called out to me from some distance away:

"*Grisha, kak diela?*"

" '*V'so fpoaradkie*" (Everything's in order), I called back.

He approached and smiled as though nothing happened. Seeing the fright in my face, he said:

"I know you're alarmed over yesterday. Had I stuck to the letter of the law, I would have had you sent to prison long ago. I haven't done so up to now only because I pity your wife. I feel sorry for her because she's so young. I want to warn you though to be careful not to talk to anyone about forbidden subjects. Not everyone will be as considerate of the two of you as I am."

The people in my brigade were tired and exhausted. They were utterly incapable of producing the quota that would have entitled them to four hundred grams of bread let alone six hundred. The amount of bread the *diesatnik* received depended on the performance of his brigade. And so I wracked my brain for days about how to alleviate our situation. Finally, I had a great idea.

I noticed that not far from where we were working many logs had been scattered about and left over from years before. They hadn't been removed and sent downstream on the river's current. When our work was finished, I ordered my brigade to bring a few of those old logs over to where the freshly cut ones were lying and cut a thin slice, no more than one-fourth to one-half centimeter in thickness, off of each end. On the freshly exposed wood I chiseled the appropriate markings and made the usual notation in my notebook. Just a few extra logs made it possible for us to fill our quota and begin receiving our full ration of bread. Of course, the overseer, thinking that we had become proficient in our work was pleased. This "good fortune" was short-lived, however, for when the snow melted, and the river overflowed its banks, some of the logs which were lying at the river shore were washed away and carried down towards the sawmills of Omsk and Tomsk.

The brigades were broken up for the season and their members assigned different work. Workmen of superior physical strength were sent to bring the logs, which weren't at the water's edge, to the riverbank, and push them into the water. Others were assigned to building rafts. The overseer made a loud announcement that anyone who knew how to swim was to line up in a separate row. They were to ride on the rafts that were carried along on the current and release the logs that jammed at the edges of the stream, preventing the free movement of the lumber.

I went to line up with the swimmers. The raft that was placed at our disposal was made of logs bound each to the next with the young twigs of oak trees. We trimmed tall, thin tree trunks and used them to shape oars. We were allocated long poles (such as firemen use) which had a hook on one end. These hook-ended poles were used to dislodge logs stuck at the water's edge. Our equipment also included two saws, two axes, two cooking pots, some military mess kits and provisions for four weeks. Eight of us set out to perform this dangerous *eplav* (rafting) labor.

As the raft was carried down stream, it was our job to steer it so that it didn't cause us to crash into the bank. Wherever logs were prevented from moving, we had to use our picks to straighten them out so that the current could carry them along. Often a single log would hold up hundreds of others. At such times our work was life threatening.

We would slide off the raft and, with the agility of a cat, leap from one log to another, picks in hand, at the ready to separate the blocked logs. The slightest movement could cause a log on which one was standing to begin to rotate. When that occurred, even greater agility was required to keep one's balance. Sometimes a man would roll off and fall beneath the logs. Such a slip could well be fatal if, at that same moment, hundreds of logs were released and began their race down river. In so doing, the logs would strike the rafter over his head, and there would be no way that he could lift his head out of the water and avoid being hit. Rendered unconscious in this way, the victim was sometimes carried along by the current, with the logs, to perish in the cold water.

There were times when the stream carried us along calmly for dozens of kilometers. At such times, we would be quite at ease. We would sit with our feet over the side of the raft and catch fish with hooks which we had forged for ourselves at the village smithy. When evening fell, we would anchor the raft on the riverbank, gather wood for a large fire, and sit around it to broil the fish. We would also cook a *zatsyerukha*, a pasty soup made of flour and potatoes, obtained from the village, to complete our evening meal. We would knead flat rolls, from the soy flour that we brought along, and bake them on a flat tin over the fire. This would be our food for the next day. After supper we would wrap ourselves in our quilts and lie down to sleep beside the fire. One man remained on watch to see to it that the fire didn't go out, and to keep a look out for any of the wild animals lurking in the Siberian taigas. The watch changed every four hours.

Once when we were out in the middle of the river, a torrential downpour began. There wasn't anyplace for us to find shelter. It rained continuously for three days. We were soaked through and through. Even the quilts with which we tried to protect ourselves were saturated.

With great difficulty, we made our way to the rivers edge, then went deep into the taiga. Our teeth chattered from the cold and wetness. We sought shelter among the centuries' old oak trees, but even there it was no easy matter to hide from the rain. The ground from under our feet had become soft and, with every step, the moss, like so many sponges, squirted streams of water. Our feet sank into these mossy pools, and there was nowhere to sit. To add to all this, tiny mosquitoes, which also hid to escape the rain, attacked us as if they were billions of locusts. They devoured our faces, which were soon so swollen around the eyes that we couldn't see where we were. We found some trees that had been brought down by lightning. Their trunks snapped in two, they lay half-upended with their crowns dug into the ground. We sat down on these trees and surrendered ourselves to fate.

I suddenly found myself shaking and shivering, simultaneously hot and cold. All through the night, I was feverish and trembling, and tortured by dreadful nightmares. At daybreak, my comrades tried to wake me. I opened my eyes but had no idea where I was or what was happening to me. They shook me: "Get up! It isn't raining any more!"

Only then did I begin to realize where I was and how I got there. I told my co-workers that I was ill and unable to get up.

I don't recall how my comrades got me to a hospital or how long it took them to do it. When I came to, I found myself in a bed. There was a white sheet under me and a white pillowcase on the pillow. That was a luxury I hadn't seen nor experienced since the day we left home. I lay on the clean white cot sick with a brand new misery, malaria. I tried to summarize all that I'd undergone from the time I left Poland with just two shirts (which by then must have been rotting in the earth as rags). It was so long since I had the pleasure of putting on a clean shirt or lying in a clean bed. Proper meals and all good things were a thing of the past and only God knew whether we would survive long enough to live like human beings again. I wondered whether I would ever be able to take off the filthy and torn quilted jacket, which I wore next to my skin within which lice made their nests and incessantly gnawed at my body. Would I ever again have a pair of shoes that weren't torn, or a good pair of trousers to cover my body? Was that too much to ask for the arduous, life-threatening penal labor we were providing?

When the doctor came to examine me, I asked him what was wrong with me. He replied that I had a severe attack of malaria. He gave me injections of "acriquinine." After I had been there for two more days, I was taken back to camp Sukhoylag.

Instead of being sent back to rafting, I was assigned to a different brigade and was once again cutting down trees. To get to work, we had to cross a river and, once on the opposite bank, had to march three additional kilometers to and from the woods. Every morning we crossed the river in two large boats, which were secured at the river bank until it was time to return home. We worked at that location the entire summer.

Towards the end of the season, cold autumnal winds began to blow bringing many rainstorms in with them. On one such rainy autumn morning, our brigade marched down to the water's edge to take the boats to the other side of the river. But the boats were not to be found in their usual place. To our amazement, we saw them seesawing out in the middle of the river. We figured that the strong winds, which had raged throughout the night, must have torn the boats loose and pulled them down into the water. Not knowing what to do, we just stood there.

Our brigadier ordered us to stay there and wait while he ran back to the village to notify the overseer and let him decide what to do. Shortly thereafter, the overseer came galloping on his horse. Seeing the boats rocking far from shore, he called out:

"Whoever swims out and brings the two boats back to shore will be rewarded with an easier assignment. He'll also receive an extra ration of bread."

One of the men quickly threw off his clothes, jumped into the water and began swimming at a relatively fast pace. At about halfway, he turned back and swam at an even faster clip to shore. The cold and stinging ice water was more than he could endure. The overseer renewed his appeal. Who'll risk another try?

I made a fast mental calculation: The man, after having gone halfway, managed to get back to shore. The energy expended swimming back would have easily served him in reaching the boats. If he could go halfway and back, he could surely have gone the whole way. He had made a foolish decision. With that thought in mind, I spent no further time deliberating. I removed my clothing and jumped into the river. Swimming the Australian crawl, I was soon beside one of the boats. I took hold of it with both hands and got in. The overseer and workers raised their voices in a "Hurrah!" Grasping the oars, I rowed to the other boat, tied it to the one I was in, and brought them both in.

"From now on," the overseer announced, "it'll be your responsibility to take the men to work and bring them back. In between, you can spend the day just waiting for them to return."

From that moment on, my situation was improved, at least for a while. After putting the men ashore in the morning, I would have the day to myself. I brought along some tin cans in which we used to boil *kipitok* and I filled them with berries. The raspberries, blackberries ("black little bears"), and wild cherries that grew in the surrounding woods had ripened by summer's end and they made a great difference for our miserable starvation diet.

Chapter 10

As usual, winter made its appearance precipitously. A lasting snow began to fall and the accompanying frost painted magnificent white leaves and flowers on the tiny windows of our houses. The streams began to freeze as well and soon their surfaces were covered with a thick firm glaze.

One morning, I informed the overseer that the river was frozen and that the boats were immovable. The workers would now be able to walk across the river and I no longer had anything to do. I was therefore reporting for a new assignment. He gave it some thought and then asked whether I knew how to harness a horse. I replied that I'd never done that before but was certain that if someone showed me just once, I'd be able to do it.

He walked me to the stable where he pointed out an emaciated little horse that reminded me of The Old Mare of Mendele's story. He told me to lead the horse out to where an immense sleigh was standing. A very large barrel was fastened to the sleigh. In the center of its belly was a sizable opening large enough to admit a pail. He then brought out all the gear and taught me how to harness the horse to the sleigh. When the horse was harnessed, the overseer showed me how to drive the sleigh to the well, fetch the water, and fill the barrel. He told me that I was now the *vodovos* (water carrier), and would be responsible for supplying water to the bakery, the dining hall and the *banya* (bath).

Gradually, I became accustomed to my new "profession." It wasn't the easiest of occupations. The barrel held about a hundred pailfuls and

I had to draw them from the well five or six times a day and empty it as many times as I served the three institutions that served the village, which consisted of about twelve hundred exiles.

As I filled the barrel and dispensed the water, I couldn't avoid spilling some of it on myself. By the time my workday was over, I resembled the very barrel in which I transported the water. The water that I spilled on my trousers and my short jacket would, in the course of the day, freeze over. After a while, I would be wearing so much frozen "armor" that I could scarcely walk, let alone bend over.

It was a great effort to get home. I walked stiffly, my gait as slow as a turtle. As soon as I entered the house, I would, with strenuous effort, stretch out on the bed. Hanele would immediately pull off my rigid trousers, which were heavy with encrusted ice, and stand them up in a basin where they reminded me of a soldier standing at attention. When the ice melted, the trousers and my jacket were hung over the oven coal box to dry so they could be worn again the next morning.

In time, I became acclimated to my new task. I became acquainted with the kitchen help and with the bakers. In the course of the day, I was able to find time to chop wood for the bakery ovens. In return, they would pretend not to see me pull the "tails" (small slices that split off) from the freshly baked loaves, which I took home. These extra little bites of bread helped us fend off our hunger. I also chopped wood for the cooks in the mess halls, and for that service, I would get to take home a small pot full of soup that was much thicker than the soup sold to the workers. Sometimes they would add a few tiny bits of meat taken surreptitiously from the dining room of the commissars.

Hanele was pregnant at the time and the day of her confinement was approaching. On a bitter cold night in midwinter, her labor pains began. In the middle of the night, I ran to fetch a midwife. She told me to bring my wife to Prakhurovka, which was about two kilometers from Sukhoylag. The hospital in Prakhurovka had but a single room, which contained three beds in total. The doctor in residence was one of our refugee exiles. There was also a nurse in addition to the midwife. They hadn't instruments or medicine available.

Hanele lay in hospital for three days suffering dreadful pain but neither the doctor nor the midwife were able to help in any way. For three days she lay screaming in excruciating pain. The entire village sympathized with her, which was very touching.

The doctor told me that my wife might need surgery and that he was helpless, having nothing with which to perform an operation. We decided to take her to the regional hospital in Ziransk. To get there, we would have to go fifty kilometers by sleigh. With such fearfully cold weather, there was a distinct possibility the journey would never be completed. There was no time to lose.

A horse was harnessed to the sleigh. I asked a neighbor, who brought a featherbed from home, to lend it to me to save my wife's life. He lent it willingly. The quilt was tied around Hanele so that the cold wouldn't penetrate to her body. Fat was applied to her face to keep it from freezing. The doctor and the midwife got into the sleigh and I got on too, intending to drive. But the doctor and the nurse insisted I get off, shouting that I would make the journey more difficult. The heavier the sleigh, the harder it would be for the horse to pull it and the longer the journey would take, all factors threatening my wife's life. I was persuaded and, with a heavy heart, I let them go without me.

The next few days were very difficult for me. I couldn't forgive myself for being dissuaded from accompanying Hanele on such a life-menacing journey, leaving her to face the bad time alone. I had a premonition that something terrible would happen.

Three days later, the midwife returned and recounted the following: When they arrived at the hospital in Ziransk, the resident physician examined my wife and determined that she would have a normal delivery. A Caesarian section wouldn't be necessary. He anticipated that she would have an uncomplicated delivery in about two hours. It was past midnight when they arrived at the hospital. Fatigued, the midwife and the doctor went out into the corridor to catch a nap beside a warm stove. They fell fast asleep. In the meanwhile, Hanele, screaming in dreadful pain, passed the child. When awakened by her screams, the doctor and midwife entered the room. They found that the baby had its umbilical cord wound around its throat. As they lifted the child, it exhaled its last breath and died.

The hospital didn't even have hot or cold water available. Had there been, perhaps the baby could have been resuscitated. As a result of the negligence and irresponsibility of the hospital administration our little daughter was killed. Hanele was kept at the hospital for eight more days. Her awful ordeal left her physically very much weakened and emotionally shattered. She was devastated by the fact that the Soviet regime could treat human life so wantonly and cruelly.

After her return from the hospital, she cried continuously. She spoke of how beautiful the baby was—her skin white, not red like that of most newborn infants, her body slender. She had long lashes on her closed eyelids and she even had a full head of hair. As Hanele spoke, she wept so that my heart ached with sorrow and I cried along with her. I felt partially to blame for this terrible loss. If I went with her and hadn't permitted myself to be discouraged, this terrible tragedy mightn't have occurred.

News of the war was scant. All we knew was that the Germans, of whom the Russians made so much, and with whom they were formerly allied, attacked Russia. They advanced with lightning speed and were already deep in Russian territory.

Because of the war, we very seldom received mail from home. Hanele's mother wrote us that our friends, Uziek and Hella, were envious of us and were extremely sorry to have returned home. She begged that the four of us stay together at all cost. Perhaps it would help us survive the war in distant, cold Siberia. She was unaware that the Soviet slave drivers had already separated us and that, despite the fact that we probably weren't far from each other, we didn't know where Bella and

Hayim had been dragged off to. Hanele's mother asked us to write and tell her whether we had enough to eat and warm clothes to wear. Finally, she asked that we ignore the return address on the envelope and send our reply to the old address. This request led us to surmise that she feared German censorship of the mail and wanted to avoid any hint of ties with Russia.

In my reply, I told her not to worry about us. We were living very well. We were eating as though it was Yom Kippur (a day of fasting). We were well dressed, just like on Purim (a day when masked actors would sometimes visit houses dressed as beggars). We were domiciled in a splendid *sukkah* (a "tabernacle" for taking Sukkoth meals, a shed-like structure with branches for its roof). My only concern was for my mother whom I missed very much. How I wish I could join her! (She knew I lost my mother when I was eight years old.)

Ever since I suffered my first malaria attack during my career as rafter, I had one attack a week, like clockwork. I took three 5-milligram "acriquinine" tablets daily. Whenever I couldn't obtain them, the attack would be so severe I had to be taken to hospital. I would lie there for two weeks with a swollen spleen and wait for the hospital to obtain the medication I needed. Upon my release from the hospital, I would be exhausted and yellow as wax due to blood poisoning induced by the malaria parasite.

On one occasion, when I returned from the hospital, the overseer included me in a group of thirty to work a forest, some forty kilometers away, in a new village. For two days, we fought our way upstream to the designated area. When we arrived, we were quartered in an immense barracks. On the following morning, we were put to work.

The village was called Bagniuvka. It was a more suitable habitation for human beings than our own Prakhurovka. Pine trees grew everywhere. Previously, every forest we worked in grew only oak trees. The air and landscape of Bagniuvka reminded us of the Otwock in Poland where the Jews of Warsaw would take their vacation. In some spots the river bank was covered with a pale yellow sand which further reminded us of those good old days when we would sun ourselves till we perspired on the bright hot sand near Otwock.

Blueberries, blackberries and raspberries grew in abundance in the woods near Bagniuvka and we would gather them daily after work. They helped considerably in assuaging our hunger when added to the hardly satisfying ration of bread. Whenever it rained, tiny yellow mushrooms called *kazenushki* seemed to spring up before our very eyes. We gathered them up and cooked them also. They provided a very tasty meal.

Provisions were brought to us from Prakhurovka twice a week. I asked the people who brought them to deliver a message to Hanele that she request the overseer to permit her to join me since I thought life was better in Bagniuvka than it was in Prakhurovka. Several weeks passed before the overseer granted my wife her request. Her arrival raised the not so insignificant problem of where to live. We had no choice but to stay in the barracks where our bed occupied a corner separated from the others with a mere quilt. This time we both worked in the same brigade. Along with the other men, I felled trees while the women, including Hanele, dragged off the branches for burning. After work we gathered berries or red cranberries, which we cooked for our evening meal on our return home.

The ambience in the barracks was very pleasant. We were young and we made time, before turning in, to sing, to recite poetry, or to tell jokes and anecdotes, all of which helped us forget our troubles during that dreary summer of labor. We comforted each other with the thought that the war would soon be over and that we would return home to those most dear to us. We would live to tell them the story of our years of harrowing experiences in far away bleak Siberia.

Hanele and I always left for work together. Once, on a warm, sunny day, the overseer had to depart early in the afternoon leaving us un-supervised. Since there was no one to watch over us, we all grew lazy and sat down to schmooze. Soon the workday was a mere half-hour from ending. Hanele suggested that she go into the woods and pick some berries so that when it was time to go home, we could leave promptly rather than first begin our gathering of berries. I thought it a good idea but warned her not to wander off too far lest she get lost.

The workday over, I took up my axe and saw and went into the woods to look for Hanele. I couldn't find her. I asked some people who were still gathering berries whether they had seen my wife. No one saw her. They said that some people had already left for home and she must have gone with them. So, I hurried home.

I went into the barracks, but didn't find her there either. I went out into the yard, to the well, and to the washroom. She wasn't to be found anywhere. I became highly anxious. I looked around and found that everyone had returned except Hanele. The sun began to set and dusk was settling in. In desperation, I went to the overseer and told him how worried I was. We hurried to the stables and he saddled up the three horses that were standing there. He helped me mount one of them, ordered his assistant to take the second, and climbed on the third one himself. We galloped to the woods and set off in three different directions.

I began at the spot where I knew she entered the woods. I rode slowly, going deeper and deeper into the forest all the while calling out her name. The echo of my own voice was all I heard in return. It grew darker every minute. I greatly feared the advent of night for these woods were populated with bear and other wild animals. I gave my horse a slap and galloped back towards the village, hoping that the other riders might have found Hanele. My fears intensified when I saw the other two. They also returned without her.

I immediately turned off the path on which I encountered the two men and galloped down a different narrow trail into the depths of the woods. Every so often I stopped and called for Hanele as loudly as I could. Receiving no response, I rode another half kilometer and called out once more. At last, I heard her very faint desperate cry. With all my strength, I shouted for her to remain where she was until I came to her.

I knew from experience that an echo can be misleading sounding as though it's coming from the direction opposite the one it's actually coming from. If, for example, the sound seems to come from a northerly point, one should go south. I therefore hurried off in the opposite direction. To be sure I was going the right way, I stopped after I'd gone about twenty meters and called out again. This time her response was much louder. Certain that I was proceeding in the right direction, I galloped on even faster and finally espied her standing on the tall stump of a tree that had been cut down.

The area around the stump was overgrown with wild thorns, making it impossible for me to ride up closer. I tethered the horse to a tree and ran to her. Her sandals were in her hand and it was soon apparent that her legs were lacerated and bloody from wandering among the wild thorns and bushes. I had to carry her on my back until we came to a path for her torn sandals didn't afford her protection from the sharp thorns. I untied the horse and we rode back to the village. It was late at night when we arrived, but no one was able to go to bed without knowing the outcome of the incident. When they caught sight of us approaching in the dark, they ran toward us with shouts of joy, happy to see us return. Now they could retire for the night, in peace.

The radio loudspeaker on the wall of a corner of the barracks informed us that England, France and the United States entered into an alliance to help Russia in the war against Germany. We received the news with great enthusiasm. Our hearts were rekindled with renewed hope that the time was close at hand for this cruel war to end. It would bring us our long sought for salvation and enable us to reunite with those we love and cherish the most.

We were no longer interested in doing anything during the evenings other than listen to the loudspeaker and catch every bit of news of the war. It wasn't possible to learn much on the radio however. The Soviet authorities censored all news bulletins. Only news that was favorable to the government was released. Most of what was promulgated was Communist propaganda. Night and day, we were served up dry reports about the collective farms, the factories and the rural soviets, and were obliged to listen to long lists of names of *Stakhanovites* who reached one hundred or one hundred fifty per cent of their work quotas. We were told of how well the *Stakhanovites* were rewarded and how bright their lives had become as a result. Only occasionally did we hear of world events or anything concerning the war. However, when the Soviet Army began to repel the Germans with the aid of the Western powers, the radio reported their victories with greatly exaggerated accounts of the exploits of the Red Army under the leadership of their blessed "Great Father," Stalin.

One evening, the loudspeaker began blaring, "Attention! Attention! Important Announcement!" Our hearts began to race as we heard the radio commentator report on an agreement that was signed in London between General Sikorsky of Poland and the Soviet Union. All former Polish citizens in the Siberian taigas were to be set free and General Sikorsky was to organize the refugees into a Polish Army. The soldiers would be trained in England and would fight with the Allied Powers against the Germans. That night no one slept. We celebrated the good news by singing patriotic Polish songs and refused to heed the overseer when he shouted to call it a night and go to bed, for we had to go to work in the morning.

The next morning, no one wanted to go to work. We all ran to the water's edge. When Hanele and I arrived, there was but one boat to Sukhoylag built to accommodate no more than twelve people. Instead, twenty crowded on. I first made sure that Hanele got on board.

A few moments later, the boat was overcrowded and pushed from shore so that in the crush no one else could get in. I jumped into the water with all of my clothes on and tried to climb onto the boat. But the oarsmen kept striking my hands and I had to let go. I was obliged to go back to shore dripping wet.

There were about ten of us who had the misfortune of being left behind. We conferred about what to do and decided to build a raft. Not to lose time, we brought the logs we needed to the river's edge and cut some thin willow twigs with which to bind the logs. It took all day to get them laced. We then pushed the raft into the water and secured it to the bank. We shaped poles into oars and in the grey of dawn we were on our way.

We glided with the current and as each one of us used his oar to urge the raft on, it sped along like an arrow out of a bow. When at one point we realized we were approaching a knee shaped bend in the river, it was too late to hold the raft back. It crashed full speed against the bank and fell apart completely. All its lacing burst simultaneously and the logs sped off with the current. The force of the crash catapulted us into the water. Those who could swim came back safely to shore but the stream carried one man further and further away. We could see him fighting for his life. I immediately raced off along the bank. After going a distance of several meters, I jumped into the water and swam as quickly as I could against the current and toward the drowning man, just as the current carried him to me. A log from the raft sped towards me at the same time. I grasped it with one hand and the drowning man with the other. I helped him take hold of one end of the log and told him to kick his feet so he wouldn't go under. Then letting him go and placing the other end of the log under my arm, I swam to shore where the others helped the endangered man out of the water. I saved him from almost certain death.

We were still about ten kilometers from Sukhoylag and had no alternative but to take off our shoes and walk in the water a little way off shore. All along the shoreline were thorns that had been growing wild for thousands of years. They had never before been trod by the foot of man. It took every ounce of strength to plod our way through the ten kilometers to Sukhoylag. Our bodies were badly bitten by mosquitoes and our faces were swollen. When we arrived at camp, we found the village in total disarray.

Everyone was beaming in anticipation of being set free. Yet there was concern over the fact that there seemed no way to escape. The overseer made dire threats that anyone who ran away would be severely punished. He issued an order forbidding anyone to leave in advance of getting confirmation of their release.

The larger families had even greater worries. How could they get away from a place that was two hundred kilometers from the nearest railroad station? The younger people and childless families decided to ignore the overseer's threats and secretly planned their escape. Summer was over and if they didn't break away within the next few days, they would become captives of the coming Winter. They would be doomed to spend the ensuing nine or ten months languishing in frigid Siberia in the worst of possible circumstances. Hanele and I felt that we had to get away no matter what. We planned not to disclose our decision to anyone. We would manage it on our own.

One morning, at the first sign of day, we picked up our sorry bundles and walked out of the village. We proceeded with running steps for the first few kilometers to get as far away from the village as possible. We figured it would be two hours before anyone reported for work. We wouldn't be missed until then. By that time, we would have covered so much ground that no one would catch up with us.

After two days of laborious progress through the wild taigas of Siberia, we reached the regional seat of the town of Ziransk. There we saw hundreds of refugees sitting beside the river. They were waiting for a ship to arrive which would take them to Asino, where they hoped to board a train that would take them away from Siberia. We waited all night on the riverbank for a steamer to appear, but in vain. We were tired and hungry as we sat there, straining our eyes, waiting for help in the form of a ship. Not only didn't it come but we were unable to buy anything to eat at any price. Hanele's feet had become blistered in the course of our continuous fifty kilometer two day march and the abraded wounds were now becoming infected.

When we noticed an empty truck going by, I ran up to the driver and asked him where he was going. "To Novosibirsk," he replied. I asked whether he would take us along.

"I'll take anyone who'll pay me."

We had several hundred rubles with us left over from what we'd been paid for our work at Sukhoylag. Since there was nothing to purchase other than a bowl of sour soup once a day and a ration of bread, we easily saved up the rest during the fourteen months of our bleak existence there. The truck driver asked for one hundred twenty rubles per person. We haggled for a very long time. When he saw the condition of Hanele's feet and that we were both wearing shoes so torn that the soles hung loose and had to be bound up with ropes, he relented some. He accepted a hundred and forty rubles for the both of us. That was nearly half our fortune.

Chapter 11

When we arrived in the large Siberian city of Novosibirsk, the truck driver let us off at a municipal eatery where the only food available was a bowl of sour *shtshi*. We greedily gulped down the watery concoction. At the very least, it would cover the lining of our empty stomachs.

Still hungry, we went out into the streets of Novosibirsk. We looked about and realized that passersby recognized us to be strangers. One woman stopped and asked who we were. I told her we'd just left the taiga wastelands and wanted to get as far away from Siberia as possible before the cold and snowstorms set in. She told us that she too was Jewish and that she was a schoolteacher. She wished to help us and kindly took us to her home where she prepared a meal, and invited Hanele to stay the night. Unfortunately, however she hadn't room enough for me. I left Hanele with her and we arranged to meet in the morning to plan what to do next.

I went to the railroad station to find out if any trains were available and to see if I could stay the night as opposed to wandering about the city in the cool of autumn. It was warm in the station and many a refugee lay sleeping on the floor. When I struck up a conversation with some of them, they told me how they'd run away from circumstances similar to ours. They were hoping to make their way to the Central Asian Republics of Tashkent or Samarkand or to some other warm city where they might stay for the duration of the war. Here was cold and hunger. There they could escape the cold, which would make life a bit more tolerable.

In the morning, I went back to the schoolteacher's house and told Hanele of my conversations at the railroad station. I thought that, since we couldn't go home, it mightn't be a bad idea to try and go to Tashkent where we wouldn't be subjected to the relentless cold.

We went to the station and when a train arrived heading for Tomsk, we purchased tickets and went on board. A short time later we arrived in Tomsk. When we alighted in Tomsk, we inquired after a municipal dining room for we knew that there we would encounter people who knew of the availability of suitable employment. We had to have something to eat and had to get some rest in order to conserve our strength for the certain troubles ahead.

We sipped sour *rosalnik* as we conversed with people who sat at the long dining room tables consuming the same tart delicacy. An elderly Jewish man informed us that it would be best if we could land employment at the municipal electric works. We asked him where the electric plant was located and before long we presented ourselves before its manager.

The manager turned out to be a very warm Jewish gentleman. We told him about all we'd been through and he was obviously moved. He had a Jewish heart, after all. He said it would be very difficult to get us settled in the city. He proposed an alternative, which he thought, was preferable. It would allow us to work while awaiting the outcome of the war and without going hungry. He figured to send us to the *prirodna khazaystvo*, the farm that supplied produce for the employees of the hydroelectric plant. The farm was located about twenty kilometers outside the city. He was certain that would be best for us. He then took us into the plant cafeteria and handed us an authorization for purchasing the evening meal. Dinner consisted of thick potato soup, and a ration of white bread. We were also given permission to spend the night in the factory clubroom. The next morning, the manager sent a truck to get produce from the *prirodna khazaystvo* and he told the driver to take us with him, giving him a letter for the farm overseer directing him to provide us with employment.

The overseer of the *prirodna khazaystvo Tomskey electrostantsia* assigned us a room with a bed, and ordered new jackets for us from their warehouse. But since it was our first day there, we were allowed to rest.

Early the next morning, Hanele was to join the ranks of those who gathered potatoes in the field and I was to be the night watchman. My task was to guard the farm against thieves who might come to steal crops. Since I was to start work at night, I had the entire day before me and was free to do as I wished.

Seeing a farmer harnessing two strong horses to a wagon, I asked him where he was going. When he said that he was going to town, I asked whether it would be all right for me to come along. "Of course," he replied, "so long as the foreman gives you permission." I hurried to ask the foreman, who readily consented.

When the driver passed the *toltshak* (marketplace), I asked him to let me off. I noticed heavy rubber galoshes on sale, so I purchased two pairs for Hanele and myself. I was very happy with this find for it meant having something to put on our feet. *Tshinias* were preferable to shoes because, in addition to being waterproof, they could be worn with leggings that would help keep our feet warm. I spent every ruble we had for these overshoes. For the time being, I didn't want to think about our being penniless.

Later, I went to work at my new job. I had to guard the storehouse where products and tools were kept; the field, to see that no potatoes were stolen; the stable for the horses; and the cow barn. All night long, I roamed the farm with two huge wolfhounds that helped me do my work.

This place seemed like paradise when compared to Sukhoylag. To begin with, the work wasn't difficult and the mosquitoes weren't as voracious. Also, we weren't far from town, where a thriving black market made all sorts of goods available (at excessive prices, of course).

Food was better here than it was in the taigas, too. We would regularly receive a six-hundred-gram ration of bread. We were given five kilos of potatoes per person per week, and every month, a half kilo of sugar with four hundred grams of oil for cooking. We were no longer going hungry. Although conditions were much better, we didn't want to stay in Siberia for another long cold winter. But we needed both money and provisions for we wouldn't get far without them.

We were determined not to use up our bread rations. We dried the bread on the stove so that we would have something to eat on our prospective journey. For now, we would subsist only on potatoes. To have money for the road, I planned on gathering additional potatoes until I had two sacksful to sell on the black market. That would provide sufficient funds to take us to our destination.

No sooner said than done. In the middle of the night, when everyone on the *khazaystvo* was deep in sleep, when no one could see or hear, I went out into the field. There were some potatoes in the field, which had been dug up earlier in the day but hadn't been removed. To protect them from the night frost, they'd been covered with sacks. I took one of the sacks, filled it with potatoes, and carried it into our room, where I hid it under the bed. From among the other sacks in the field that night, I chose another one that was fairly clean. In that sack, I collected our zwieback, adding more each day.

After doing the same thing several nights in a row, we had enough potatoes, and at the end of the week, a sufficient supply of dry bread with which we could start out. During this interval, we boiled up a pail full of potatoes twice a day adding some onions, sauteed with our usual allotment of oil. Of course, I got the onions from the very same field and we didn't go hungry.

Given the "fortune" we amassed, we began to make plans for running away. We decided to do it on our scheduled day off. On the night before, when everyone was asleep, I took out everything we were going to bring with us: first the potatoes, then the zwieback, and finally our belongings. I took them some distance from the farm to a spot in the woods that was at the edge of the road and covered them with fallen twigs and leaves.

Before daybreak, we slipped out, picked up all our things and went out on the open road. When a peasant came by in a small wagon, we stopped him and got him to agree to take us to the city in exchange for a few rubles. The peasant was on his way to market. When we arrived there, I took all our things off the wagon, placed them to one side, and left Hanele to watch them while I went out into the market with some of our potatoes. The housewives besieged me. Each demanded that I sell my potatoes only to her. I asked eighty rubles per measure and the potatoes were grabbed up even before I finished quoting my price. Bit by bit, I sold everything. I now had quite a few rubles in my pocket and that before the military guards noticed what I was selling. Now that I was rid of the "contraband" there was no longer anything to be afraid of, so we dragged our bundles and ourselves to the train station.

Many refugees were already waiting around the station who, like us, were hoping to make their way to Tashkent, once described by Ilya Ehrenburg as "the city of bread." But there was no hope of getting on board a train. All tickets had been sold out weeks in advance. We found out that for a large sum of money a freight car could be rented and attached to the next train bound for the warmer *respublikas*. We were more than willing to pay our share if it would help us escape the cold of another Siberian winter. We would have to interest a party of about thirty-five people to pull off such a venture. And, although every one of the refugees wished to get away from Siberia as soon as possible, it proved to be very difficult to assemble a group of thirty three more people to rent the freight car. It would cost one hundred thirty rubles per person and very few were fortunate to have that much money, for most had none at all. But we managed to scrape together the requisite number. Two members of our newly assembled group undertook to go to the railroad official in charge of renting the car. The official escorted all of us, with our luggage, to the railroad yard. There, on a side rail, stood a freight car. The official directed us to load our things and told us that in the evening a locomotive would arrive and our car would be coupled to a train that was to take us to Tashkent.

After we loaded our things onto the train, we found that we still had several hours to wait. I left Hanele on the train to keep an eye on our things and hurried off to market to buy some things that might stand us in good stead on such a long journey to so distant a place. I bought some tea which I was told could be sold en route at an inflated price. Although I paid an exorbitant price, I was assured it would be worth ten times as much in Tashkent.

The train dragged on like a turtle through town and country. Cars were constantly uncoupled and new ones added as we went along. It took three weeks to finally reach the warm Uzbekistan region and its capital city, Tashkent. The city was teeming with Polish refugees making it resemble a Persian fair. The hundreds of thousands of people raised a great din. Refugees from every corner of the great Soviet nation came together and swarmed like bees around a beehive.

We all sought a place to sit down or at least put down our bundles, but in vain. The railroad station was so thick with people and their belongings that there wasn't room to put one's foot down. Every few minutes another train arrived to add yet more people to the crowd before steaming off to make room for the next train. A bit farther away on the larger square near the station so many people lay on the dirty grass, it was impossible to make one's way through them. We climbed over their legs as we held onto our packages and attempted to get as far as possible from this unending human mass. Finally, we noticed a bit of open space in the midst of this swarm of people and we quickly threw down our bags to prevent anyone else from taking the spot. Weary, we sat down right on top of our things. The zwieback we'd taken with us had long ago been consumed. We were without bread but glad to have made our way to a warmer province where it was possible to sleep outdoors without freezing.

After having slept under the open sky, I got up early in the morning, leaving Hanele with our things, and went to the local market to buy something to eat. The city of Tashkent was actually seven kilometers from the railroad station. After a solid hour of walking, I found myself in the city where I asked for directions to market.

Once there, my attention was drawn to the Uzbeks sitting on the ground with their legs crossed under them with sacks full of *uruk* (a dry, very sweet, peach-like fruit having a sweet, almond-like kernel). Some of the Uzbeks had red rags spread out before them with ripe, tasty looking pomegranates piled up high. Asking prices were reasonable considering that this was a black market.

I began by selling the tea, which we brought with us, for about three times our cost. I purchased a kilo of *uruk* and two very large *lepiashki* (flat rolls), which the Kirghiz called "*non*". I then hurried back to Hanele. I spent more than half a day at the market and I was certain she would be famished and impatient for something to eat.

However, when I arrived, Hanele came over with a large piece of bread in her hands. She smiled and explained how an elderly gentleman who was sitting near us noticed that I left early in the morning and hadn't returned for a long time. Seeing that Hanele was faint with hunger and still hadn't anything to eat, he asked her to watch his things for a while until he returned. Since she was already watching our own things, she replied: "Very well, I'm sitting here anyway."

A short time later, he reappeared with a large loaf of bread and a little kettle full of *kipitok*. He cut the loaf in half and gave one piece to Hanele in payment for watching his things. She didn't want to accept it, not wishing to be paid for so small a favor. But he was insistent, explaining that he didn't lack for money. He could allow himself anything he wished for because he left home with many possessions. Whenever he sold one of these items, he was able to buy enough on the black market to sustain him for a month. Even if the war were to last ten more years, he wouldn't die of hunger, he said.

"And where is he now?" I inquired, curiously.

"He's gone to the municipal bathhouse to bathe," she explained, "and he asked us to watch his things again."

I laughed over what happened, and we settled down to eat the *uruk* and the fresh white rolls that I bought, with great gusto.

The next day, I looked over what little we owned and saw that we still had a new nylon nightgown that Hanele had treasured for all this time. It was especially precious because it was a gift from her mother. I was wearing a wedding ring that hung loose on my finger because I had lost so much weight. Hanele had her wedding ring also. In addition, I had a small bag of mushrooms, which I dried in Siberia and kept aside for a rainy day. I also had the two sacks in which I carried the potatoes that I sold when we left the *Priradna Khozaystva*, as well as the sack I used for the zwieback we ate on our travels. I gathered everything together and set off for the city once more to see what I could get for them.

I went into the municipal dining hall and displayed my wares. A Russian woman that I showed my wife's nylon nightgown to was so taken with it that she enthusiastically shouted:

"*Taka krasyva plativa! Ya yestshi ni kagda nye vadalye!*"(I've never seen such a pretty dress!).

She immediately began bargaining with me.

"How much do you want for this?" she asked, holding it in her hand.

"I don't want money, I want produce," I replied.

"What kind and how much?"

"I want a bar of soap, and about five kilos of bread."

She haggled with me and I let her have the nightgown for four kilos of bread and a one pound block of soap.

My next stop was in the kitchen of the dining hall, where I showed the cooks the bag of mushrooms. They all wanted to purchase it from me. I bargained with them for a long time until someone was willing to pay the price of two good meals (which included soup, Ragu, and two kilos of bread) and an additional one hundred rubles.

I went back to Hanele and showed her what I was able to obtain. I only then noticed that my gold wedding band was no longer on my finger. I searched everywhere I'd been in the course of the day, but in vain. I couldn't find the little gold hoop.

We realized that just hanging around the streets, like most everyone else was doing, would serve no purpose. All we had left were the three sacks of potatoes and zwieback. When they were gone, we would die of hunger, and no one would even take note or care. As for the prospect of obtaining employment, that was impossible. The city was overrun with people. We took our luggage and elbowed our way back to the railroad station with the idea of taking a train further inland. We hopped onto the first train that arrived and it eventually brought us to Samarkand.

Samarkand was a city of little clay houses fenced in by a tall clay wall. Each of its "huts" consisted of a single room wherein an entire family was sheltered. The land all around was also of a drab, clayey gray. There were no pavements. Everything was imbued with the same gray hue. The only exceptions were the small government buildings. They were only one story high but appeared to have been dipped in snow, they were so white. They stood out and could be seen from a considerable distance.

We walked over to one of the little white buildings. The sign over the entrance read "Gorsoviet" (municipal administration). We went inside. An Uzbek, who obviously had plenty to eat, came toward us and, in a mutilated Russian, asked us what we wanted. We said that we were refugees from Poland recently freed from Siberia. We had been wandering about for several weeks and finally, with a great deal of difficulty, found our way to Samarkand. We were homeless, without food, and looking for work. It was here that we hoped to establish residency. He pointed to some long benches where several other refugees were already seated and who, like us, were also seeking refuge. We sat down and waited without knowing what for or for whom. In the meantime, more refugees arrived. There was no more room on the benches, so they sat down on the floor.

A truly primitive wagon, with two grotesque high wheels, arrived, drawn by a camel. The Uzbek said something to the driver in his native tongue and he, in turn, counted off nine of us, Hanele and myself included. He directed us to take our bundles and go on board the wagon. The driver drove off with us without our knowing where we were going.

The wagon lumbered on for about two hours. The wagon floor was so steep that we kept sliding backward and were in constant peril of falling off. This was because the two shafts were harnessed high at the camel's neck and this tilted the entire body of the wagon.

The road outside the city was of the same gray clay found in the city. From time to time, we saw the clay houses of farmers who lived in the desolate, impoverished districts of the collective. Finally, we came upon vast fields that stretched for miles around. Growing in those fields were thin, brown twigs with large, round buds that were white as snow. When we came closer, we saw that the men and women who worked these fields of twigs had sacks hanging from their necks. They were picking the white buds, which turned out to be cotton, with both hands, and deftly deposited them in their sacks.

The wagon drove into a very large yard and the Uzbek driver, addressing us in his own tongue, told us to get off. We were left standing beside a huge warehouse within which everything needed for administering the farm collective was stored. The driver went up onto the roof and, forming a round horn with the palm of his hands, sang out an exotic, long drawn out tune:

"*H-a-a-k-i-m, h-a-a-k-i-mm!*" Several seconds later, there was an answer, which seemed like an echo: "*Y-a-h-shi, y-a-a-shi!*"

The Uzbek then descended from the roof and explained that he had just given demonstration of the telephonic device by which anyone on the collective could be summoned and how, in general, communication took place. He then directed us to sit on the ground and wait.

A few minutes later, a man arrived. He was dressed in white linen trousers, tied with a rope around his waist instead of a belt. Over these, he wore a long cotton *tshupan* or caftan with wide multicolored stripes and he had on a *dopa* or skullcap, which was commonplace in this region. He greeted us in broken Russian with a *Zdrastvoyeti Tovarishtshi* (Greetings, comrades!) and introduced himself as the foreman of the collective. He quickly unlocked the warehouse, weighed out a kilo of flour for each person and made us understand, by speaking half in Kirghiz and half in Russian, all the while gesturing with his fingers, that what he gave us was a five day supply. Unless we wanted to die of hunger, we should divide the flour into five portions and not use it up all at once. He then handed each person a blanket and had us sign a receipt for each item. Finally, he led us to our quarters. Hanele and I were assigned to one of the clay huts. Single people were housed in clay barracks.

Our house, or *kibitka*, was but a single windowless room. A rectangular opening served as both entrance and window. The floor was of the same clay as outdoors. Instead of a kitchen there was a hole in the floor where a fire could be started and over the hole was a clay chimney. Two bricks built in over the hole served as support for the *kazan*, or kettle, in which the cooking was done.

There was no wood with which to build a fire. Instead, the twigs of the cotton plants were used. After the cotton was picked, the twigs were pulled up and each person carried his own bundle of twigs home and left them in the yard to dry in the sun. When dry, they burned like straw and great heaps were required for cooking. The Uzbeks called the cotton twigs *guza poya*.

The kilo of flour was divided into five portions and then each portion was halved. One half was cooked in the morning, before going to work, and the other half in the evening, when we returned.

After bringing water to a boil, the flour was dropped in and stirred into a paste. Two such meals constituted our daily fare. No other food was provided.

Our work was to gather cotton off the little bushes. A little later, I was given a horse and wagon in which I was to deliver cotton to the city, where there was a huge depot to which dozens of cotton-filled wagons arrived every day. It was my job to load the wagon at the farm and then unload it in the city onto piles that were already several meters high. Taking a large basketful, I had to climb the steep pile of cotton that gradually grew to a height of several stories. At the top, I emptied the basket. I then climbed down, refilled the basket, climbed up and climbed down again.

It was grueling work. What with the tropical heat on the one hand and malnutrition on the other, we were always weary. Our strength seemed to be ebbing and we realized that we wouldn't endure for long.

On our fifth day at the collective, we had proof. The victim was a healthy appearing Pole who worked in our group and who looked to be made of steel. Nonetheless, he became distended from starvation taking on the appearance of a barrel. When he was no longer able to work, he languished in the barracks for two days and then expired.

We were obliged to bury the deceased ourselves. After the victim was buried, a deadly fear overcame us. We could see that the same fate awaited us all. We got together to figure out what to do. We decided that on our day off a delegation would call on the Salsoviet (rural governmental administration) to lodge a complaint.

I and two others went to the Salsoviet and told them of our dreadful circumstances, of how hard we worked and how we were compensated with a mere two hundred grams of flour a day. We weren't even given shortening or salt. As a result, we were becoming swollen with hunger and one of us had already died of starvation.

"We've come to ask that you do something about getting us more food or, alternatively, send us to a different collective where we might fare better."

Upon hearing our request, one of the officials with a fat, well-fed face, flushed bright red, banged his fist on the table and began to upbraid us:

"Where," he howled, "do you get the nerve to demand more? Do our citizens get more than you do? If they don't complain, what right have you to make demands?"

I attempted to cool his rage by replying in as calm a tone as I could manage:

"Comrade manager, it's true that the citizens of the collective don't receive more than we do, but you can't compare them to us. Every citizen member of the collective has his own garden that measures ten hectares. He is permitted to cultivate it when his work for the day is done. He can plant potatoes, corn, and other vegetables. Every citizen member has a cow or two goats. Many raise chickens in their yards and they enjoy additional privileges, which makes life easier for them. We subsist entirely on a hundred-gram pap twice a day, just the paste without a bit of fat. How can that provide us with the strength needed for such arduous work? How long can we survive on that? That's why we were forced to come here and ask that you do something to alleviate our situation and help us sustain our miserable lives."

As I was about to finish speaking, he was no longer able to contain himself.

"You talk of a miserable life?" He screeched at the highest possible octave.

"What should our men say, those who have fallen on the front in defense of the fatherland? Can they come complain about their miserable lives? You should be happy we saved you, rescued you from the feudalism of Poland, which didn't provide you with nearly as much as we do! Where were you when our people ate clay instead of bread? For twenty years we ate clay and no one complained! Now it's time for you to eat clay without complaining…I can't stand the sight of you any more. If you don't take yourselves out of here at once, you'll not even receive your two hundred gram allotment of flour."

Weary and dejected, we scarcely managed to trudge the twenty kilometers back to the collective. Immediately upon our return, we gave report of what our delegation had accomplished. Disappointed with our results, those who came to hear us dispersed with their heads bowed in resignation and tears in their eyes.

Moved by hunger and despair, everyone began on their own to look for ways to ease the hunger pangs gripping at their bowels. The only person with whom we could actually communicate was a Kirghiz member of the collective who drove a tractor. He spoke Russian better than anyone else on the farm and he was willing to help us. He took us into the field and taught us which grass was edible: clover, wild *shchav*, and mint.

Thereafter, we picked these three plants, filled our *kazan* with them, boiled them up, and then added a bit of flour. We filled our stomachs with this mixture twice daily. It did help to dispel our feeling of hunger and was healthier and more satisfying than flour alone. The tractor driver also pointed out the more affluent of the collective's farmers. He introduced us to some of them so that we might ask them for their help.

One family, which owned two goats, proposed that my wife collect a sack full of grass for them after work for they were unable to take them out to pasture often enough. In return, she would receive a glass of milk and, on occasion, a small cup of potato soup with some egg drop floating on top. On such evenings, our meals were truly festive.

Sometimes, on our days off, we would walk to the city to meet with other refugees from whom we hoped to hear news of the war. We would also exchange stories of the dreadful living conditions to which we were subjected. This was how we found out that some refugees purchased vodka on the black market and took it back to the collective for sale, thereby earning a few extra rubles. The profit could then be used to buy food. This was yet another way to cope with the ever present hunger. I began to take an interest in such dealings. I found that I could barter one kilo of flour for a bottle of vodka, which could be exchanged for two kilos of flour on the farm.

These kinds of dealings were fraught with risk, for if anyone was caught trafficking in vodka he was severely punished. I decided to take my chances however figuring that there could be no greater punishment than to become swollen with hunger and die. It seemed to me that trading liquor would be our only opportunity to escape death by starvation.

The next time our weekly rations were distributed, I took our two kilos of flour and went to the city where I obtained two bottles of vodka. With the help of the tractor operator, I sold them that very same evening and went home with four kilos of flour. The following week, I used the four kilos to obtain four bottles of vodka, which brought me eight kilos of flour, an amount sufficient to keep us from being hungry. However, our good fortune was short-lived.

The *kolhoz*-members who bought the liquor failed, on more than one occasion, to report for work. When the foreman initiated an investigation, he found them lying about in the field, dead drunk. He ordered a more detailed inquiry as to how the vodka found its way into camp and who was responsible for distributing it among the farmers.

While we were away at work, the foreman searched all the lodgings. Several bottles of liquor were found hidden in the homes of some of the refugees. They were immediately dismissed from work, arrested, and taken to the city prison. Fortunately, I had the prescience to dispose of my bottles on the same day I brought them from market. Had I not done so, Hanele and I would have been among those arrested. After that, I no longer wished to take on the risk of illegal trade. For the time being, we had enough flour to sustain us.

On a subsequent day off, we again went into town to find out what was going on in the outside world. There were rumors that in certain cities Polish organizations had set up stations to recruit men for General Sikorsky's Polish army. Those who were recruited were sent to England for basic training and then assigned to duty on one of the fronts to fight the Nazis. When I heard the happy news, I wasted no time thinking it over, and started out for the nearest registration station. It was sixty-five kilometers away and I would have to go there on foot. I trudged along the dirt roads of Uzbekistan for two days before arriving at the Polish registration office.

Thousands of Polish citizens were already waiting to join Sikorsky's Polish army. As they stood in line, word about the registration procedure was passed from one man to the next. Only "pure" Poles were being accepted. Jews (who had readily identifiable Jewish names) were barred, unless they could prove that they held previous rank in the Polish army.

Any hope of my being accepted was dashed, right then and there. I felt envious of those who were permitted to join. They were going to receive new uniforms, including new shoes and underwear. It would have been for me the fulfillment of my dearest wish, something I dreamed of continuously. It was worth going to war to once again feel the cleanliness of fresh underwear next to my skin.

For a number of years, I'd been wearing a dirty jacket, in which literally thousands of lice were nesting. Although our jackets were collected for disinfecting from time to time, it was about as much help as cupping is to a dead man. After every disinfecting, the lice seemed to bite harder than before as if in revenge for being subjected to the intense destructive heat of the delousing process.

When my turn came, I went inside. Several Polish officers sat alongside long tables. There was a physician and a civilian who registered each volunteer on a prepared form. He recorded the information asked for on the questionnaire: name, address, birthplace, age, and military classification. The form was passed from hand to hand, each officer entering his own notes. After that, the physician directed the candidate to undress and examined him, especially the eyes. When he finished, the doctor told the man to get dressed and sent him into the next room. There, two-kilo loaves of bread were laid out on another long table. And on yet another, were several samovars filled with boiling hot, sweetened tea, with accompanying tin cups. Each man received a whole loaf of bread, which he carried over to the next table. There he sat down to eat, after pouring himself a cup of tea.

Every fifteen minutes, a sergeant in Polish uniform entered the room and read off a list of names. He told some to go home. They would be notified if needed. He told others to go to the warehouse in the yard and handed them a list. At the storehouse, they received underwear, shoes and uniforms. Specially scheduled trains would then take them on the first leg of their journey to England. It was obvious that those sent out into the yard were Polish in both appearance and name, while those sent home were Jewish. For my part, I was happy that I wouldn't be hungry going home. I had enough bread left over to last me the entire journey.

Although I (together with the other Jewish volunteers) was disappointed with the anti-Semitic attitude of the Polish commission, I wasn't entirely unhappy at the outcome because I wasn't at all certain that Hanele would have been permitted to accompany me. I would never have abandoned my dear wife, to leave her all alone and friendless in such a heartless land.

The few refugees who worked on the collective began to scatter, hoping to improve their fortunes elsewhere. We were among the last of the Europeans left living among the Asiatic Uzbeks. And so we, too, decided to leave the collective. The next time we received our two kilos of flour, Hanele kneaded it and baked some flat rolls on the fire. We rose early the next morning and went off to the city with no idea as to where we were bound.

Chapter 12

We went to the railroad station, boarded the first train in, and traveled to the city of Osh in the Soviet Republic of Kirghizia. In Osh we wandered about on dreary clay streets again, not knowing where to turn. As we walked wearily on, we had a very pleasant surprise. We met one of my father's sisters. Her husband and their only son, Fishl, were with her.

My aunt Perl, her husband, Avrom, and their son had lived in Grodzysk. In 1939, when the war broke out, they fled their home hoping to escape the Nazi assassins. Taking their wanderers' staffs in hand, they suffered much the same hard fate as we did and they just barely made it to the Kirghiz city of Osh.

When we saw how they were dressed and what they looked like, we realized how we must have appeared. There was no need of a mirror. Back home, my aunt had quite a buxom appearance. Now she was pale and shriveled. My cousin Fishl was very thin and looked jaundiced. My uncle Avrom could scarcely stand on his feet. People in much better condition would be considered ready for their graves.

Despite everything, we were happy to have found relatives. They took us to a dark little *kibitka*, in which they were living. They were very discomfited on account of their not having anything to offer us in the way of welcome. We asked them how they managed. They described how they sold everything on their backs and then wandered from one collective to another. It was with their last ounce of strength that they eventually made their way to Osh. They were promised work in the city but so far none materialized. They resolved not to seek work on a collective, no matter what the circumstances. At night, Fishl would go out beyond the city limits to gather up sugar beets from the field of a collective farm. These they cooked. They hadn't any other food to eat. My uncle complained that he couldn't digest the beets and was, as a consequence, ill with stomach troubles. My aunt and Fishl were themselves quite ill and couldn't work on a collective even if they wanted to.

That night we slept on the clay floor of their home. Getting up very early, we bade them a fond farewell, made note of their address, and promised that as soon as we were settled somewhere we would let them know and that we would maintain contact with them. Sad at heart, we went away.

Leaving the city behind, we found ourselves on a road called Pomirska Doroga. It stretched five hundred kilometers all the way to the Chinese border. As we went along, we searched both sides of the highway for a collective where we might find work and a place to rest our weary heads. After much hunting, we arrived at a Salsoviet Khazaystvo (Rural Government Administration) which agreed to employ us. We were provided housing in a small clay *kibitka* and promised one hundred twenty rubles per month. We were also promised the right to purchase four hundred grams of bread and, in the field where we would be working, a daily ration of thin soup called *shurpa*. We were being called upon to do field work, harvesting melons, potatoes, various other vegetables, and strawberries. I was asked whether I knew anything about carpentry.

"Yes I do," I replied.

"Well then, you can build a *larok* (small store) for the distribution of bread."

Hanele and several other women were assigned to picking strawberries. They were told that tasting the berries was strictly forbidden and that there would be a very harsh penalty for eating even just one. I was given a saw, a hammer and an axe and led to a small stand of cultivated trees. There weren't any natural forests in Kirghizia, so trees had to be planted and cultivated on the collective. I was asked how I planned to make use of the young trees. After thinking awhile, I had the idea that it might be possible to weave a wall or door with the saplings, given that they were young, thin, elastic, and all of a similar height. When I told the foreman, he liked the idea and suggested I get right to work and see whether it would succeed.

The first thing I did was to chop down a number of trees, trimmed off the branches, and dragged them over to a small house which had a blind wall, without doors or windows. I figured that it would be easier and faster to have to weave only three walls. Moreover, the house would be stronger if the woven walls were attached to a solid wall that was already standing.

I selected the eight thickest tree trunks, dug eight holes, and planted the trunks firmly upright. I placed three poles on each of two sides, and two poles in the middle of the rectangle. When the eight poles were finally in place, I wove a wall much as one weaves the covering of a Sukkoth tabernacle. When I finished weaving the first wall, I fastened it more firmly to the *kibitka* wall by propping it up with two small trees, which I attached by hammering them in with large nails. I did the same with the opposite wall so that I now had two woven walls firmly attached to the wall of the *kibitka*, three firm walls in all. For the fourth wall, I marked off the space for a door by driving in two shorter poles and then wove the rest of the wall and the door.

Working on the ground, I wove the roof the required length and breadth of the house. That finished, I had several other workers help me lay the roof on top of the walls. I then used nails to secure the roof to the walls. Finally, I mixed clay and straw together and applied it to the roof to make it rainproof. When I showed the foreman my handiwork, he expressed great admiration for what I had done. I never expected my job would turn out so well.

Many good things were available on the collective, but none of them for workers. The taking of a potato or anything else from the field was met with severe punishment. We would be fortunate to suffer no more than expulsion. It wouldn't have been so bad if everything had gone along in normal fashion. But the Soviets are specialists in abnormalities. During the very first few weeks, we were content, expecting that this would be the place where we could finally wait out the war. Alas, "Man proposes and God disposes."

Although the four hundred grams of bread and the bit of slop we received in the field wasn't enough for proper nourishment, we were satisfied, for we knew from painful experience that things could be worse. We were soon to learn however that we couldn't be certain of even that small allotment.

Every day a wagon was sent to the municipal bakery in the city to fetch bread. When the bread arrived, it was weighed and everyone purchased his ration. All too often, the driver returned empty-handed saying that for one reason or another the bakery was short of bread.

It wouldn't have been too bad if, on the following day, the ration we missed were made up. But that would have been an impossibility in Soviet Russia. They had a stock excuse for such situations: *Diyen prezhil diyen propol* (a day lived through is a day lost). We fasted two or three times a week therefore. If bread was brought the following day, it was usually brought late in the evening, after work. So we went hungry all that day as well.

Because of the machinations of the administration, we became exhausted with hunger and could scarcely stand up. The Kirghiz could easily go without their ration of bread because they had land, some had a cow or even a couple of sheep, and they all had stores of food which they had acquired one way or another. We however were solely dependent on the miniscule portion of watery soup bought in the field and our meager ration of bread. We would stretch out in the shade, near the entrance of our *kibitka*, and lie there exhausted, faint with hunger. The lack of food made us dizzy. We didn't even have strength enough to swat the flies that constantly beset us.

A young Kirghiz family lived next door to us. The woman of the house, seeing us lying there wasting away, took pity and brought us a little jarful of the soup she cooked for her own family. These ministrations were the only things that kept us alive. As I lay famished at the entrance of our little house, I felt sure that if I didn't do something drastic soon this place would become our grave. Something had to be done to strengthen us and keep us from accepting death by starvation.

A thought flashed through my mind and henceforth gave me no rest. Behind our *kibitka* there was a *kopiyets* (storage cellar) where the day's harvest of potatoes was stored. At night, the *kopiyets* was secured with an enormous snap-lock, which was hung on two very strong doors. If only I could open that lock! That would remedy our terrible affliction and we wouldn't ever go hungry again. I remembered that when I was a child, I used to play with a snap-lock and worked it with a nail, opening and closing it without ever using a key. Why not try the same with this huge lock?

At nightfall, when it grew a bit cooler outdoors, and the coolness of the air helped us regain some of our strength, I got up from the ground to hunt for a large nail. Finding one, I waited until the entire village was in deep sleep. My heart raced as I stealthily made my way to the earthen cellar and began to manipulate the viscera of the lock with the thick nail I found. With the point of the nail, I located the little tongue that closes the lock. As I pressed harder on the languet, the lock flew open. I snapped the lock closed and repeated the operation.

I was convinced that my plan would work. I slipped quietly back to our hut and picked up a sack. I asked Hanele to come with me to make sure that no one was watching. I opened the lock and lifted one lid of the cellar door. Hanele closed the door behind me, and stood watch until I filled the sack and came back out. I closed the cellar door, put the lock back on and snapped it shut. We returned to our *kibitka* with a sack full of potatoes. From then on, we cooked as many potatoes a day as we could eat.

One day, cousin Fishl suddenly appeared. He was red-eyed from weeping. He told us that his father died of dysentery induced by eating sugar beets. He was buried in a mass grave along with other refugees who died of typhus and dysentery. Fishl also said that he and his ailing mother were without means of subsistence and were helpless and desperate. I immediately conceived of a plan that would enable us to help my unfortunate aunt and cousin while also helping ourselves.

Hanele cooked up a pail full of potatoes and the three of us sat down on the ground to eat. As we ate, I made Fishl the following proposal:

"You may as well spend this night with us. In the gray of dawn, before the collective begins to awaken, you'll go home with a sack of potatoes on your back. You'll sell the sack of potatoes in the city and we'll share the money. With your share of the money, you'll have the funds necessary to buy food for yourself and your mom. You'll come here twice a week and we'll have another sack of potatoes ready for you. We'll continue this game as long as we can. Who knows, perhaps we'll manage to survive the war this way."

We followed our plan for several months and it worked well. Life became somewhat more tolerable now that we were no longer solely dependent on the ration of bread. With the money Fishl brought us we were able to buy some things on the black market: part of a loaf of bread, some sugar, salt, and, from time to time, some butter for cooking.

One day, Fishl arrived in a state of bewilderment. With tears in his eyes, he told us his mother died of typhus and, like his father, the authorities were about to bury her along with Kirghizians who died of various contagious diseases. He didn't want his mother buried in a mass grave where he wouldn't know her whereabouts. There were some Jews willing to help him remove the corpse from the hospital provided there was someone to help carry the body to the cemetery. It would have to be done immediately however before all the dead were removed for mass burial.

I rushed back to Osh with Fishl. The dead were lying in a large cellar awaiting a truck which was to take them to the mass grave. We looked around for the Jewish watchman. It was arranged that he would pretend not to see anything while my aunt's body was taken out. When we inquired as to his whereabouts, we learned that on the night he and my cousin made their agreement, the Jewish watchman fell ill with typhus and was being kept in isolation in the hospital. Without his help we could accomplish nothing. A Kirghiz was already on guard at the morgue and we couldn't communicate with him.

Fishl and I remained standing near the morgue trying to think of some way to keep my aunt from being buried in a mass grave. As we stood thinking about what to do, a large truck that had been sprayed with carbolic acid arrived. All the corpses were loaded onto the truck and driven off to their common grave. Deeply grieved, I returned to the Salsoviet and threw myself into my work hoping to forget our daily tribulations. However, my thoughts attacked me like so many flies and I obsessively thought of how in less than three months I lost an uncle and aunt and how my cousin, who was the apple of his parents eyes, was left an orphan.

One day, as I was digging the hard, dry earth with my primitive hoe, engrossed in my sorrowful thoughts, the foreman of the Salsoviet suddenly appeared before me. With a very stern mien, he ordered me to immediately go to the administration office for my *roshtshot* (accounting) and, he added, that early next morning my wife and I were to take our things and leave, and never return. That was all he said to me. I didn't dare ask for an explanation. I surmised that while we were at work, he must have gone into our *kibitka*, which had no door and therefore was always open. He must have seen the potatoes hidden under a blanket, under our bed.

I went to the office as I was commanded to do. I then went home where we cooked our last meal of potatoes and packed our things. Early next morning, we went to Osh, where we met my cousin Fishl, who no longer had his house. It was taken from him after the death of his mother.

He was living with a friend who worked in the city. He was determined not to work at a factory or collective farm because he objected to working like a slave and being paid close to nothing. He preferred to frequent the marketplace, buying and selling for profit and, in that way, to eke out his poverty-stricken existence. Hanele and I decided against the risk of becoming "speculators" and, Heaven forfend, become separated to pine away in different prisons. We thought it preferable to choose a more difficult but more likely way of surviving the war.

Once again, we went out onto the Pamir road, which leads to the border with China. After about fourteen kilometers, we came upon a collective willing to employ us. It was an immensely huge agricultural collective, providing for the needs of the commune as well as the population of the nearby city. Besides raising agricultural products, fruit and livestock (sheep and chickens), the collective was also engaged in carpentry and housing construction. It had its own blacksmith shop and a tremendously large bakery.

Our first assignment was to provide help in building *kibitka*s. The work was done in a primitive fashion reminiscent of the time when Jews were slaves in Egypt. A large hole was dug in the ground and filled with water. A wagonload of short straws was emptied into the waterhole. Then a *tikmen* (a primitive shovel-like hoe), which was used in digging the hole, was used to return the soil back into the hole. Next, the Kirghiz workers rolled up their pants above their knees and jumped barefoot into the hole where, with their *tikmen*s in hand, they trod on and mixed the clay and straw together until it became a thick mass. The *tikmen*s were used again to fill hods with the mixed clay and straw.

The hods were carried to wherever the *kibitka* was being built. The masons took their trowels and threw one layer of the clay mass on top of another and then used their trowels to smooth a wall, in accordance with the pitch and thickness of strings put in place beforehand. That was how "houses" were built in Kirghizia in the twentieth century.

Hanele and I were given the honor of carrying the hods from the hole in the ground to the masons. The wet clay was frightfully heavy. On the very first day, we both developed blisters on the palms of our hands. On the second day, the work was even more difficult because the blisters became abraded turning into extremely painful, raw wounds. We complained to the foreman and requested an easier assignment for a few days, just long enough for the wounds to heal. He burst into laughter and replied with a popular Soviet saying: "*Rada privikatsh, kak niye privikniesh toh zdokhniyesh*" (you had better get used to it, if you don't you'll croak).

The food at this commune was better than at the Salsoviet. We were still allowed only four grams of bread, but we received it regularly. The *shurpa*, cooked in the field, where we worked, was also better. It was thicker and sometimes contained potatoes. Whereas the previous *shurpa* was completely free of shortening, this one was laced with mutton fat.

While the masons were in process of shaping the walls of the *kibitka*, carrying the clay hods to them was more or less tolerable. But, when it came to laying the roof, the work became much worse. The hod full of wet clay had to be carried up a tall ladder and one had to be a virtual acrobat to keep from falling off. The person in front had to bend down to his ankles so that he wouldn't be taller than the person behind. The person in back had to carry the hod on his shoulders while gripping the ladder with both hands. As he pushed the hod up with his shoulders, he had to push at the carrier in front of him to keep him from falling backwards and keep him going forward. Happily, when the house was finished Hanele and I were sent to do farm work such as harvesting corn from the fields. We were assigned dozens of different tasks like these in the course of a year.

On this collective, radio loudspeakers gave us news of the war. The reports became more encouraging and we joyously looked forward to returning home where we would tell everyone the story of our difficulties in Russia, happy for it to be all in the past.

We heard that a Polish legation had been established in the city of Osh for dispensing aid to Polish citizens. On our next day off we went to Osh to register for aid. When we arrived at the legation office, an awful sight met us. The legation was located in a *kibitka*, which stood in a very large yard surrounded by a high clay fence. Hundreds of enfeebled, ragged refugees lay on the bare ground, so weak they couldn't wave off the huge horse flies that ate at them. Swollen with hunger, they spent many days and nights dragging themselves from all over the *oblast* (region, province) to what they thought would be their last hope of staying alive.

The office opened at ten in the morning. The personnel lit a fire under a *kazan* and cooked up a soup. Together with a piece of bread, it was dispensed to all the unfortunates waiting in the yard. Most of them no longer had strength enough to stretch out their hands and grasp the precious gift. Other applicants voluntarily ran over and fed them as they would little children.

As we waited to enter the *kibitka*, we formed a very long line in the yard and, after several hours, we were registered. We received two kilos of white flour, half a kilo of sugar, and half a kilo of American "Crisco." After that, we passed through another room, where the women were given a dress and the men, either a pair of trousers or a used jacket. Hanele received a worn dress and I got a jacket from an English military uniform. Although the garments weren't new, they were a treasure of inestimable value to us. We were told that if we returned in a month's time, we would again be eligible for assistance.

In the course of our work on the collective, Hanele and I were sometimes separated. This happened when one of us was sent far from the farm on special assignment. On one occasion, I was sent twelve kilometers away to help harvest wheat. At another time, Hanele was sent to a construction project along with several Kirghiz and Russians. At such times life was very lonely for us. Hanele and I were the only Jewish refugees in the commune and we had nothing in common with the Kirghiz and Uzbeks. During those periods of separation, I threw myself into my work in order to forget.

One late summer day, Hanele and I were both at work in the same field. She was raking up the chaff left behind by the tractors that were threshing the rye and piled it up into tall stacks to dry. Several Kirghiz men and I were tilling the soil with our *tikmens*, preparing it for the next sowing. Suddenly we heard a horrific scream emanating from my wife. With *tikmen* in hand, I ran to her and saw the head of an enormous snake hissing at her from beneath the stack at which she was working. I moved stealthily to one side and brought the sharp edge of the *tikmen* down suddenly and hard upon the head of the snake, severing the head from the body. The snake's body continued to coil and recoil spasmodically for some time, as its severed head kept opening and closing its mouth, as though trying to catch its breath.

Without warning, the Soviet government issued a new directive: all collective farms were to raise pigs to supply pork for the Soviet market. The Kirghiz are pious Muslims and are as careful as Jews to avoid pork. They are forbidden to even look at a hog. However, the order was very strict and no collective was exempt. Our manager hadn't an alternative but to arrange for the breeding of swine.

He had a large yard prepared, fenced it in with a clay wall, and had a small two-room house built. One room was to be for the animals and the other for the individual who would care for them. A Russian woman who was a specialist in hog breeding was brought in from the city. The government provided the first thirteen animals and the Russian specialist began working with them. After having worked with the *treyfe* (unclean) piglets for two weeks, she became very dissatisfied with her wages. She simply left the collective one day, abandoning the porkers.

The commune was gripped with dismay. The Kirghiz were all afraid to take on the defiling work. Then the manager realized that he had an *Urus* (white, European) on the farm. He sent for me and put me in charge of the thirteen squealers.

I was fearful of undertaking such responsibility. Should any of the piglets die, I would be accused of sabotage, as has happened more than once in the Soviet Union. Whenever something went wrong, those in charge were labeled "Saboteurs" and sent to join the white bears. The manager reassured me, saying that no one was born skilled.

"If you work at it, you'll learn in good time," he said. "And if you need some help initially, you'll go to a nearby collective where there's a specialist in the raising of swine. You'll be given good instruction there."

And that's just what happened. I acquired a brand new profession, that of "hogs herder."

People were treated like worthless slaves at the collective, but animals received truly humane attention. For example: I received thirteen kilos of barley meal daily, along with a pod (sixteen kilos) of potatoes for the thirteen little pigs in my charge. A human being received only four hundred grams of bread. In raw flour, that's only two hundred fifty grams. The workhorses were allowed as much oats or whole barley as they could consume and, on top of that, as much hay as they could stuff themselves with.

I cooked potatoes in a large *kazan* twice a day. The barley meal was then added to the potatoes. When the mixture cooled, I transferred it by the pail full to the pigsty where the baby pigs swilled it down in an instant, only to begin screaming again, as though they'd been scalded. When they ate their first meal of the day, I chased them out into the wide-open field. There they would turn over the soil with their snouts in search of roots. Occasionally, they would stray over to a planted field and destroy it before I even noticed. When that occurred, I would be sternly rebuked for not properly carrying out my responsibilities and for allowing the hogs to destroy government property. Such breach of duty could have subjected me to severe punishment.

I complained to the manager and pleaded with him to relieve me of this responsibility because four hundred grams of bread didn't give me sufficient strength to chase the pigs around. They were faster than I was and much better nourished. This job was much more taxing than the fieldwork. At least, in the field I received a little pot of soup. Now that I was isolated from the field, I was forced to subsist only on the miserable little ration of bread. "Surely you can see that doesn't provide the strength required to chase after those quick little pigs," I concluded. At that, the manager insinuated that I was a blockhead.

"You have thirteen *tshutshkas* (pigs in Kirghiz). You could pretend to have fourteen," he said.

His suggestion hit me like a bolt of lightning.

The very next morning, after I went to the *ambar* (storehouse) where I was issued my daily allowance for the pigs, I removed two kilos of potatoes and peeled them. Hanele browned a considerable quantity of flour and cooked up a *satsheruha* (a "scorched" soup). We ate to satiation to the point where our ears actually wobbled. That was the beginning of a more satisfying life for us.

On one of Hanele's days off, I left her to tend the animals while I went in to town to obtain the monthly assistance provided by the Polish delegation. Along the way, I encountered the "specialist" swineherd from the neighboring collective to whom I was sent for my initial instruction on the breeding of hogs. We talked like professional colleagues all the way to town. He gave me some candid advice and, like a true specialist, told me what I could do to fatten my piglets and see them grow before my very eyes.

"Get up very early," he said, "and take a sack with you to the *kaniushna* (horse barn) before it's cleaned. Fill the sack with horse manure. It'll be full of the whole barley that the horses haven't been able to digest. Put the manure into the *kazan* but don't mix the flour into it. Strain the flour through a fine net and stir the bran into the manure. Next, peel the potatoes and use them for yourself but put the peelings into the *kazan*. Add water and cook the mixture, stirring it as it boils. Feed this concoction to the pigs and, within two weeks, you'll notice a tremendous difference in them."

I tried following the specialist's advice and was soon convinced his idea was priceless. The pigs were truly growing before my eyes, obviously becoming larger and fatter every day, and every day, I collected dozens of kilos of flour and potatoes, which I stored away.

After a while, the hoard was becoming too large for me to keep hidden and I began to puzzle over what I should do with so much flour and potatoes.

Not far from us, there was another collective where some refugees were living in horrific conditions. I decided I could afford to make their lives a little easier. I invited them every evening and asked them to bring their metal plates and spoons along with them. Each day, I cooked them a *kazan* full of potatoes and dumplings that helped keep them alive.

Among these refugees, there was a woman with a small child without any means. I proposed that she come to our farm at dawn during each of her days off and knock twice on our window, which looked out on a field just outside our fence. I would then pass a sack of flour out the window, which she could take to the city to sell, and we would share in the proceeds. With her share she could buy milk on the black market. She would not only have enough for her child but also enough for herself so that their nutrition would be improved.

The Muslim holiday of Ramadan approached. In observance of this holiday the faithful would fast for thirty days, eating only at night. The Muslims would get up about two hours before sunrise, say prayers and eat hurriedly before the sun began its ascent. Then they would fast all day. At night, they would slaughter a sheep, cook it and celebrate with a feast. The poorer Kirghiz, who didn't possess sheep, were given a horse. They slaughtered the animal and distributed a kilo of horsemeat to everyone.

We hadn't seen meat of any kind for a very long time. When we were given our share, we started to cook it over a fire of *guza poya* (twigs of the cotton plant) which burns very rapidly. We grew tired of repeatedly adding these twigs to the flame, which characteristically flares up like so much straw, and voraciously ate the meat before it was sufficiently cooked.

The next day Hanele had severe abdominal pains. We didn't know the cause of her distress. There were no doctors on the commune, only a nurse who served the entire collective. I went to get the nurse. She examined my wife and said that she was suffering from an attack of appendicitis. She instructed her to lie quietly and assured us the trouble would subside.

That night, Hanele was burning up with fever and groaning with pain. Early the next morning, I ran to get the nurse again. She saw my wife lying there with parched lips on account of her high temperature and determined that she be taken to the hospital in the city, some fourteen kilometers away.

I hurried to see the manager and asked him to provide us a horse and wagon to transport my wife to the hospital. His response was that all the horses and wagons were at work and that he couldn't let me have any before evening. When I shouted at him that then it might be too late, he answered cold-bloodedly that that he couldn't help. He remained adamant, and I left in despair.

As I went away, I tried to think of how I could help my ailing wife. I went out onto the large yard of the blacksmith shop. Outside the smithy were several two-wheeled handcarts that the blacksmith had just repaired. I quickly took one of the carts, hitched myself to the shaft and hurried to the yard of our *kibitka*. I asked the nurse to help me place my wife in the cart and come with us to the hospital. Once again, I harnessed myself to the cart like a horse. The nurse pushed from behind. By the time we reached the hospital we were bathed in perspiration.

Immediately upon arrival at the hospital, Hanele was examined. It was determined that she wasn't suffering from appendicitis, as the nurse thought, but had contracted typhoid fever. They berated the nurse for her incorrect diagnosis: Where did she acquire the know how for making diagnoses? The two-day delay could have jeopardized my wife's life.

Every day thereafter, as soon as I finished preparing food for the pigs, I locked them up and rushed off to the hospital to see how Hanele was doing. Because of the danger of contracting the disease, I wasn't permitted to see her. I waited for hours beside a closed window, through which I could see her lying exhausted with cold compresses on her forehead.

A nurse reported to me on a daily basis. I was told that the high temperature could very well continue for three more weeks before a turning point could be expected to occur. If my wife came through the crisis, she had a chance of living. I could see that she was becoming more debilitated day by day. I looked at her fair head. The lovely, thick hair, which graced her head like a beautiful crown, was shaved off. I dreaded the very thought that her life could be in mortal danger. At night, I couldn't fall asleep for fear that God forbid I might lose her.

The tropical winter was arriving and a series of heavy rains began to fall. The downpours would wear away the clay roofs of the *kibitkas* and they began to leak so much that there was nowhere to hide from the rain. One night, I nearly wore myself out trying to keep dry. I tied all four corners of our quilt to the head rails of our metal bed hoping to create a sort of roof, but to no avail. The quilt was soon saturated and all the rainwater leaked right on top of me. I pushed hard against the wall of one corner of the house and remained standing that way for the rest of that exhausting night. As soon as the first gray of dawn appeared,

I prepared the feed for the swine, locked them up, and started my walk to the hospital in Osh.

The rain slackened somewhat, but the roads were under so much water that it was very difficult to make progress. The clay roadbed had been transformed into slippery, sticky, thick mud, which clung to my shoes and made it very difficult to get to the city. With whatever strength I had remaining I finally arrived to be struck with an even greater realization of how much damage the rain caused that night.

Dozens of *kibitkas* had been washed away. The roofs of many houses that were still standing had fallen inward and the walls of many homes were collapsing. The Kirghiz were standing near their half or wholly ruined homes with sacks or rags on their heads. They were afraid to stand too close lest the heavy partially destroyed walls fall in on them and cause injury.

Soaking wet and exhausted, I arrived at the hospital where I had a pleasant surprise. The nurse informed me that my wife weathered the crisis safely but that she was extremely tired and weak. I immediately went over to the window and looked in. Hanele lay on her bed obviously weary and worn-out by three weeks of elevated temperature. When she noticed me, she tried to raise her hand in greeting, but lacked the strength. Her hand fell limply back upon the quilt and she greeted me with a weak smile instead.

That day, I spoke with the doctor. He said that although the crisis was over, there was still great danger because the illness had completely drained my wife of energy and that she would need good care if she were to regain her strength.

When I left for the city the following morning, I took a bar of soap that I'd received from the Polish aid delegation. I intended to sell it on the black market and buy something nutritious to help Hanele recuperate. As I wandered about the bazaar with the bar of soap in hand looking for a customer, I suddenly felt someone take hold of the arm in which I was carrying the soap. I swiftly turned around and saw an

NKVD lieutenant holding me firmly in his grip. Fear turned me speechless. All at once, I was filled with thoughts of what great trouble I was in and how severely I'll be punished for speculating on the black market.

To my great surprise, the man didn't take the soap from my hand. Instead, he let go of my arm, stepped back a pace or two, and opened his arms wide as if to embrace me. He called out my name in great glee. Stunned, I stared into his face and recognized a former comrade. Before the war, we belonged to the same group of the Pioneer organization. I then fell into his arms. We were genuinely glad to have met each other.

He wouldn't let go of me. He invited me to a teahouse where the Kirghiz enjoyed a pot of tea. They drank from a small vase as they sat with their legs crossed beneath them. We drank our vase of tea, and told one another how we came to be in Osh. He also told me how he came to be a lieutenant in the NKVD.

In 1938, when the bloody revolution against General Franco was in progress in Spain, he volunteered to join a foreign brigade formed to help the leftist Republicans in their struggle against Franco's fascism. Shmaye was the son of a Jewish "bourgeois," a real estate broker. He lived on Nalovki Street in a pleasant, spacious apartment in relative comfort and security. His father was troubled over the fact that his son was veering towards the political left and they often quarreled over it. When the Communist Party of Poland began to secretly organize volunteers, supplying them with false papers, and smuggling them out of Poland to France and from there to Spain, Shmaye was among the first to go. While fighting in the front ranks in Spain, he was severely wounded in the right shoulder and was confined to a Spanish hospital for many weeks. When the leftists lost their revolution, the USSR agreed to admit a number of wounded fighters, Shmaye among them. Soon after he recovered from his wounds, the Soviet government hired him and he eventually attained the rank of lieutenant in the NKVD.

I interrupted his account, explaining that I was on my way to see my wife who was in the hospital recovering from typhoid fever. And after my visit, I would have to walk fourteen kilometers to return to my commune. We bade each other farewell. He gave me an address where I might find him and urged me to contact him any time I encountered any difficulty, for he felt sure he could be of much assistance and help in making our lives easier in the Soviet Union. I thanked him and went right off to the hospital.

I made a firm decision that I would never see him again for I became convinced of the falsehood of the communist ideology that was being put to so cruel an effect. I didn't want to have anything to do with him nor would I be seeking favors from anyone with Communist party affiliation. I also detested anyone who would help the Soviets carry out their barbaric machinations, even if it happened to be my former compatriot and friend with whom I had so blindly fought in the cause. I had been completely deluded by beautiful slogans and I was even ready to give up my life to see communism realized. It turned out that the glorious slogans were nothing but a device to ensnare people and exploit them for the government's barbaric ends. The more we resisted their spurious favors and the further we could get from these inhumane oppressors, the better it would be for my wife and me. The only thing we wanted was to survive the war and escape this accursed inferno.

Chapter 13

Seemingly overnight, the Soviets decided that the refugees, whom they couldn't control, were just too much trouble. Under the pretense that they refused to work and that they promoted speculation and a black market, it was concluded that the only way to keep them in line was to make them Soviet citizens. This way they would have to conform to Soviet law. They would be forced to work wherever the government assigned them and would have no right whatsoever to leave their employment. It was again announced that all refugees were to report to a government office and apply for Soviet passports. No one would be permitted to live anywhere or to be found on the streets without a passport.

No refugee reported voluntarily. We were afraid that once we obtained Russian passports, we would forfeit our right to return home after the war was over. We would remain in servitude in that murderous land of enslavement forever. We all knew Soviet citizens were considered the property of the Soviet government.

In those years, the workers in the factories and on the collectives were mostly women, elderly men, and children. The younger men were all fighting on the front. By acquiring new citizens, the state forcibly added new blood to the work force. The Soviets saw this as a splendid opportunity for the infusion of fresh manpower in the hinterlands. They deliberately forced children from ages nine to fourteen from their homes and sent them to specially organized schools that trained them in physical work. When they were far from home, the nine year olds were sent down into the coal mines and taught to dynamite coal, load coal, and do other things which would be considered heavy manual labor for even adult males in good physical condition. Many youngsters were killed doing this work, yet their parents didn't even know where they were carried off to.

Since none of the Polish refugees voluntarily applied for Russian passports, the Soviets had to employ their old well-tried methods. One night, they sent out trucks over the entire country. NKVD officers went from place to place dragged refugees out of their beds as they slept, packed them off into the trucks and forcibly took them to the local administrative offices where they had installed cameras. Everyone was photographed and his or her photograph was affixed to a passport form. The form was filled out and forced on the individual who was, thereupon, declared a Soviet citizen. They delivered a speech to the effect that since these refugees were now citizens of the Soviet Union, they were subject to Soviet law, and must faithfully serve their "beloved fatherland." And so, we became the property of our subjugators.

The day finally arrived when I could take Hanele home from the hospital, where she had been confined for a month. She was pale and wore a kerchief on her head where her hair was only just beginning to grow back. I hoped she'd be able to spend a few days at home and regain a bit of strength, but that was not to be. She was home but two days, when she was assigned to a construction brigade that was sent twelve kilometers from the commune.

I pleaded with the foreman that if he absolutely had to put my wife to work, couldn't he at least give her something to do on the farm and give her the opportunity to get a little stronger. There was no lack of work on the farm. Why was it necessary for her to go so far away when she was still so weak after her illness? My effort was in vain. Indeed, the foreman became very angry that I even dared question his orders. I didn't see Hanele again for three months, not until the brigade completed its work.

Shortly thereafter, the Soviet policy of enforced citizenship began to take effect. All new citizens were ordered mobilized into a *trudovoy armi* (work army). They were to report "voluntarily" to the capital of their respective *oblast*. Once there, they would be sent to do work in support of the war industries.

I was forced to pack my things, leave my wife behind, and travel to a designated address in Osh. A large group of refugees was being assembled and sent as laborers to Kzil Kiya (Red Hills), a Tupik town of coal mines at the very end of the railroad line.

Mountains reaching high into the sky surround the town. This range of mountains was bare, having no vegetative growth whatsoever. The burning sun baked them into a red brick color, hence the name Kzil Kiya. Deep beneath the red mountains, lay rich deposits of coal and, as was later discovered, uranium. Beyond the mountains, in one direction was the Soviet border with Iran. Some of the other mountains in another direction border on Turkey. I was assigned to work in the coal mines of Kzil-Kiya.

We were quartered in an immense barracks where forty beds were lined up as in an armory, one next to another. After we were assigned our specific cots, we were sent to the baths. After that, we were handed a ration of bread. With bread in hand, we were led to the mess hall where we could purchase some sour *shtshi*.

When everyone finished eating, an overseer lowered us by way of a windlass, deep underground and showed us the shaft where we would start work the following morning. He then told us to go back to our barracks for rest. In the morning, we were to rise when we heard the whistle sounding, eat breakfast, and report to work.

The whistle blew early and awakened us all. An enormous kettle of *kipitok* had already been prepared and we washed down whatever bread we had left over from the previous day's ration with some of the boiling water. We then gathered at a designated area where we were given our specific assignments. Two new workers were detailed to each of the brigades where we were given instruction in carrying out our duties. I was to work with a group of *kanagani* (horse riders).

I was given a wide belt, which I fastened around my hips, onto which I hooked a heavy, rectangular battery. A length of electric wire led from the battery to the hard hat on my head. A searchlight was attached to the hardhat and this was what we depended on to light our way in the dark shaft. We went down into the shaft where the horses were already waiting. We harnessed them to small railway cars, each of which could be loaded with approximately half a ton of coal. The cars traveled on rails and two *kanagani* attended each horse.

I was in mortal fear as we went 1500 meters below the surface. I thought I would never get out alive-that way down there was where I would find my grave. My co-worker who was assigned to teach me the job, told me to stand up on a "bumper" at the end of the car, a step about six centimeters wide. I was to hold on tightly and, while standing, bend as low as possible whenever the car was in motion. That is, if I didn't want to have my head severed from my body by the beams fastened to the "ceiling." Some of the beams put in place to resist the immense pressure from above, and keep the "ceiling" from collapsing, hung quite low. Since the cars traveled at considerable speed, I might not notice the danger in time and could lose my life. As he completed his explanation, he let out a brief whistle at the sound of which the horse carried us deep down into the bowels of the shaft with the speed of an arrow.

The light from our headgear cast shadows that floated on the beams and rafters of the walls and ceilings. They seemed like huge, satanic monsters and were quite frightening as they changed from small to giant dimensions and danced before us like so many wild demons. My fear for my life increased with every moment that passed. My heart beat so fast that I was sure it would burst.

At last, we saw a light in the distance. When we reached the electric illumination, the horse stopped. My co-worker jumped off the bumper and, with one hand, disengaged the horse and harness which was fastened but by a single hook to the front of the car. Holding the hook in his hand, he led the horse and his harness to the other track, to cars already loaded with coal, and he rehooked the harness to the row of loaded cars. We then got up on the bumper of the last car. He whistled, and we were off in the opposite direction. We delivered the cars, filled with coal, to a turntable from which a special hauling machine called a *lebyotka* pulled the cars up out of the shaft.

Sometimes, as we traveled back and forth, a car would derail. The first time I saw this happen to a loaded car, I was frightened. I was certain it would require ten people to get the car back on track but not so in Sovietland. The *kanagan* told me that a person could put a car back on track all by himself. Since a full car weighs nearly a ton, I asked how that could be. With a smile, he proved that it was possible.

As a rule, when a car is derailed only three of its wheels go off track. The fourth wheel remains on a rail. The *kanagan* pointed to a small thick board, with one side shaved thin that was always on hand for just such an emergency. My co-worker took hold of the board and inserted its thin edge under the wheel that was still in place. That would keep it from sliding around on the rails. Then, he walked to the other end of the car, put his shoulder against it and gave it a sudden lift. With a groan, the car put its other three wheels down on track. I admired my co-worker's technique.

On another occasion, he told me to try it. I attempted it, but was unable to do it on my own. He then got up on the bumper, on which we stood, while the cars were moving and said: "Try it now." I did so easily. He then explained that two could always do it. It was only a bit more difficult for one person. "In time, you'll find that it can be done by one person and you'll eventually be doing it too." After a while, I became accustomed to working in the shaft and my fears disappeared.

Hanele and I wrote to each other and kept in touch. She wrote of how hard she worked how hungry she was, and how lonely she felt. She wished that we could be together. It would make it so much easier to endure the suffering.

I asked the manager of the mine to permit my wife to come and live nearby. He said that if I found a place to live, he would have no objections and would grant us the necessary permit. Whenever I had a free moment, I hurried to the housing office and requested a place for my wife and myself. After considerable effort, I was finally given housing and had Hanele come to Kzil-Kiya.

We settled in our new home, which was at Number 242 Djalska Dolina. All it was, was a large room with a small cookstove and a large window. We acquired a small iron bed, a table and a single wooden chair. That was all we had in the dwelling, which was no more than ten meters from the market. We drew water from a well about fifty meters away.

The miners of Kzil-Kiya received a bread ration of eight hundred grams. Hanele, who was given work in the barracks, received only four hundred grams. Her work consisted of cleaning the barracks, carrying in coal and water, and seeing to it that there was always a supply of *kipitok* boiling in the kettle for the miners to drink. Since they worked three shifts, it was kept boiling twenty-four hours a day. She received half the ration that a miner did because, it was explained, she didn't work in the mine and therefore didn't require as much food. Actually, her work wasn't any the easier.

In addition to bread cards, other cards were issued monthly, entitling the bearer to purchase four hundred grams of sugar, two kilos of pearl barley, and four hundred grams of meat. Although those things were listed on the card, they were almost never available. If any one of these products became available in a *larok*, it would be nearly impossible to make one's way into the store, for the lines outside would stretch for miles. We would be lucky to obtain even one of these products in the course of a month, and if we did, we nearly never got any of the others. The cards expired at the end of the month and throughout the USSR the rule was always the same: "The day you've lived through is the day that's gone." Nothing was available retroactively.

The shaft I worked in was always wet on account of underground springs, which constantly seeped through. Huge pumps were used to draw out the water. Due to the continuous moisture, my malaria began to reappear and I soon suffered from very severe attacks. They occurred twice a week, every third day, like clockwork. I knew the precise day and time of each attack.

At the beginning of every siege, I felt extremely cold. The ague was so severe and made me shake so much that I was unable to keep my teeth from chattering. No matter how hot it got outdoors, nothing that I covered myself with warmed me up. After shivering for several hours, I was suddenly overcome by a feeling of extreme heat. This plagued me for twenty-four hours, sometimes leaving me unconscious. When the attack subsided, I would lie there so weak that I couldn't get up.

My work time was changed every ten days in accordance with a planned schedule. The mine was worked in three eight-hour shifts. Therefore, I would sometimes work eight o'clock in the morning until four in the afternoon. Ten days later, I would be in the mine either from four in the afternoon until twelve at night, or from twelve at night to eight in the morning.

According to the established rules, a person who was ill was excused from work only if he had an elevated temperature. Illness unaccompanied by high fever wasn't considered illness unless the individual suffered a crippling result. If a person missed work or was even fifteen minutes late and couldn't prove he had a high fever he was labeled *prigulshtshik* (tardy). Anyone so classified was punished by being deprived of half his bread ration for a month. If he "malingered" a second time, he was imprisoned, and forced to perform the same labor as before, this time, under the watchful eye of armed guards who brought him and who escorted him back to prison. Moreover, prisoners received only three hundred grams of bread. Anyone punished as a *prigulshtshik* a third time received a prison sentence of five years.

It sometimes happened that I would begin shivering while on my way to work and I knew another malaria attack was coming on. I reported to the nurse as soon as I reached the mine. I would let her see that I had the shakes and would ask her to excuse me from work and give me a statement confirming that I was undergoing a malaria attack. I could then go to the doctor for an injection of "acriquinine."

The nurse first took my temperature. If I didn't have as much fever as stipulated in the regulations, she would send me to work saying that she couldn't give me a statement until I had sufficient fever. Despite my illness, I had to go down into the mine to work. When the fever finally had me burning like a flame in Hell, I went out of the mine and back to the nurse. She took my temperature again and this time gave me the note excusing me from work.

My malaria worsened considerably since my first attack in Siberia. During that time, a five milligram acriquinine pill brought relief but that was no longer the case and I was given increasingly larger doses by injection. The most recent doses of twenty-five milligrams were not much use. Following the injection of so large a dose, I was temporarily deafened and had to remain lying down at the doctor's office until I recovered sufficiently to drag myself home.

For a while, I also contracted a bad case of dysentery. The diarrhea was severe and I was unable to retain anything. The muscles involved were weakened and I became incontinent. Thick mucus mixed with blood poured out of me. Hundreds of people were dying of the malady. The only medication that had any effect was Sulfadine, but it was not to be obtained at any price. The doctor sent me to a hospital where there were many other patients suffering from the same illness. Every day I saw people carried out who had succumbed to the disease. Strangely, the physician treating patients with this life-threatening malady forbade them to eat anything other than curdled milk.

In addition to being so sick, I was tortured with a hunger that I could scarcely endure. When Hanele came to visit, I complained about how hungry I was and told her I had to have something to eat. She became alarmed and asked:

"Don't you know the doctor has forbidden you to eat anything, that it's dangerous for you to eat?"

"I feel it's more life-threatening not to eat," I replied.

On the following day, Hanele brought me a bowlful of wide noodles that she kneaded from the barley meal she brought with her from the collective. At the bazaar, she traded a piece of bread for some white cheese, sprinkled it with a little sugar, and smuggled it all in to the hospital.

We went out to the hospital yard at a spot where no human eye could see and I wolfed down the whole dishful of noodles and cheese. I felt satiated and was immediately aware of renewed strength flowing into my body. And wonder of wonders, on the very day after I ate this satisfying meal, my physician confirmed that the bloody discharge had stopped. After observing me an additional day, he discharged me and I went back to work in the coal mines.

The malaria however continued to plague me and several days after my return to work, the doctor prescribed a change of assignment so that I could avoid standing in water since this was what aggravated my illness. As a result of the doctor's orders, I was given a task working in a dry area. Instead of being a *kanagan*, I became a *plitovoy*.

I stood on a large iron plate where the loaded coal cars were lowered by a pulley. I had to untie the grabs from the cables and turn the cars around on the plate so that they would be in position to enter the tracks. There, the *kanagani* took over and set the cars towards the exit of the mine.

We were paid one hundred fifty rubles a month for our work. With that, we were expected to pay for our rent, electricity, and our ration of bread. If any cash was left over, it was used to purchase whatever might be available in the local shops, especially items for which we had ration cards. Of course, the one hundred fifty rubles were paid only to those who completed their work quota. I seldom received the full amount. More often, I earned from ninety to one hundred rubles. Hanele received seventy-five rubles for her work, for which, fortunately, there weren't fixed norms. She simply had to complete her assigned tasks in the course of the day.

Prices in the government markets, given our miserable compensation, were relatively modest. For example, the clayey black bread, obtainable without ration cards, cost ninety-five *kopecks* per kilo. Somewhat lighter-colored bread, known as *zakalatah*, was priced at two rubles and twenty-five kopecks. The white rolls baked on the anniversary of the October Revolution, although not every year, cost five and a half rubles. Nothing else could be purchased in government stores, with one exception. About twice a year, barrels of vodka were brought in. People would queue up for miles with their pots and pails and bought the bitter brew by the pailful. Then they drank themselves senseless. It was a way to forget their troubles.

If anything else was needed, we had to hunt for it on the black market, where prices were outrageously high in comparison with government outlets. A kilo of bread cost one hundred twenty rubles. A kilo of dark barley groat flour was one hundred rubles. A kilo of corn flour, ninety-five rubles. A pair of patched old shoes went anywhere from nine hundred to two thousand rubles. A glass of milk was fifty rubles, oil for frying or cooking, four hundred, real butter, six to seven hundred. Obviously, we would have to be billionaires to live at black market prices.

I hadn't worn a shirt on my back since the two I took with me from Poland wore out. I always emerged from the mines blackened and greasy with coal dust and would go directly into the bath to wash. After bathing, I had to put my tattered and dirty jacket back on against my naked skin so that I was never free of dirt. The seams of the jacket were chock-full of biting lice and nits that I could never get rid of. Sometimes, as I waited on the plate for the cars to be loaded and lowered to me, I would take off the jacket and delouse it in order to alleviate the itching that was so very bothersome. When I received the signal that the cars were ready, I would put my jacket back on.

Although I worked in the coal mines, I was obliged to buy my own coal, and coal was hard to find. During the summer months, I took a large, heavy lump of coal from the shaft and carried it the more than two kilometers home. A lump of coal that size was sufficient for boiling up *kipitok* in the morning and, if we were lucky enough to obtain some barley groats, to cook them as well.

The climate in winter in those parts is very strange. It's generally unbearably hot during the day but very cold at night. Heavy snow could fall during the night to a depth that reached above the knees. But in the morning, when the sun came up, it immediately became insufferably hot and the snow would melt so fast one could see it steaming. Deep puddles formed and gave off so much heat it was unbearable. Incessant heat tormented us until sunset. The minute the sun went down, it grew dreadfully cold. Freezing winds began to blow and we found it necessary to light the stove for protection against the frost. On such nights, the stove had to be filled with coal if the house was to remain warm.

Because we were so poorly nourished, we were very sensitive to the cold and to the sudden change from hot to cold. And the houses were built in such a way that they failed to retain heat. Consequently, we had to keep the stove going throughout the winter nights and were obliged to order a small wagonload of coal. Our turn for its delivery was to have been in October. But as with everything else in the Soviet economy, the coal wasn't delivered on the specified date but several weeks later. In the meantime, we just froze.

Hanele was pregnant again and we were very concerned not to have what happened the previous two times happen again. When the doctor determined that she was pregnant, we asked the mine director to give her work that was easier than carrying heavy pails of water, or sacks of coal for heating and for boiling the large kettles of *kipitok* for the dorms. We were afraid that she might God forbid suffer a miscarriage. But the director had himself a good laugh over our request. We pleaded with him in vain.

We turned to the chief physician at the polyclinic and told him about what Hanele had been through, losing her babies twice. She was afraid that something similar might happen should she have to continue to carry the coal and heavy pails of water. It was too dangerous for her to do these things.

The doctor, a refugee himself, heard us out. He was very considerate and immediately wrote up a statement demanding her release from work.

When we brought the statement to the director, he read it and angrily tore it into bits. He knew Soviet law better than the doctor did, he scolded, and he wouldn't release my wife before she was into her ninth month. We then decided that no matter what the authorities did, she wouldn't go back to work and jeopardize the pregnancy.

Several days later, after midnight, there came a knocking at our door. Two NKVD agents were there. They asked for my wife's passport and demanded to see her "food ration card" without which she couldn't obtain bread. When she handed them over, they pocketed them and instructed her to appear early the next morning at NKVD headquarters where they would return her documents.

When she arrived at their office the next morning and they noticed her, they politely asked her be seated. One of them then delivered a long lecture. "The fatherland" was being greatly wronged by her. They threatened that if she didn't return to work and work eight full months, she wouldn't get her food card and would have to go hungry until such time as she realized that she was only hurting herself. Not until the end of the eighth months could she have a doctor issue her a certificate of release from work. On no account would she be released at the present time. She didn't go back to work. We decided that we would just have to get along on my eight hundred grams of bread.

Every day, when I went off to work, I carried a small kettle with me which I left in the mess hall, near the mineshaft. On the way home, I bought some *shtshi* and took it back with me to my starving wife. Before going home, I ate my own portion in the mess hall. That is how we survived the first eight months of the pregnancy, on *shtshi* and eight hundred grams of bread.

One midnight, Hanele began to have labor pains. Fortunately, I was off from work and at home. We dressed quickly and began a slow walk to the hospital, some four kilometers from where we lived. The journey, which should have taken about half an hour, dragged on for more than three hours because we were forced to stop every ten or fifteen minutes. The labor pains made it difficult for Hanele to walk. She wanted to squat and relieve herself. I forcibly kept her from doing so, for I feared she might, God forbid, drop the child in the middle of the dark field. There wasn't a living soul passing by, and there were no homes near the field where one might call on someone for help. Dawn was beginning to break when we finally dragged ourselves into the hospital. Hanele was admitted immediately and one hour later, on the seventeenth of March 1944, she gave birth to a little boy.

I went to the mine and informed the supervisor that my wife had given birth. She was coming home soon and I would need an outfit for my newborn son. According to Soviet law, a newborn was entitled to a quilt and three meters of linen to be purchased from the closely guarded government stores. He wrote out a requisition, which I took to the *ambar* at the mine. I was able then to buy these items at government prices. I took the linen to a Kirghiz woman who made two little undershirts for our baby and used the rest to make three diapers and a tiny bonnet.

I lost no time in going to the marriage bureau to register the child. On strength of the birth certificate I was issued, I was given an additional ration card for two hundred grams of bread.

Before Hanele and the baby were released from the hospital however, it was determined that the child's blood was infected with the malaria parasite. This was on account of our both being long time carriers.

We had neither crib nor cradle for the child when it was time to take him home. I found some boards and a few nails and made a box. I gathered some fresh grass and left it out in the sun to dry. I placed the "hay" in the box, covered it with a new diaper, placed it on the table, and that had to serve as a bed for our newborn child.

When my wife and child came home, we placed him in the small box and stood watching him as he slept. I was reminded of the story of Moses and of how he floated all alone in the river, until Pharaoh's daughter rescued him from certain death.

According to doctor's orders, the baby was to be brought to the hospital twice a week for injections against malaria. The baby seemed to have an instinctive sense of where he was being taken, and thrashed about in our arms whenever we walked in the direction of the clinic. He coughed and gasped with pain when the needle full of acriquinine was injected.

Hanele also suffered severe attacks of malaria. The situation was especially tragic when she tried to nurse the child. The high fever accompanying the attack would either dry or spoil her milk making it unfit for consumption. The baby would scream with hunger and we were unable to help in any way. In desperation, we sought out a Kirghiz woman who was nursing an infant of her own. With great urgency, we requested that she nurse our child and save him from starvation. She agreed to do so but the infant refused to take the woman's nipple, and kept trying to take his mother's breast instead. To keep him from drinking the impure milk, Hanele applied acriqui-nine to her nipples. The baby would get hold of one with his mouth, and be pacified for a moment, but as soon as he tasted the awful bitterness of the acriquinine, he gasped badly and started to cry. It was extremely painful to see our child go hungry because he wouldn't nurse from a strange woman's breast.

In order to nourish the child properly, Hanele herself had to be better nourished. Yet we hadn't any additional source of food. I cut off a fourth of a kilo of bread from my ration, added it to the two hundred grams of the baby's ration, and exchanged it on the black market for a glass of milk for Hanele. Such a meager diet was far from enough.

When we were arrested in Minsk, I still had the addresses of my brother, who now lived in Palestine, and of two of my wife's aunts, who were living in America. I also had photographs of the entire family. I knew that if the NKVD found us in possession of foreign addresses, our lives would be in danger. They were known to torture anyone with a foreign address. They coerced them into confessing espionage and the possession of the addresses of contacts. To avoid arousing their wildly paranoid suspicions, I pretended to use the bathroom. While there, I tore up all the addresses and photographs, threw them into the toilet bowl, and flushed them down.

But now, when we were in such dire straits, and the western world joined the war to help Russia conquer a common foe, I thought it might no longer be as dangerous to contact someone for assistance. At the very least, we could have a much needed aid package sent to us. But how could I recover those addresses?

That was the topic of conversation with some friends who had a son our son's age. A brother in America sent them food packages all the time and it proved to be of great help in improving their nutrition. They gave us the address of the American Jewish Joint Distribution Committee and I copied it down. Our friends advised us not to write any more than that I was asking for help in looking for my brother, who lives in Haifa, and that I would appreciate their sending me his address. Nothing more was to be said because mail was censored by the Soviets. The American Joint Committee would then take care of the matter for us.

I followed our friends' advice to the letter and in less than three weeks, I received a food package from the JDC. The parcel contained a two-pound can of Crisco, two pounds of coffee, a five pound package of white flour, a pound of dry noodles, several tins of canned meat, and a new woolen blanket. We rejoiced as we opened the package. We embraced and kissed each other and burst into tears.

The next day, we received a postcard from the JDC informing us that they received our letter and were forwarding a package. Immediately upon receipt we were to notify them so that they might continue to assist us. They also said that they contacted the Jewish Agency for Palestine requesting them to ascertain my brother's address and promptly forward any available information. We were happy to find so many generous Jews in the world who hadn't forgotten their less fortunate brethren.

Our lives improved, of course. Now that our child was better nourished, he was developing satisfactorily. The only impediment to our happiness was malaria, a disease that tortured all three of us. Our little baby suffered from this tropical plague even more than we did.

We sold the two pounds of coffee and bought two kilos of farina. We cooked some for our son, with a glass of milk we bought him every day. He would lose his appetite because of the malaria and couldn't eat the cereal we tried to feed him. We made up all sorts of tricks to distract him, as we tried to get him to swallow a spoonful. We called in the neighbor's little dog, Kukla. As we talked, we fed one spoonful to the dog and one to the child. We told him to eat up, just like Kukla. When he swallowed what we fed him, we were happy.

Despite his physical suffering and limited ability to eat, our baby was developing nicely. He resembled Hanele, having a fair complexion, fine blonde hair, and a pair of sky-blue eyes. Whenever she took him to meet me at work, the miners would stop to marvel at his beauty.

The baby was our sole consolation. When we played with him, we forgot our troubles. We prayed to God that we survive the war, bring our son out of that accursed communist hell, cure him of his terrible disease, provide him a decent education, and see him grow up a free man in a free country.

Once, following my frequent attacks of malaria, I worked the night shift. While sitting on the plate awaiting the signal from the "shaft" above mine that the loaded car was ready to be lowered, I dozed off. I dreamt I was standing in a yard in Warsaw and a horse was kicking wildly as he ran straight towards me. I grew afraid and pressed hard against a wall. The horse came right to me, reared up on its hind legs, and began to wave its forelegs above my head. I tried to cry out, but I was unable to produce a sound. I awoke from my terrifying nap and found myself in a cold sweat, but pleased that it was only a bad dream.

As I straightened up, the signal came that a car filled with coal was about to be lowered. I watched as the men fastened the grab to the cable, and then pushed the car onto the steep ramp towards me. To my horror, in the next instant, I saw the grab of the car pull away from the cable, and the car hurtle down the tracks straight towards where I stood. I tried to run away but it was too late. The car landed on the plate, at full speed, and pinned me against the wall.

When I regained consciousness, I was lying on a hospital bed. I had an excruciating pain in my back. My eyes bulged out like two large lamps, engorged with blood. I tried to move, but couldn't. Every part of my body hurt. I groaned and yelled and suffered so. The doctors administered opium to ease my anguish. I dozed off and was besieged by nebulous, pain filled nightmares. I don't know how long it was before I realized what happened to me. I recall only seeing the hurtling car I tried to avoid.

I asked the miners I worked with to tell me what happened. They obliged by filling in the details. The car, which was loaded with coal, pushed me up against a wall that was supported by heavy beams. The miners came running, pushed the car aside and took me out. I was unconscious. They shouted for help. Before long the nurse arrived and had me taken out on a stretcher. A first aid squad was already waiting up on ground level to rush me to the hospital emergency. Once there, the doctors rushed to bring me back to life.

Little by little, I improved. Hanele came to see me every day, with the baby in her arms. I was able to get out of bed for a while and attempted to take a few steps. At first, it was very difficult to take even a single step because everything still hurt. I continued to practice day after day and extended it every time, until walking came more easily. I was eager to leave the hospital preferring to be home with my wife and child.

At the end of three months, the doctor discharged me despite the fact that I was still in great pain. His instructions were to go home and stay in bed for a week. Afterwards, he would decide whether I could return to work. Eight days later, the doctor certified me as fit for work. However, I wasn't to be sent back to the mine but given less strenuous work outdoors.

My new job was to empty the cars of an oily gray rock that had to be removed before getting to the layer of coal beneath. Two of us would receive the loaded cars from below and ride them up to the top of a hill. Then we took hold of the side of the car, which was cradled on an iron rod, and tipped it over, hurling the rocks down to the bottom of the hill. We then rode the car back downhill. The work was far from easy but it was better than working below ground in the shaft. I was out in the fresh air all day, which itself was a great advantage.

The box that served as a bed for our child was becoming too small and I began to inquire about where I could find a child's bed. Hearing that a Kirghiz had a crib for sale, I went to check it out. It was infested with bedbugs but I had no alternative and bought it. I scraped off all the joints with a knife blade, boiled up some water, and scalded the bed several times. When I was satisfied the bed was perfectly clean, I dried some grass and placed it in the crib, making a roomy bed for our child to sleep in.

Chapter 14

One day at noon, when I went to the mess hall to eat a bowl of *shtshi*, it was announced over the loudspeaker that the war had come to an end. Hearing the happy news, we were overcome by a warm wave of joy. We tossed our caps in the air and jubilantly shouted hurrahs. All the town's sirens were sounded in order to let everyone in on the news. The mine manager entered the mess hall and announced loudly: "Today is a great *praznik* (holiday) and you're all free to go home and celebrate the victory."

We went outdoors and the miners streamed out of their dark shafts. The trucks that served the mine industry filled up with people who then drove them around town. Those riding the trucks filled the streets with the sound of patriotic communist songs that they caroled in chorus. I too, jumped onto a truck, one that was headed in the direction of my home so that I would arrive there that much sooner to share the joyous news with my wife and child.

In the midst of jubilation, doubts began to creep into my heart. Now that the bloody war was over would the Soviet government be so generous as to free us and allow us to return home? We were forced into Soviet citizenship and slavery. We knew that since the days of the Bolshevik Revolution not even a fly could escape from within the iron curtain. So how would we ever free ourselves from their satanic claws?

After a day of celebration, everyone returned to his or her daily routine. Here and there someone occasionally mentioned the extraordinary event but the enthusiasm gradually died down. Living conditions didn't change in any way. The women who worked in the coal mines were forever talking among themselves about the two most important things they would like to have right away: enough bread to appease their hunger and the safe return of their husbands, sons and fathers from the front. Unfortunately, neither of these hopes was destined to come true.

Instead, the military garrisons that fought in the western territories were sent thousands of miles from their homes. Those who lived in the southern parts of Russia were banished to the north to perform hard labor, while those who resided in eastern Russia were dispatched to the mines in the south so that they would be as far from their families as possible.

Because some of these troops marched into western countries and had an opportunity to see the colossal difference between conditions there and those in the Soviet slave state, the government feared that the returning military would infect the citizenry with their new perception of the world. This might, in turn, lead to insurrection. Veterans were therefore kept isolated in the Siberian taigas and coal mines where they would have little contact with the general population.

Rather than becoming easier, redeeming bread rations became much more difficult. During the war, people were obliged to stand on bread lines for hours on end. But things were very much worse now. Hundreds of soldiers were sent into the towns and they, too, had to stand in line for their bread. This doubled the number of people standing in line because no new outlets were opened. Many people would spend the night holding a place to be among the first to receive their rations when the *larok* opened.

The Jewish refugees clung to one another for support and every day someone had another astounding story to relate to encourage themselves and others and to keep from losing hope. None of these accounts emanated from a credible or dependable source. We would scoff at such accounts and considered them to be highly unlikely *yidn viln azoy* tales (the way Jews would like it stories).

One day, a young fellow appeared in the shaft and told us exuberantly that a Polish delegation arrived in Kzil-Kiya to register former Polish citizens. We at first ridiculed and scolded him:

"You've just cooked up another *yiva* duck haven't you?"

"No," the young man beat his chest.

"This is no *yiva* duck, this is the truth. I spoke to them myself. You can go and find out for yourselves that what I'm telling you is the honest truth!"

I was very skeptical but several of us set out for the indicated address. It was at some distance from the city. On the way, we encountered many other refugees and asked them whether the story we heard was true. "True," they confirmed, "as true as it is now day."

When we arrived at our destination, hundreds of Polish citizens were already queued up to register. Our names were recorded and placed on an "option" list, which they were preparing. Anyone who signed up was considered to have renounced Russian citizenship and automatically regained Polish citizenship.

The delegation informed us that the following week they would receive a shipment of products, which they would distribute to supplement whatever we were receiving for our labors. When an "option" was negotiated, they would arrange for our repatriation. When we heard these words, we were infused with a spirit of hope. The mere assurance that preparations were being made for our repatriation instilled us with courage and endurance.

Meanwhile, I received a letter, and two days later, a package from my brother. The parcel contained food, soap, and other goods. That same week, we also received some things from the Polish delegation, such as two kilos of flour, some sugar, and more Crisco. The Polish delegation also supplied us with shirts, trousers, and dresses for women. We also got a tiny little snowsuit with a hood to go over the head, for our son.

We lost no time in preparing to leave. Since we received food and clothing from the Polish delegation and an occasional package from abroad, we now seldom ate the clayey black bread. Instead, we cut it up into slices and dried it on the stove. We collected the toast in a sack so that there would be something for us to eat on our long journey back home. We hoped that either today or tomorrow we would at long last be going home. Our desperate longing for the happy moment was premature, for it was a long time in coming.

In their impatience to see their expectations fulfilled, people were again spreading false *yiva* news. One man swore, for example, that he saw long lines of rail cars waiting to pick us up on the tracks of the local station. Another brought us the "duck" that he heard the chief of the coal mines issue an order to the effect that the *roshtshot* (accounting) of the Polish refugees was to be prepared forthwith in advance of their departure for home. None of these stories held even a grain of truth.

Finally, a full year after we registered, we received a summons to appear at the Polish delegation office with passports in tow. Representatives of the Soviet government would be present to examine the passports and, if everything were in order, would issue permits to return to Poland.

We went there with our passports and, after the Russians scrutinized them, they were stamped with an authorization to depart for Poland. Our addresses were recorded in detail and we were instructed to have our things packed as soon as possible because, in three days, a truck would came to transport us to the train.

Our joy was indescribable. We hugged and kissed each other right there in the yard of the delegation office. We wept and we rejoiced. We put our hands on one another's shoulders and danced in a circle. Dancing and singing, we marched out into the streets and made them resound with patriotic Polish songs. The Kirghiz and Russian passersby stopped and stared wondering what was happening. We explained that we were going home. Some of the refugees made up a song, and everyone spontaneously broke out singing it:

Home, home, we're on our way home!
I'm a young man from Warsaw, bold,
Keep the fortune you say is gold.
May you and your country burn in hell,
At last little brothers, all is well.
Home little brothers; we're going home!

The Soviet citizens regarded us with envy. Some even expressed regret.

"At least you have someone to act on your behalf. No one's concerned to help us improve our lot."

The day we yearned for and dreamed of for so long, finally arrived. We stood outside with our luggage and waited for the truck that was to pick us up. It arrived on time and we boarded. Along the way, it took on other refugees and when it was packed full, it brought us to the railroad station. Forty people and their bundles were crammed into each car of the freight trains set aside for us. Inside each car, there were benches along both sides, leaving the center free for standing and moving about. Ten people laid down on each bench and ten under each bench. Each person placed his bundles under his head. When everyone was loaded on, the locomotive whistle sounded and the long freight train began to move. We didn't protest the fact that we were packed in like so many cattle. We were anxious to leave the Soviet *Gehenna* (hell) and arrive at the Polish border without further delay.

The train dragged on slowly because from the Asian side up to the Ural Mountains, the boundary between Asia and Europe, only a single track was laid. Trains, in either direction, had to stop and wait for the train going in the opposite direction to pass. The oncoming train went off on a siding, and followed it a little way, until it returned to the main track. When the other train turned north, ours proceeded south. Such transfer points occurred about every two hours.

There were no toilets on the train. Whenever it stopped, we jumped down and relieved ourselves in the open field, men, women and children, all together. We were afraid to go any distance from the train for fear it might depart and leave us behind in the wasteland.

When we stopped at a capital city of an *oblast*, we got off to see whether there was anything to buy. At some of the larger stations, we might sometimes find a restaurant where we could buy a bowl of soup. In any case, there was hot *kipitok* to be had at each station. We filled our pots and kettles with the boiled water and ate some of our dried black bread with it.

The convoy would stop several hours at the larger stations. More freight trains bringing refugees from other places pulled in. We ran over to each train to inquire about Bella and Hayim, from whom we hadn't heard for seven years. We did find my wife's sister and brother-in-law on one of those trains. They had a newborn infant scarcely two weeks old with them. We were all overjoyed. At long last, we found one another again and would be going home together. They found space for us on their train albeit not in the some car. We moved our things into a nearby car and traveled the rest of the way on their train.

The closer we came to the European border the colder it got. It was particularly hard on Bella's infant. The baby caught cold and cried and coughed badly all night long in the unheated freight car, especially when it had to be changed and exposed to the frigid air. The child grew worse and worse as the train proceeded. There was no doctor on board and there was nowhere to buy medicine. We were just then traveling through the wild steppes of the Tatar Republics, an abandoned wasteland reminiscent of scabs on a scurfy head, where each peasant hut was a hundred kilometers from the next and at a considerable distance from the tracks. The hillocks and wild grey grass kept us widely separated from the Tatar settlements.

One freezing cold night, when the infant had been crying and coughing continuously, it suddenly fell silent. Everyone thought it fell asleep exhausted by its nightlong ordeal. When the train stopped the next morning, our brother-in-law came into our car and informed us, in a tear-filled voice, that the child expired during the night.

We didn't know what to do with the innocent little body. The engineer insisted that it be buried at once because keeping a dead child on the train among the passengers was forbidden. We had no alternative but to walk a few meters from the train and dig a little grave. We wrapped the baby in its swaddling clothes and buried it. Dozens of refugees gathered about the grave. Our brother-in-law said *Kaddish* for his son and there was sadness in everyone's eyes as we returned to the train.

Our own little son, who was two years old by then, also was sick throughout the journey. His malaria attacks came regularly and he often suffered a high fever. As we approached a station and the light from the electric lamps flooded the car through various cracks, they cast huge moving shadows on the walls. He would scream terribly and we didn't know whether it was on account of the fever or because he was frightened. At first, I thought it was the fever. Later on, I realized he screamed only when large shadows appeared. So I watched over him every night and whenever I saw the approaching light, I covered his little head with his quilt. This helped to keep him calm. The fever persisted longer than it ever had before. This alarmed us greatly. We began to fear that after all we'd been through, we too might lose our little one.

We brought acriquinine along and administered it to him regularly. But the fever didn't let up. We got off at every station, and whenever we saw a train arrive, we ran from car to car looking for a doctor. Finally, I found a Jewish physician among the refugees of one of the freight trains. He accompanied me to our car, examined our child and found that the fever wasn't due to malaria but to measles. However, he hadn't any medicine and couldn't give him anything that might help. He advised us to keep the child warm and said that in a few days we would be arriving at the borders of Poland, where it would be possible to get aid.

After three weeks of dragging along in the freight train, we arrived at the Polish border. Soviet police were the first to enter our train. They asked for our Russian passports, which they immediately confiscated. Then they asked whether we had any money to declare. Those who showed them their money had it taken from them. "You won't be needing Russian rubles any more," they said. Then they ordered everyone to open their packages, inspected the bundles, and robbed them of whatever took their fancy.

The train then proceeded slowly for a short distance and stopped again. The Polish border patrol came up to us and asked whether we had anything to declare. "We have nothing. The Russians asked before you did," we replied. They grinned and descended from the train.

It began moving again. We were on Polish soil at last, and traveling on Polish rails. We were delighted to be back on Polish earth and putting increasingly greater distance between the barbarians and ourselves. The train was now traveling at high speed and some of the returnees were so pleased, they started singing a patriotic song. I was preoccupied with my own thoughts, impatient to arrive at our first stop so I could get off the train and seek out help for our sick child.

As I was thus engrossed, a sudden racket of machine gun fire and a hail of bullets terrified us. The car didn't even have windows through which we could see where the shooting was coming from. When the train stopped in the former German city of Stettin, we got out and saw that dozens of bullets had struck. Fortunately, no one was hurt. Refugees who arrived there before us informed us that the shooting was the work of the anti-Semitic Polish organization calling itself AK (*Armiya Krayowa*), a nationalist army that was supposedly fighting the Soviets. It found that its arms were too short to strike effectively, and turned instead to the task of annihilating any Jews that may have escaped the claws of the Nazis. We were also told that the AK murderers were making it a practice to route Jews from the trains, take them out into the woods and unceremoniously execute them. And so, on our return to Poland, we were reminded of a fact we chose not to remember during our sojourn in Russia, that Polish anti-Semitism always was and continues to be the most virulent in the world.

As we were getting down from the train, a number of Poles gathered around and stared at us, a veritable sight to behold. Some couldn't refrain from calling out:

"Would you look at that! So many Jews still left. And to think, people say Hitler killed them all…"

We paid no attention to them. They might as well have been just so many barking dogs.

The first thing Hanele did upon alighting from the train was to take our child in her arms and hurry away to seek a medical center where he could be helped. There happened to be a first aid station right at the depot. A doctor examined our son and said he should be taken to hospital immediately. Hanele didn't want to waste any time and went to the hospital right away. My brother-in-law, my sister-in-law and I gathered up our bundles and went to inquire after lodging.

Many Germans were afraid that the Poles might take revenge. Every day saw some of them abandon their homes, taking only clothing and small household goods back to Germany. Some of the younger Poles realized that they could earn a few *zloty* if they met every incoming train and, for a gratuity, offered the returning repatriates the addresses of recently abandoned living quarters. We accepted just such an offer from a young man. We paid him what he asked and he led us to an abandoned apartment. It consisted of two rooms and a kitchen. The apartment was fully furnished with just about everything needed for housekeeping, including cooking utensils and dishes, all left behind by the fleeing Germans.

Assured that we had where to rest our heads, I left our belongings with my brother and sister-in-law and sought out the location of the hospital my wife and child went to. After several hours of searching in the unfamiliar city, I finally found my way to the hospital. The doctor who examined our son on the freight train made the correct diagnosis. I could see that our son was entirely covered with red spots.

I told Hanele that we found a place to stay. As soon as she heard that, she wanted to take our child home. However, the hospital doctor said he wouldn't release the child until he was cured. Not wanting to leave the child in the care of strangers, Hanele demanded that she be permitted to remain in the hospital until the child was well. After considerable argument, permission was granted. Eight days later, when Hanele and my son were safely home, I had gotten us fairly well settled-in.

There was generally no problem obtaining food. Although some goods were scarce, there was as much white bread as anyone would want. It wasn't the black, clayey bread we had in Russia and, so far, at least, we didn't have to stand in line for hours on end to purchase it. Flour, groats and potatoes were readily available. If we only had the money, we could live well and most certainly have enough to eat.

I registered at the employment office and was immediately provided with work. It was to dig ditches for the municipal water system. Another man and I assisted a plumber. We were sent wherever water pipes had been damaged. We dug a ditch until the pipe was exposed. When the plumber repaired it, we closed up the hole that we previously dug up. We had hopes of living a peaceful, happy life. But, as the Yiddish saying goes: *Der mentsh trakht und Gott lacht* (Man plans and God laughs).

Since my brother-in-law and sister-in-law were childless, they decided they would take the train to Warsaw to find out what had become of our homes and members of our family. When they returned from Warsaw, they brought devastating news. Warsaw was in desolate ruin and everyone in the family had perished. While still in Russia, we heard rumors that the Germans were murdering Jews in Poland, but we never could have imagined the horrible reality. Bella and Hayim's report shocked us to the core and the pain of it will be with us forever.

The road to Warsaw was a threat to life. The AK gangs rampaged throughout the country unchecked, murdering Jews wherever they could. On the way to Warsaw, Bella and Hayim twice saw Jews pulled off the train at a station stop, dragged into the woods and shot. In Stettin, too, the situation grew increasingly dangerous for the handful of Jews who had escaped death. A day didn't go by that we didn't hear of some lawless mob of Polish anti-Semites harassing a few defenseless Jews. They attacked Jews who came to the market place to sell what little they owned to have the wherewithal to stay alive. They beat them and robbed them of whatever they had. Even those who came as customers were barbarously attacked.

The younger returnees organized *kibbutz*im in preparation for migration to Palestine, where they hoped to build new lives for themselves. The Polish gangs attacked them as well, robbing and sometimes killing them. Every morning, upon leaving home, we found a dead Red Army soldier lying among the bombed out ruins or a Jew who had been done away with as he was coming home from work at night. The gangs also began to break into Jewish homes at night to rob and plunder their property at gunpoint. Everyone became fearful. Some decided to stay close to the German border and hoped to save their lives that way.

Before long, the Poles developed yet another industry. They began smuggling frightened Jews into Germany. They demanded exorbitant prices for taking a Jew across the German border. Only the very wealthy could pay such a price.

To make certain the robber bands didn't break into our home at night, we fastened a heavy iron bar on the door so that it would be well secured from the inside. We were afraid to keep the lights on at night, for we wanted to prevent anyone from noticing that our apartment was occupied. All night long, shots could be heard in the street as though the war was still in progress. People were afraid to go to sleep, afraid that they might be caught unprepared for the worst. Rummaging in the attic, among old pieces of metal left behind by the Germans, we found a bayonet. We kept the bayonet at hand to defend ourselves should anyone break in.

My brother-in-law conceived of a plan by which we could get to the German border and save our lives. He knew where the smugglers assembled those who made arrangements to be taken to the border. They were to be taken there by truck from that location. His plan was for us to go there and steal into the truck. If the smugglers caught us and demanded pay, we would say we haven't any money, but they'll have to take us anyway for we would cause a disturbance. The police would become involved and they would be apprehended and severely punished.

The plan didn't appeal to me. First of all, under no circumstances would we take our child along on such a hazardous venture. Secondly, what made him think the smugglers were so inept that they couldn't handle the challenge? They might overpower us, in which case, the result could be fatal. "I don't want to do that," I said firmly, "but if you want to risk it, go ahead. We'll find some other way."

He was determined, however, and on that same evening, he and Bella packed a small valise, with a few things, and left to carry out his hazardous scheme. Several days later, we received a letter informing us that they were already in Germany, in the American Zone.

As time went on, the house we lived in had fewer and fewer tenants as increasing numbers of people left Stettin to go to the German border. Soon, all the other occupants were gone and we were the only family living in the three-story house.

I came home every evening and locked the entrance to the building. I went up to the third floor, walked into our apartment, fastened the two locks and let down the heavy iron bar so that it crossed the middle of the door. We would remain sealed up that way until I left for work in the morning.

A Jewish Committee had been set up in Stettin endeavoring to meet the needs of the Jewish community. This committee provided the *kibbutzim* with food and clothing. And now that the community was in a state of disruption because so many were running away, there were some representatives from Palestine attached to the committee. They came to help the *kibbutzim* escape from Poland and then find a way for them to gain illegal entry into Palestine. These brave young men from the *Briha* (Hebrew for "flight" or "escape") accomplished their mission by very secret means.

When I returned home from work one night, I sealed the downstairs door and went upstairs to our apartment, as usual. After our evening meal, we prepared to go to bed early so that we wouldn't need to turn on the lights. We hadn't quite dozed off, when we heard a loud commotion in the yard. We held our breaths and strained all our senses to try to discover what was going on.

At first, we heard several men talking to one another. We couldn't grasp what they were saying from that distance. Somewhat later, we heard knocking at the downstairs door. When no one answered, they increased the tempo of their pounding. When that didn't help either, they began to kick at the door and yell, as though possessed, that we better open up or it would go badly for us. By that time, we realized who they were and what they wanted.

"Open up!" they roared.

"We know there are Jews living here! If you don't open up, we'll break down the door. Then, none of you will get out alive!"

Interspersed with their threats, were some of the ugliest expressions in the Polish language. We stayed very still and, with baited breaths, listened to the racing of our hearts. Hanele tried to persuade me that we should take our child up to the attic and hide there.

"No," I countered, "that's not a good idea. There's no door in the attic that we can reinforce the way we did the one here. We're behind two strong locks with a thick bar in the middle of the door. Even if they break down the door downstairs, we'll be safe here because it would take more than the strength of a Samson to break that bar. We have a greater chance of surviving here than anywhere else. And if we get through this night safely, we'll not spend another minute in this damned country."

I got out of bed and crept to the window to look down into the yard. I could see three hooligans hard at work, with iron bars in their hands, trying to raise the downstairs door off its hinges. Apparently, they were unable to break the lock. I went to the door and put my ear to it to try to hear whether anyone was coming upstairs. I stood there with bayonet in hand, ready for any eventuality. No matter what happened, I was determined not to yield.

Suddenly, the sound of several revolver shots reached our ears. After that all was quiet. We couldn't understand what could have happened down in the yard below. We waited a few minutes, in what seemed like an eternity, after which I went to the window once more to see what was going on. This time, there was no one to be seen in the yard. I went back to bed but couldn't close my eyes. We watched over our son the rest of the evening. How like a little angel he looked, sleeping soundly, unaware of the danger lurking all around him. This was the worst but last terror-filled night we would spend on the accursed soil of Poland.

Chapter 15

I rose at the first grey of dawn. But instead of going to work, I went to look for a way to escape the nightmare we could expect to experience in the days to come. I told Hanele to seal the door behind me and not dare open it to anyone until I returned and she could hear my voice outside the door.

I hurried over to the Jewish Committee and asked to see the secretary. In a single breath, I told him of the night of terror we just experienced.

"After last night, my wife and child, and I cannot take the risk of staying here any longer. If you don't do something to help us soon, whatever happens will be on your shoulders."

Silence reigned. The secretary exchanged silent glances with the two other people sitting at the table who heard my story. Suddenly, one of them, an elderly man, inquired:

"What's your name?"

"Hershl Altman," I responded quickly.

"Might your father's name be Sholem Altman?"

I looked at him in astonishment, my eyes searching his face.

"Yes," I replied. "How did you know?"

A smile appeared on his face. He seemed pleased to have to offer an explanation to the other two.

"His father, Sholem Altman, is a highly regarded leader in the Poale Zion movement. Many long years ago I worked with him in Warsaw, where we organized the very first labor unions. After a long period abroad, he returned to become the secretary of the Painters' Alliance, which had its headquarters at 38 Djika Street in Warsaw."

The elderly gentleman and the secretary of the committee assured me that they would do everything possible to keep us from living through another night as I described. They asked me to remain seated. The older man left the room but was back about ten minutes later with a young man. The young man, I discovered later on, was from Briha. He wrote down the address of a *kibbutz* on a small piece of paper, told me to go straight home, pack everything, and go to that address with my wife and child. From there, we would be taken across the border, along with a number of other people from the *kibbutz*. I sped home breathlessly, and we packed up everything. In less than two hours we were at the *kibbutz*.

The *kibbutzniks* were sitting on their luggage on the floor and waiting for us to depart for the border. We were given instructions on how to conduct ourselves in order to cross the border safely. The same young man who told us to come to the *kibbutz* said that we should get rid of any Polish documents, addresses, or photographs, which would identify us as Jews, or citizens of Poland. We were to forget our real names. We were to choose a German name, and an address where we purportedly lived before the war, and commit each of those to memory. Without a pause, he suddenly asked me: "What's your name?"

"Hans," I replied.

"And where do you live?"

"In Hamburg, on Koenigstrasse, number twenty-two."

"Good!"

He then asked my wife the same questions and, satisfied with her answers, continued to coach us.

"Remember that you're Germans who've run away to Stettin to escape the bombardment and that you're coming *nach heimat* (back home). You'll be sent across the border together with some Germans. Keep to yourselves so that they don't find out who you really are.

Right now, we'll take you to the transit camp where Poles will register you and put you aboard trains. During registration, make your answers brief. Don't dare speak an extra word. If they address you in Polish, shake your head as if you don't understand. They won't ask you much anyway because we've bribed them. But just to be sure, follow our instructions exactly. The moment you arrive at the transit station you're on your own."

Our group numbered twenty people altogether. We lined up and marched off to the transit camp. It was right alongside the railroad station. We were led into a four-story building that once housed a German school. All four floors were filled with itinerant German workers contracted by the Poles to clean up the city but now on their way home. Our group was escorted into the cellar. We spread our blankets on the hard concrete and prepared to spend the night in very crowded conditions. Early the next morning, we formed long lines and waited for the registration to begin.

Several Polish officials were seated at the registration tables. They were ready to register everyone on their long lists. When our turn arrived, they asked us questions in Polish. I pushed Hanele and the baby ahead of me and answered for the three of us.

"*Das ist meine frau, und meine knabe*" (That's my wife and child).

"Name?" he asked in German.

"Hans Altman, *meine frau* Hilda, *und* Karl."

I reeled off my address as "Frankfurt, Koenigstrasse 22." When I finished reciting the memorized monologue, the official's face broke into a smile. He turned to me and said, in Polish: "We know you're not Germans." I shook my head and waved my hands around. I grimaced to show that I didn't understand a word he said. I stepped aside, and the next person stepped up to be registered. We were handed a hunk of bread spread with marmalade and were told to board the trains that were ready to transport us deep into Germany.

We arrived in the city of Hanover, which was in the English sector. We were told to disembark and taken to a school, where we were each provided with a wool blanket. Mattresses were laid out on the floor and that was where we spent the night.

In the morning, we received bread cards, to be used to buy bread, and tokens with which we could obtain meals in a restaurant. The mayor of the city came and delivered a speech in which he said that he was sorry there wasn't any housing available. For the time being, we would have to live at the schoolhouse until we made our own arrangements.

None of us felt very comfortable among the Germans. Moreover, we were fearful on account of our false status. We had false names, fake addresses and affiliation. We tried to figure out what to do to avoid living among the Germans like so many scared rabbits. After much debate, I suggested that we confer with Dr. Auerbach, who was then living in Dusseldorf, and was, at the time, one of the most prominent attorneys in all of German Jewry. Surely he would know how to extricate us from the unpleasant situation we found ourselves in. The idea met everyone's approval and a decision was made to send a delegation to make request of Dr. Auerbach to receive us. Two others and I were unanimously approved to carry out this mission. Everyone contributed a few marks for train travel expenses, and we departed for Dusseldorf. We knew Dr. Auerbach lived in that city but we didn't have his home address. We spent a long miserable day in the unfamiliar city before we finally found someone who knew his address.

When we rang the bell of his residence, he received us warmly and listened very attentively to what we had to say. He then informed us that we had nothing to fear. His advice was to call upon the mayor as soon as we returned to Hanover. If we were as frank with the mayor as we were with him, nothing untoward would happen. In the event we were dissatisfied with the mayor's response, we could always turn to the occupation authorities. The British would surely do what was right.

We thanked Dr. Auerbach heartily, and returned to Hanover. We called everyone together and reported what we were told. Their happiness and joy was indescribable. Our words infused one and all with a renewed spirit.

On the following morning, our delegation went to see the mayor and explained the whole matter to him. We told him that Dr. Auerbach advised us to call on him and seek his help. On that very same day, the mayor brought two Jewish representatives before us, and we beleaguered them with the many questions that troubled us.

We were asked to assemble in the large auditorium of the school, where the two Jewish spokesmen reassured us that we had nothing to fear. The authorities understood that we couldn't have gotten out from under the claws of the anti-Semitic Poles without using false names. We were now in a safe haven where we would be helped to establish ourselves and be allowed to live in peace. They then requested that we line up to be re-registered and obtain temporary documents showing our true identities. After re-registration, we were assigned places to live. Families were allotted separate residences, while single people were domiciled in rooms rented from German families. Once again, we began to feel like a free people.

Life in Germany stabilized quickly. The British occupying power saw to it that the ruins of the houses destroyed by war were promptly removed. German contractors proceeded to rebuild the city at a feverish pace. Seemingly overnight, the streets of Hanover sprouted new buildings. The streets took on an air of normalcy. More and more shops made their appearance and offered a variety of goods. Living conditions were continually improving. A committee, supported by the Jews of England, opened an office and, with a generous hand, supplied the needs of the refugees streaming in from the Russian taigas as well as of some of the survivors of the Nazi extermination camps.

There were rumors that the United Nations Relief and Rehabilitation Administration (UNRRA) camps were being readied in the American

Zone for escapees from the dreadful concentration camps and Siberian forests. When we heard of these rumors, we began to think about how we might get over to the American Zone. Some of our acquaintances told us the Briha was involved in transferring survivors from the English Zone to the American. But no one knew where Briha had its headquarters. We inquired continuously, hoping to contact Briha, but no one had information. Obviously, they were carrying out their work in the strictest secrecy.

One day, I was riding on a streetcar that was so jammed with passengers that there was no room inside and I remained standing outside on the platform. A young man caught my eye. I could see he was Jewish, but he was obviously not one of us. Unlike the refugees, he wore better clothing and his skin was tanned by the sun. He noticed that I was observing him, smiled broadly and inquired: "*Yehudi?*" I replied in the affirmative and we started a conversation as we rode along. I told him briefly that I was in the city with my wife and child, having just returned from Russia, and that we were having difficulty making a life for ourselves. There weren't many Jews in the city and I couldn't see a future for us in such a cold, foreign place. It would be much better if I could get over to the American Zone, where most of the survivors were living. I heard that the Briha was transferring Jewish refugees to the American sector but, so far, I was unable to find anyone who knew how to get in touch with them.

He interrupted me with a smile. "You've found the right address." He took a notebook from an inside coat pocket, wrote something on a page with a pen, and handed me the piece of paper, saying, "Come to this address with your wife and child at any time. From there you'll be taken to the American Zone."

When I returned home and told my wife of my unusual encounter with the wonderful young man, I was beaming. I showed her the address from which we would cross over to the American Zone. We started to pack immediately, so as not to lose time.

Early the next morning, we each strapped on a rucksack, containing our meager belongings, took our child by the hand, and boarded a streetcar that would take us to the address we were given. It was far outside the city, a secluded one-story building that had a kitchen on the street entrance level. Food was being cooked in great pots and served to refugees in an adjacent large hall furnished with a long table and very long benches. The refugees sat along both sides of the table as they ate their meal. On the floor above, was an immense room with some twenty beds made up with clean white sheets, white pillowcases and green military blankets. At one end of the large room was a long, narrow lavatory equipped with several showers.

Upon our arrival, we were led upstairs, assigned beds and shown the washroom. We were told to make ourselves comfortable and to come downstairs for the evening meal at six o'clock. A splendid meal was prepared. Some twenty people were served a hearty, delicious soup, meat, two vegetables, and an apple dessert. We were free to eat as much of the bread as we wanted. After the meal, we were advised to go upstairs, and try to get a good night's rest because very early in the morning, before daybreak, a truck would arrive to take us across the border to the American Zone.

At about four in the morning, we were awakened, instructed to wash quickly, and then go downstairs with our luggage. When we entered the dining room, we found buttered white bread and hot coffee all ready to be served. After breakfast, promptly at five o'clock, a military truck drove into the yard. We crammed in with our baggage. The open side of the truck was covered with a tarpaulin, and we drove off.

By dawn, we had traveled a considerable distance. When the sun had fully risen, the air within the truck became extremely warm and uncomfortable. We knocked at the driver's partition and asked him to open the tarpaulin and let some fresh air in because we found the heat stifling. He stopped the truck and removed the cover. The drive was far more tolerable after that.

Several hours later, the truck stopped again. The driver said that he had to replace the tarpaulin because we were approaching the American Zone. He warned us to remain quiet. We weren't to talk or cough or sneeze because, insofar as the border patrol was concerned, he was transporting goods, not people. He assured us that once we were inside the American Zone, he would once again remove the tarpaulin and, this time, leave it off. We resumed our journey.

When we felt the truck stop again, we held our breaths and sat perfectly still. After some time, we heard English being spoken, in loud tones, alongside the truck. We couldn't understand any of it and were afraid we'd been discovered. The conversation continued for some time, and we finally heard the driver turn on the ignition. The truck started up and traveled a short distance, then stopped once more. The tarpaulin opened, the driver stuck his head in, and announced, with a smile, that we were within the American jurisdiction. He removed the tarpaulin, as promised, and drove on. Darkness had fallen by the time we pulled into an enormous transit camp in the American sector.

We saw a long, wide street and huge wooden barracks on both sides. The truck came to a halt and we were asked to climb down. We were led into one of the barracks. It contained a great many collapsible canvas, military cots. Everyone appropriated a bed and tossed his things on it. Tired out by the journey, some of us sat down on the cots, and others lay down to rest.

Caldrons of steaming hot soup were brought in, and everyone was served a bowlful, along with several little packages of crackers. We were informed that we would only stay overnight. In the morning we would be sent to permanent camps. Weary, we laid down to rest with our clothes still on. We didn't even unpack our things. We were so tired; we soon fell asleep.

I don't know how long we'd been sleeping, when a blinding light, which suddenly flooded the barracks, awakened me. I sat up on my bed in surprise and looked about to see what was happening. I saw about a half-dozen American soldiers come in with large cartons, which they set down on a long, large table in the middle of the room. Taking blankets from the cartons they placed one on each bed. If the occupant was asleep, the soldier carefully covered him so as not to awaken him. After distributing the blankets, they left little packages of cookies and candy on the children's cots. Their work done, they quietly slipped out of the barracks and turned off the lights as they departed.

I remained sitting in utter surprise. I was literally moved to tears at sight of the heartfelt, humane attitude that these considerate American soldiers displayed towards the unfortunate and weary Jewish wanderers. I thought of the anti-Semitic Polish hooligans and-not to mention them in the same breath-these kind, merciful young Americans and came to the conclusion that there were still some good people in the world. A warm feeling suffused my spirit and I fell asleep calmed and reassured. I was glad we had left behind the cruel, corrupt Poles and their accursed communist masters.

The next morning, we were again loaded onto trucks, which took us to a permanent camp called Ziegenhain. It was situated two kilometers outside the town of Ziegen in the Kassel district. The camp was fenced in with barbed wire. The guard towers used by the Nazi villains in their armed supervision of their victims were still standing. Although we were free to move around as we wished, camp police were stationed at the gates to ensure that no outsider was admitted without the express permission of the American occupying power.

About 1200 refugees were quartered in the camp. They soon became active in a number of political and cultural pursuits. A variety of Zionist movement groups were formed. All the political events of the period were discussed at their meetings. A special office of culture was established. It lost no time in designating one of the buildings to be used as a school. Children were enrolled and the teaching of regular subjects began. A radio loudspeaker system was installed. It broadcast news from the press and local camp activity three times a day.

A group of young people, myself included, desirous of making a cultural contribution to the education of the community, established a theatre workshop for the performance of Yiddish drama. We were able to make use of a large theatre, which could easily accommodate eight hundred people. We put up notices on the theatre doors that we were seeking talented people for a theatre ensemble.

Among our early founders, was a gifted young director named Elie Bulman. With unsurpassing devotion, he put together and directed, from memory, a number of one act plays familiar to us from pre-war days. We attracted another wonderful young man who wrote songs that were so heartfelt they touched everyone's soul. His name was Alex Fogelbaum. We also had with us a young writer, Vielka Brode, who undertook to help us in our work and assisted us greatly in the writing of theatre prose.

We organized an ensemble of twenty-two people and called our first meeting. We elected a committee of four to be responsible for the theatre and its management. Those chosen were Bulman, Shpagatner, Fogelbaum and myself.

The first thing we did was to apply to the cultural affairs office to supply us with plays to perform. They promised to do so but said it would take time because there were no Yiddish books left in Germany following the Holocaust. The committee promised to ask the American Jewish Joint Distribution Committee to handle the request and was confident they would send us some material. We decided to name our workshop the *Sholem Aleichem Dramatic Club of Camp Ziegenhain* and went right to work. Purim was approaching and we received a request from the cultural affairs office that our first theatrical performances have some association with the holiday.

Our friend Fogelbaum quickly thought up several Purim songs. Back in Warsaw I had seen performances of Sholem Aleichem's one-act play, *Mentshn* (People) as well as *Yiddishe Parnosses* (Jewish Livelihoods) so I proceeded to write down whatever I recalled. What I couldn't remember I made up. We named our revue *Laugh Calories for Purim* and rehearsals began.

When we were ready for our final rehearsal, we invited the culture committee and the camp commander, who was an officer of UNRRA, to see the performance. They were most enthusiastic and this bolstered our confidence.

We discovered that we had a fine artist in the camp and we asked him to do the stage sets for our performances. The camp commander ordered the theatre painted and renovated. When everything was ready, we had playbills printed in town and hung them on walls all over camp to announce the grand opening of the Yiddish theatre. The text on the posters was in Yiddish transliterated into Latin characters.

The first performances of the *Laugh Calories for Purim* revue were highly successful. It had to be presented three times to give everyone an opportunity to see it. Some people came to two, others to all three performances.

The culture committee was so pleased with our production that they threw a banquet in our honor. We were highly praised for our daring and successful undertaking. As an expression of its gratitude, the committee awarded four hundred marks to each of us: Elie Bulman, for direction, Fogelbaum, for his lovely Purim songs, Yakov Vaystuch for musical direction, and me, for piecing together the two one-act plays from memory.

Imbued with courage, we immediately set to work to prepare a second revue entitled *Yisroel Buft* (Israel Calls), to be presented in conjunction with the Passover holidays. The revue was dedicated to the theme of Palestine. No country would take in the survivors of the Nazi annihilation campaign. Because they had nowhere to go and languished in the UNRRA camps, a move to create a Jewish homeland for the refugees was initiated in the United Nations.

Our friend Fogelbaum composed two songs for the revue. These songs became instant hits, right after Passover, spreading from

Ziegenhain to all the Displaced Persons Camps in the American Zone. Whenever the talented Fogelbaum performed these songs himself, the audience wouldn't let him leave the stage.

In the meantime, the Joint Distribution Committee forwarded the texts of Sholem Alecheim's one-act plays and Jacob Gordin's full-length works to the culture committee. Now that we had good material to perform, we really got to work. To begin with, we prepared a program we called *Father, You Laugh, Alas for Your Laughter*! It consisted of the following one-act plays of Sholem Aleichem: *Mentshn* (People), *Agentn* (Agents), *In Tsvevn a Seks und Sechtzik* (Double Sixty-Six), and *Oyler Haba* (World to Come).

After presenting these with great success, we began to feel like real professionals and undertook a production of *Got, Mentsh und Tayvl* (God, Man and Devil). After that, we presented his *Der Meturef* (The Madman). When these plays did well, we hired a German truck driver and went around to all the DP camps in the American Zone. There was a thirst for Yiddish theatre everywhere we went. We gave performances in the following camps: Schwarzborn, Hofgeismark, Hesenheke, Herzog, Rachel, Fridlar, Wetzlar, and a number of others. We spent the entire summer wandering about in the truck, like gypsies, serving the DP's hunger for a Yiddish word. We took great pleasure in the thundering applause with which the enthusiastic audiences greeted us.

During that time, I learned that my father, his wife and their daughter had survived the war in Belgium. I wrote him immediately and he started preparing papers that would permit our settlement in Belgium. At the same time, Briha began organizing groups of Zionist youth from within the camps to steal them into Palestine.

Bitter debates broke out in the United States on the question of what to do with the DPs. The British Mandate was to expire shortly and the Zionists demanded the liberation of Palestine. They hoped that it might become a haven for the tens of thousands of homeless Jews residing in the DP camps. To further the cause, we arranged giant demonstrations and displayed huge banners demanding that the the gates of Palestine be opened. Dozens of reporters arrived to photograph the demonstrations.

Briha took people out of the camps day and night making every effort to get them to the shores of Palestine. The number of people left in our camp grew fewer and fewer and there was talk of the camp being liquidated. Before long, the liquidation of the camp was for real. On that very day, a truck arrived to transfer us to another camp in Kassel, and our son fell ill. With our sick child, we sat high up on a truck packed full of people and their baggage. Our child lay on some bundles and we were all very uncomfortable. He was feverish and began to vomit. We asked the driver to let my wife and son sit beside him on the driver's seat so that the child might be more comfortable. The driver consented. As soon as we reached the city, Hanele took him to seek medical assistance while I continued on to the camp to find lodging.

The new camp was called Jaegerkaserne. By the time I landed a room and unloaded our things, it was late in the evening and I hadn't heard anything from my wife and child. I went down to the camp office to telephone the doctor that Hanele intended to go to. I learned that the doctor hadn't been able to establish the cause of the illness and told Hanele to take our son to a hospital. A telephone call to the hospital elicited the information that our son was being detained because he was ill with scarlet fever.

The hospital was situated some distance outside the city. It would therefore be some time before Hanele would arrive home although she left the hospital quite a while earlier. She didn't show up until after midnight. She was tired and unhappy as she told me that the hospital authorities were adamant in their refusal to let her stay with her child while he, in turn, refused to be parted from her. With his last ounce of strength, he held on to her and it was heartbreaking to listen to him plead that she not leave him. Hanele was also afraid to leave our son in German hands. Knowing of their cruel murder of countless Jewish children, she couldn't bring herself to trust her ill, defenseless child to these people.

There was no sleep for us that night. At break of day, we arose and hurried off to the hospital. The trip began with a long trolley car ride. A barge then took us across a stream after which we walked about two kilometers before we finally arrived at the hospital. We weren't allowed in but were directed to a window outside, at which we could stand and look in on our son. The nurse warned us to make sure he didn't catch sight of us.

While we were still several meters from the window, we could already hear him moaning and calling "*Ma-ma, m-a-m-a!*" We slackened our pace and tried to steal a glimpse. I saw him standing up in his crib. A bandage on his head covered his ears and neck. His little face could scarcely be seen. His little hands gripped the safety rail of the crib as he continued to murmur "*M-a-m-a, Ma-ma.*"

Hanele stood behind me and took a quick look, then pulled back so that he wouldn't discover her. We stood at the window for hours. Every groan and call of "*M-a-m-a*" cut through our hearts like a knife. We asked the nurse why our son's head was tied up and why the bandage covered his ears and neck. She explained it was routine in the treatment of this particular disease. It was done to avoid a respiratory infection since any complication could make the illness life threatening,

We came by the window day after day to steal a look at our son and observe his progress. For the first two days he kept calling for his mother. On the third day, we found him asleep in his little bed and waited for him to awaken. He no longer called for his mother. We watched as a nurse fed him something by the spoonful. He ate in silence. After that, he sat up in bed and played with a toy. We could see he was improving and, for the first time, we felt relief.

We bought him the very first toy he ever owned a clown suspended on a string between two pieces of wood. Pressing the sticks together made the clown turn somersaults. We asked the nurse to bring the toy to him and we went back to the window to see his reaction.

The nurse brought him the toy and showed him how to make the clown do somersaults. He immediately imitated her and when he succeeded in getting the clown to turn over, he broke into smiles. We were so happy to see him smiling that we forgot to stay hidden. Suddenly, he raised his eyes and saw us. Throwing the toy aside, he again began to wail: "*Ma-ma, ma-ma!*" We couldn't forgive ourselves for being so careless. We waited some time away from the window, listening to his plaintive cry. After about a half-hour, the nurse managed to get him to calm down and the crying ceased. Only then did we leave for home.

The long awaited day when we could take him home from the hospital finally arrived. When we went to get him, he looked at us with estrangement in his eyes as though he couldn't decide whether to go with us. Untrusting and curious, he stared at the two of us as though he couldn't forgive us for having left him with strangers in a strange place. Several days after returning from the hospital, he finally responded to the loving affection and tenderness we showed him. He was once again at home.

In our new UNRRA camp, Jaegerkaserne, we couldn't organize a drama group. Most of our members were gone, many of them by way of illegal *aliya*. Others were sent to different camps. All the camp populations were shrinking. We too were preparing to leave and join my father in Belgium. Nevertheless, I tried to find something to do in my free time. My good friend, Fogelbaum, became a member of the camp administrative committee and tried to get me a position, but there weren't any vacancies. Eventually, I joined the firefighter brigade of the camp.

Any young man would have found fire fighting attractive and enjoyable. We had two hours of practice each day, riding around the camp with all our paraphernalia and conducting fire drills. The rest of the day, we were off.

There were twenty-eight of us divided into three shifts of seven, and another group from which substitutes could be drawn. Each shift served eight hours. Our two-hour practice period over, we sat in the firehouse and enjoyed each other's company. We would kibitz and sing songs, scarcely aware of the day's passing. During the entire time that I was a fireman, I didn't put out a single fire mostly because there wasn't one.

We had an agreement according to which a different man went home each night while the others remained on duty. Since our brigade was responsible for night watch only once every three weeks, I seldom slept in the firehouse.

The American occupying authorities issued a temporary document certifying that we were stateless. The Belgian consulate affixed our visas to this document and we were thus fortunate to be able to depart for Brussels.

The author, Hanele, her father, and her sister, Bella
Warsaw, Poland. December 10, 1937

The author, Hanele and Ben Tsion
1937

Hanele, the author, and their son
Ziegenhain, Germany 1947

From left to right:
The author, Hanele, and their son, Bella and Haim
Ziegenhain, Germany 1947

Demonstrations for Israeli Independence in Lager Ziegenhain
1947

A sample program

The organizers of the Drama Circle
From left to right: Wodnicki, Altman, Bulman, and Spagatner

The Players
The Sholem Aleichem Drama Circle of Lager Ziegenhain

Chapter 16

The express train to Brussels went by way of Paris and stopped at the Gare du Norde, Brussels. I could see my father, his wife and their daughter through the window of our car. They eagerly searched for us among the passengers to welcome us to Belgium. We disembarked and greeted them heartily. After claiming our baggage, we all went to my father's house. They still lived in the same house at Number 18 Rue Grisar, in Anderlecht. Everything seemed to be exactly as it was before with no changes whatsoever. Every piece of furniture stood exactly where it did when I left ten years earlier in 1938.

My father let us have the guestroom, which was furnished with a convertible leather sofa. That's where we slept at night.

When I went out into the yard, I noticed one thing that was different. The factory, which was so noisy and busy making hats was transformed into a shop for the production of ladies'purses. A post-war innovation was put into practice. Instead of making handbags of leather, the manufacturers were using plastic. Such bags were less expensive than the leather ones and were easier to market. Almost all the Jews of Brussels were engaged in this new business.

After rejoicing that we managed to come through the horrible war unharmed and finding each other after being separated for so many years, it was time to turn to the realities of life. I had to think about what I might do in Belgium to become independent and settle down with my family.

My father offered to teach me the trade. When my stepmother found out what my father proposed to do, she again began placing obstacles in our path just as she had in the good old days. She interrupted my father as he spoke and began to present her own arguments: My father was not the sole owner of the factory. He had a partner. My father therefore didn't have the right to teach me the business on company time. It would be much better if I went elsewhere to acquire the skills of the trade. Once I acquired them, I would be able to work anywhere I wanted to.

Not wanting to be drawn into a conflict between my father and his family again, I complied with all their decisions. My father arranged to have one of his friends teach me. Since the highest paid workers in the industry were those who attached the locks to the hand bars (a stamper) of the handbags, I was taught this line of work. When I became proficient, I asked my father to employ me as a stamper.

My stepmother once again interposed her own calculations. It would be wrong to take work away from someone who was in their employ for years, so it would be advisable for me to look elsewhere. Seeing that I wouldn't get anywhere with her in the way, I wondered whether I shouldn't try to do something on my own.

I purchased several meters of plastic, cut some small purses from my own pattern and sewed them together, bought some small locks and attached them, and then went around to stores and attempted to sell my change purses. As I obtained orders, I bought more plastic yardage and thought I finally found a way to make a living. No matter what I did was wrong. Since I had to cut and sew material in my father's factory, my stepmother quarreled with my father demanding that he keep me from using his equipment. I was obliged to give up the manufacture of the little purses and look for employment outside the family business.

On top of everything else, the visa I had obtained was only a tourist's permit. As a tourist, I hadn't a legal right to employment in Belgium unless I could prove that I possessed a skill no one else had, in which case, I would be issued a work permit. I couldn't find any such work and continued to have difficulties becoming established. I could have obtained employment that was legally prohibited to me, but then I would be breaking the law. It would be rare to find an employer willing to do that for Belgian law was very strict. An employer who violated it was subject to severe penalties. I faced the prospect of never being able to work in Belgium since I had no special qualifications that would legitimately entitle me to a work permit.

While still in the UNRRA camp, we wrote to some of Hanele's relatives who lived in America and asked that they fill out papers vouching for us and invite us to immigrate to the United States. They sent us the requisite documents but because of immigration quotas, our visas were held up as we waited our turn. We could expect it to be several years before we could go. In the meanwhile, I had to find employment to support my family and myself and not be a burden to my father. No matter how diligently I looked for work however I could find none.

At the time, there was but one Yiddish newspaper in Brussels. *Undser Vort* was a daily, the organ of the Poale-Zion Party of Belgium where my father was the moving spirit. He never gave any indication at home of a shortage of hands at the editorial offices of the paper. I accidentally noticed an advertisement in the newspaper for a typesetter of Yiddish. With the advertisement in hand, I went up to the editorial office, which was on Rue Bara, one street away from where we lived. Calling upon the editor (his name was Avrom Riba), I applied for the position.

He asked whether I was a typesetter. I replied that I wasn't, but that I had a good command of Yiddish and was willing to learn. He asked me my name. When I said "Hershl Altman," he inquired:

"Is Sholem Altman a relative of yours?"

"Yes," I answered, "he's my father."

"Strange." He scrutinized my face.

"I've never heard him mention that he had a son."

I interrupted him curtly.

"Two sons," I said. "And there are many other things you've not heard from him."

He hesitated a while, and then told me to report for work early in the morning.

"And I believe," he added immediately after, "that if your intentions are serious you'll learn the job."

I arrived home feeling pleased and in good spirits. I told Hanele that I finally found employment with the newspaper called *Undser Vort* and that, if all went well, I would start in the morning. I didn't say a word about it to my father. I was annoyed with him for not having done anything to help me find work and for having helped bring matters to such a pass that we would once again be obliged to leave Belgium, despite the fact that this time we had nowhere to go.

The newspaper was still being published in primitive fashion, being set by hand rather than on linotype. The first thing I was taught was to throw the type from yesterday's edition back into the case, which was divided into many little sections, one for each letter of the alphabet. I was shown how to stand in front of the case and where each letter belonged. In order not to get the letters mixed up, I pasted paper markers on each section. I acquired the skill very quickly and only a few days later was tossing seventy to eighty lines an hour back into the case, letter by letter.

At the end of the week, the editor called me into his office and handed me my wages, five hundred francs. Obviously pleased with me, he said I would earn more as I advanced. He promised that the following week I would be taught to hold a composing stick in hand and set type.

My father still didn't know where I was working. One day, he unexpectedly entered the editorial office and saw me there, standing in front of a case and setting type like a real compositor. He lost his composure completely. He came over to me and asked crossly,

"Why didn't you tell me you were working at the paper? Why did you keep it a secret?"

I responded with the same question.

"Why did you keep it a secret that I could find work on the paper? Were you afraid that if I obtained employment in Belgium, I might God forbid want to stay here?"

He didn't reply and remained out of sorts with us for some time.

The editor, because I was making a real effort to learn the trade, filled out a form to the Belgian authorities on my behalf. He requested that I be granted a work permit because I was a typesetter of the Yiddish language and that there were no Yiddish compositors available in all of Belgium. On those grounds, I received a work card and was pleased to be in a position to take care of my family.

We started to look for a place to live for I was earning enough not to have to depend on anyone else's help. As soon as I received my first wages, Hanele began to take care of our housekeeping expenses so that my stepmother wouldn't feel we were imposing on her. We made every effort to be as independent of them as possible.

A short time later, we had an opportunity to take over a fully furnished apartment from acquaintances of ours that were migrating to Brazil. We purchased the place and all its contents and moved right in. But even after we lived apart from them, my stepmother, with my father's assistance, did everything she could to cause us to leave Belgium.

The United Nations had just voted on the creation of a Jewish state and Israel had, in a propitious hour, become an independent nation. Even before the establishment of the Jewish State, my father was officially in charge of immigration to Palestine. Certificates of Immigration were his to distribute to Zionist youth who planned on making *aliya* (immigration to Palestine). My father was forever proposing that we move to Palestine to settle and promised that as soon as we made the decision, he would assign us a certificate.

When Israel became a reality, my father was given further authority to distribute visas to people wishing to move to Israel. My father then repeatedly hinted that we ought to prepare to go there because he would have no trouble in issuing a visa whenever we were ready. We could be among the first to immigrate.

At virtually the same time, the United States passed a law permitting Displaced Persons who were war refugees to enter the country above the established quotas. At just about the same time, one of Hanele's uncles, who lived in Australia, sent us papers vouching for us and opened the prospect of immigrating to that country. He very much wanted us to join him there. We faced a most difficult dilemma. All at once, we had a choice from among three different places, and we had trouble making a decision.

My brother wrote from Israel that he built a two-room cottage for us near his own home and that he was impatiently awaiting our arrival. The British Embassy informed us that visas to Australia had been set aside for us and the American Consulate notified us that our visas were ready and we should come to collect them. It was a most difficult task to make the right decision.

It was all happening so fast that we didn't even have passports ready to which to attach the visas. We didn't want to apply for Polish passports. We no longer had any ties with that country. We made a decision to apply for passports as stateless persons and to consider ourselves stateless no matter where we decided to go.

We considered the pros and cons upon which our choice of country should depend. We would very much have liked to go to Israel. But after all our horrendous experiences, we didn't have strength to go to a country engulfed in flames and spilling blood in its struggle for liberation. Although our uncle in Australia would have loved to have us, when we informed him of our three choices, he replied that he was of the opinion that America was more suitable than Australia. One might do well in Australia from an economic standpoint. However, life there was difficult in other respects. He referred to Australia as "a glutton's place in the middle of a cemetery." It offered little in the way of Jewish cultural life. America, on the other hand, had the largest Jewish population in the world and economically things were better there than anywhere else. We decided that we would go to America and began feverishly to prepare for the journey.

We took the train to Paris and there had some difficulty with our passports. It took three days to resolve the problem. From Paris we went to Le Havre to board the SS America bound for New York.

In the interval between arriving in Paris and leaving for Le Havre, I ran around from one steamship company to another and caught cold. By the time we boarded the ship, I could no longer stand up and had considerable fever. I went to bed in my cabin and was obliged to remain there for the duration of the crossing, which took nine days. I not only had a cold, but also suffered from seasickness the entire time. As luck would have it, the ocean was extremely stormy all the way. In addition to being debilitated by the fever, I couldn't eat. The ship rocked so much that as soon as I ate anything it came right back up. The only thing I could retain was seltzer.

On the ninth day, in March of 1951, on a Friday, Hanele came down from the deck to tell me the New York skyline was coming into view. With her assistance, I dressed and got up on deck where it was a magnificently beautiful, sunny spring day. The ship sailed calmly and slowly on mirror-smooth waters. Visible in the distance was the Statue of Liberty, a proud lady, torch in hand, reaching for the blue skies. Soon we saw wide strips of land upon which hundreds of automobiles went gliding by at great speed, as though they were being propelled by an unseen wind. These rushing automobiles were my first great surprise as I approached the shores of New York. In Europe, the auto wasn't nearly as visible as it was in the American wonderland.

The ship arrived in the harbor and was being anchored. High above us, on the shore, hundreds of people eagerly awaited their relatives and friends. Scanning those hundreds of faces, Hanele recognized her aunt who sent us our immigration papers. Above the great din, my wife called out to her. Her aunt finally noticed us and smilingly began to wave to us. The greeters on shore weren't permitted to approach the incoming passengers. Certain procedures had to be undergone first.

Every immigrant brought a sealed envelope containing x-rays of his internal organs. This was for proof that their internal health was good. The envelope also contained a letter from the consulate, certifying that the consular physician affirmed that the x-rays belonged to the immigrant presenting them.

Several physicians were on hand to examine the immigrants. Each envelope was opened and the letter read. The physician then observed the person, placed an official stamp on the letter and proceeded to the next passenger.

When my turn came, the doctor broke the seal on my envelope, read the letter, and when he finished reading looked at me sharply and asked me a question in English. I didn't understand and, with considerable effort, tried to tell him so. He then asked whether I understood German.

"Ja" I replied.

"How much did you pay the doctor for your x-rays?" he asked sternly.

"Nothing," I said. "These are x-rays of the consular physician in Belgium. I didn't pay anything for them."

He ordered the three of us to be seated off to one side. When all the other passengers had been examined, he turned several other passengers and us over to two civilian officers. They took us by ferry to the "Isle of Tears," Ellis Island.

I was alarmed by the fact that I was sent to Ellis Island instead of being released like most of the other passengers. I figured that the doctors must have uncovered some dread disease on account of which I might be refused entry into the country and would probably be deported.

That first night on the Island, I was unable to sleep and kept thinking of my unhappy fate. I would surely be sent back to Europe. What would become of my wife and child? During the course of the night, I decided that should I be sent back to Europe I would insist that my wife and child not suffer because of me. They, at least, should remain. I was doomed but a better fate awaited them here.

Early in the morning, I told Hanele what I decided. After listening to what I had to say, she raised her voice at me. She would hear of no such one-sided plans. If worse came to worst and I really was to be sent back, she and our child wouldn't remain here without me. Whatever my fate, it would be theirs also.

After breakfast, I was called to the telephone. I was very surprised. Who would be calling me here? It seems that our uncle (Hanele's aunt's husband) was moving heaven and earth to obtain our release. He established that the examining physician hadn't found a trace of illness in me. However, when he saw how exhausted I looked, he suspected some dreadful disease and that I must have bribed a European doctor to supply false x-rays. We were sent to Ellis Island to await clarification of the matter. Since it was Saturday, I would have to wait until Monday morning to be taken to a clinic for new x-rays. If what they showed proved to be the same as on the ones in the envelope, I would no longer be detained.

On Monday morning, I was summoned and taken by ferry to a clinic in New York. New x-rays were taken and they showed that all was well. We were released shortly thereafter.

Hanele's aunt and uncle were waiting for us in their luxurious Cadillac. They helped us load our things into the car trunk. It was the first time in our lives that we sat in so sumptuous an automobile. It carried us through the streets of New York to their splendid home in Forest Hills on 71st Road. It was a magnificent fourteen-room private house, surrounded by a beautiful garden, which included apple and peach trees.

Our uncle had us stay in three rooms on the third floor of his house. Prior to our arrival, he furnished a bedroom for me and my wife and a separate child's room for our son, who was now nearly seven years old. The third room was a living room in which we could spend our time pleasantly.

Our aunt and uncle lived there with their three daughters and an only son. One of the girls was sixteen, another was fourteen, and the youngest was only three. They employed a live-in Gentile woman to do the housekeeping.

We developed a very good relationship with the family. Our aunt, who was Hanele's father's youngest sister, was a pretty, gentle woman with a very sensitive heart. She did everything she could to make us feel at home. She never failed to call us to the table at mealtime. Whenever they went out anywhere, we were always invited to come along, whether it was to call on friends of theirs, to see a movie, or just go for a car ride. We were always together. All four children, from the youngest to the eldest, were happy to be with their "green" cousins.

Our uncle was a very tolerant, successful, well-to-do businessman who dealt in real estate. He was a contributor to the community and was very generous with us.

After we rested several days, my uncle took me downtown to begin a search for employment. He had many contacts in the printing business and tried to get me work in the field. Wherever he took me, the first question asked was whether I knew English. Since I didn't, it was impossible for me to obtain a job as a typesetter.

Our uncle decided that it was paramount that we go to night school to study English. One evening soon thereafter, he took us to a school in Queens and registered us for night courses, which we attended every evening.

I got up every morning and went downtown with my uncle. I bought the *Jewish Daily Forward* and looked in the "Help Wanted" ads for some temporary work that I could do until I became proficient in English. Then, perhaps, I might obtain a job in the printing field.

I changed jobs as often as I changed socks. I worked as an operator sewing military overcoats for the Korean War. I made army caps, men's hats, and other things.

Having begun to earn a living, I thought that we were with our aunt long enough and that it was high time we took on responsibility for ourselves. We should no longer continue as guests of the family.

At table one evening, I told our aunt and uncle that we were looking for a place to live so that we could be independent. They protested, urging us not to. My earnings were insufficient to both pay rent and provide for all the other needs of my family. They asked us to stay with them for at least a year. That would enable us to save up some money. Only then should we look for lodgings.

However, I felt we could manage on our own. We had lived with them eight months and that was more than enough. It was too much to keep accepting room and board for so long. I began to look for some place without letting them know. I found an apartment in a run down section of Williamsburg in Brooklyn. It was on the top floor of a neglected building. There was neither central heating nor a refrigerator. The rent was forty-five dollars per month. The landlord was a Jewish man. Realizing that the apartment was not suitable for us, he didn't want to rent to me. He reasoned that since I was a greenhorn, I probably didn't know the difference between one section of the city and another. I argued with him: What difference did it make to him whom he rented to so long as he was paid the rent he asked? He shrugged his shoulders as if to say I was obviously not in my right mind and reluctantly accepted the money that I pushed into his hand.

The apartment was very dirty and in disrepair. Hanele and I cleaned it for two weeks. We installed an icebox instead of a refrigerator and brought in a kerosene stove. When the place looked decent, I told my uncle we finally had a place to live and we asked that he ride over with us to see where we planned to move.

When my uncle saw the dilapidated neighborhood and went up to the fourth floor with us and viewed the three neglected rooms, the icebox and the kerosene stove, he shouted:

"You had better go at once to get your money back! Don't you dare move into this shabby slum!"

I was determined. I told him we would move because we had benefited enough from their generous hospitality. We would be forever grateful for it and would always remember how much he and his wife had done for us by bringing us to America and providing us with a warm home for eight months. It was high time we became self-sufficient. True, this wasn't a first class apartment, but it wasn't the worst either and would do for a start. We'd lived in places that were much worse and would hope that in time we'd be able to afford a change to something better.

Our aunt and uncle pleaded with us in vain. We moved out. They were very much offended and were in a huff for about three months. It hurt us to have them angry with us and we decided to buy them a present by way of apology. We purchased a beautiful clock framed into a model of a ship, artistically reproduced in pitchwood. They were very happy to see us and our friendly relations were restored.

When we moved, another sister of my wife's father provided us with the furniture we needed, such as a table and chairs, and gave us cooking utensils and dishes. But it wasn't too long before we discovered that the apartment really wasn't for us.

It was winter. We lit the kerosene stove and turned up the flame because it was very cold in the house. The stove became red hot and it seemed as though the glow would extend all the way down to where the reserve kerosene was stored. I tried to reduce the flame by turning down the wick, but found it impossible to do. Apparently, the heat damaged something. A great fear took hold of me. I was afraid that if the stove continued to burn and the heat made its way down to the reservoir, the kerosene would explode. Hanele and our son went to bed in their clothes and I sat down to watch the stove in the event things became more dangerous. I could warn them and we would run from the building.

Fortunately, there wasn't much fuel left in the reservoir and after another half-hour, the stove began to cool down. We never used the kerosene stove again.

For the rest of the winter we suffered from the cold. We weren't able to live in that apartment for more than seven months. By that time, Hanele's sister, Bella, and her husband arrived in New York from a Displaced Persons camp. We rented eight rooms in a private house where we could all live together by dividing up the space. This house was equipped with every modern convenience, such as a refrigerator and central heating. There was a veranda, which was covered over with the thick branches of a large tree growing in the yard. It was in this comfortable home that Hanele brought us the joy of a new baby daughter. We named her Dvoyrele, in memory of Hanele's mother, who was so cruelly murdered along with Hanele's younger sister, little Halinka, in the Majdanek concentration camp.

EPILOGUE

It has now been thirty years since we arrived in this golden land. As I look back on the first day that we trod this blessed earth, I feel compelled to sum up what we've accomplished here, but I simply don't know where to begin. Shall I begin with a hymn of praise and gratitude for the land of Columbus that has granted us the privilege of citizenship? Shall I sing to the freedom of its democracy that we have now so long enjoyed? A democracy, in which we sank our roots and for which we shall be forever thankful for giving us these many years of freedom and contentment?

Now, thirty years later, I'm retired and living on a pension from Uncle Sam's social insurance fund known as "Social Security." It provides me the assurance that the years of my old age will be spent in dignity. With an inner calm, I can soberly appreciate the vast difference between the earlier circumstances of my life and the genuine freedom of this country. There is no equal to it anywhere on earth.

Granted, I haven't become a millionaire, but never once have I gone hungry. We've encountered our share of difficulties, but we've always had an opportunity to overcome them. Sometimes I worked for less than desirable employment, but I always had the choice of exchanging it for better. I was always free to do what I thought would be best for us. No one could compel me to do anything that wasn't to my liking. I even attempted to go into business. After working in the millinery trade for a year, I opened a factory of my own and for ten years, we prospered.

We educated our children "so that they might find favor in the eyes of God and good people," as the saying goes. My son, whom we miraculously brought out of Russia, has won various scholarships towards his education. He earned three degrees: a bachelor's, a master's and a doctorate. He now teaches philosophy in several highly regarded colleges in New York City. He is married and has presented us with a grandchild who brings us much joy. Dvoyrele, our daughter is also married. She is a graduate of Bronx Community College.

When we go to bed at night, we sleep peacefully, certain that the NKVD will not rob us of sleep by banging on our door, nor will they rob us of bread and cause us to go hungry. Every bite of bread tastes good to us for we know it's been earned, not under slavery and duress, but through honest work, voluntarily performed. If, occasionally, and because we are surfeited, some dish doesn't particularly please us, we remember the "good old days" in Russia where we were distended with hunger. As if by magic, the food acquires a most delicious taste. We then consume it with a hearty appetite, for we feel it a terrible sin to throw food away when so many starving people still toil away in countries enslaved by communism.

When we lay down to sleep in a clean bed, made up with white and tidy linen, I try to compare our situation now with the "seven fat years" we spent in utter deprivation in the Soviet "paradise." We slept on a filthy straw sack, without sheets, without a white-encased pillow, and without a shirt. We had lice gnawing at our wasting bodies.

I know why I'm grateful to my new, adopted country. I murmur softly to myself, as if in prayer, the verses of the song written by the great Jewish American patriot, Irving Berlin: "*God bless America, My home, sweet home!*"

As a citizen of the country that offers the greatest measure of human freedom, I can travel wherever I like, doing whatever I please and spending my time wherever I wish. I've begun to take advantage of these valuable liberties. Twice, with Hanele and our daughter, I visited Israel, the liberated Jewish homeland. I finally met my brother and his family. His family now, *kein ayne hore* (may no evil eye bring them harm), consists of his wife, two sons and a daughter who have, in turn, given him six precious grandchildren. I was delighted to meet my cousins who like us experienced the horrors of the Soviet Union. They escaped death to find a warm and comfortable home where generations have only dreamed of settling, the Jewish homeland, Israel.

In Haifa, I once again met one of my closest companions in Warsaw, my dear and loyal friend, Friedrich Garfunkel, with whom I shared the joys and sorrows of the best years of my youth. Unfortunately, I completely forgot to write about the many memorable events connected with this dear friend of mine. When I visited with him in his large bookstore, Renaissance, we talked for a very long time about our mutual experiences in the old home of our birth. I'm resolved that if enough years are granted me, I will devote myself to immortalizing them all. Friedrich Garfunkel's story is a fascinating book all by itself.

As soon as we were more or less settled in America, I joined Branch 678, the Mendelson branch of the Workmen's Circle and was a member there for two years. When my cousins, Manya and Leyzer Glikshteyn arrived from Grodzisk, they invited Hanele and me to join the Grodzisk Society. Before long, the Grodzisk *landslayt* made me a member of their administrative committee and soon thereafter elected me president. I held the position for several years until I resigned and turned it over to an older member. Since then, I've been recording secretary. My spare time is taken up with the duties of this office.

My adopted country is experiencing difficulties at present. It is in the throes of economic uncertainty, internal and external instability, and an extraordinarily widespread crime wave. However, I believe to the depths of my soul that a nation such as ours will surely overcome every obstacle. Like the night fog at dawn, every evil now besetting the land will disappear and the glory of mighty America will again be a shining example of honor, justice and brotherhood for all.

Printed in the United States
39877LVS00006B/61